David Hon

Blackwell Bible Commentaries

Series Editors: John Sawyer, Christopher Rowland, Judith Kovacs

John
Mark Edwards

Revelation
Judith Kovacs & Christopher
Rowland

Forthcoming:

Genesis
Gary Philips & Danna Nolan Fewell

Jeremiah
Mary Chilton Callaway

Exodus
Scott Langston

Lamentations
Paul Joyce

Judges
David Gunn

Jonah
Yvonne Sherwood

1 & 2 Samuel
David Gunn

Haggai, Zachariah and Malachi
Richard Coggins

1 & 2 Kings
Martin O'Kane

Mark
Christine Joynes

Job
Anthony York

Luke
Larry Kreitzer

Psalms
Susan Gillingham

Romans
Paul Fiddes

Ecclesiastes
Eric Christianson

Galatians
John Riches

Isaiah
John F. A. Sawyer

2 Corinthians
Paula Gooder

John

Mark Edwards

Blackwell
Publishing

350 Main Street, Malden, MA 02148-5020, USA
108 Cowley Road, Oxford OX4 1JF, UK
550 Swanston Street, Carlton, Victoria 3053, Australia

First published 2004 by Blackwell Publishing Ltd

Library of Congress Cataloging-in-Publication Data

Edwards, M. J. (Mark J.)
  John / Mark Edwards.
    p. cm. – (Blackwell Bible commentaries)
Includes bibliographical references (p.   ) and index.
  ISBN 0-631-22906-X (hardback) – ISBN 0-631-22907-8 (pbk.)
1. Bible. N.T. John–Commentaries. I. Title. II. Series.

  BS2615.53.E39 2004
  226.5′07–dc22

                                        2003019601

A catalogue record for this title is available from the British Library.

Set in 10 on 12.5 pt Minion
by SNP Best-set Typesetter Ltd., Hong Kong
Printed and bound in the United Kingdom
by TJ International Ltd, Padstow, Cornwall

For further information on
Blackwell Publishing, visit our website:
http://www.blackwellpublishing.com

Contents

Illustrations

The Blackwell Bible Commentaries series, the first to be devoted primarily to the reception history of the Bible, is based on the premiss that how people have interpreted, and been influenced by, a sacred text like the Bible is often as interesting and historically important as what it originally meant. The series emphasizes the influence of the Bible on literature, art, music and film, its role in the evolution of religious beliefs and practices, and its impact on social and political developments. Drawing on work in a variety of disciplines, it is designed to provide a convenient and scholarly means of access to material until now hard to find, and a much-needed resource for all those interested in the influence of the Bible on Western culture.

Until quite recently this whole dimension was for the most part neglected by biblical scholars. The goal of a commentary was primarily, if not exclusively, to get behind the centuries of accumulated Christian and Jewish tradition to one single meaning, normally identified with the author's original intention. The most important and distinctive feature of the Blackwell Commentaries is that they will present readers with many different interpretations of each text, in such a way as to heighten their awareness of what a text, especially a sacred text, can mean and what it can do, what it has meant and what it has done, in the many contexts in which it operates.

The Blackwell Bible Commentaries will consider patristic, rabbinic (where relevant) and medieval exegesis, as well as insights from various types of modern criticism, acquainting readers with a wide variety of interpretative techniques. As part of the history of interpretation, questions of source, date, authorship and other historical-critical and archaeological issues will be discussed; but since these are covered extensively in existing commentaries, such references will be brief, serving to point readers in the direction of readily accessible literature where they can be followed up.

Original to this series is the consideration of the reception history of specific biblical books, arranged in commentary format. The chapter-by-chapter arrangement ensures that the biblical text is always central to the discussion. Given the wide influence of the Bible and the richly varied appropriation of each biblical book, it is a difficult question which interpretations to include. While each volume will have its own distinctive point of view, the guiding principle for the series as a whole is that readers should be given a representative sampling of material from different ages, with emphasis on interpretations that have been especially influential or historically significant. Though authors will have their preferences among the different interpretations, the material will be presented in such a way that readers can make up their own minds on the value, morality and validity of particular interpretations.

The series encourages readers to consider how the biblical text has been interpreted down the ages, and seeks to open their eyes to different uses of the Bible in contemporary culture. The aim is a series of scholarly commentaries that draw on all the insights of modern research to illustrate the rich interpretative potential of each biblical book.

John Sawyer
Christopher Rowland
Judith Kovacs

I am indebted to the editors of this series, Christopher Rowland and Judith Kovacs, together with an anonymous referee, for their assistance in the arrangement of material and for pointing out a number of lacunae in earlier drafts. Thanks are due to the following institutions for permission to reproduce works of art relating to the Gospel: The National Gallery, London, for Sebastian del Piombio's *Raising of Lazarus*, Rembrandt's *Ecce Homo* and El Greco's *The Expulsion of the Traders from the Temple*; the Ashmolean Museum, Oxford, for Lanfranco's *Christ and the Woman of Samaria* and a Dominican master's *John and Mary at the Cross*; St Bartholomew's Hospital, London, for Hogarth' *Pool at Bethesda*; the Courtauld Institute, London, for Bruegel's *Christ and the Woman Taken in Adultery*; the Victoria and Albert Museum, London, for Blake's *Christ in the Sepulchre, Guarded by Angels*. Among the employees of Blackwell

Publishing who have helped with the preparation of this text are Jean van Altena, Kelvin Matthews, Alison Dunnett, Rebecca Harkin and Lucy Judkins. Any inconsistencies or omissions that remain must of course be ascribed to me, though it will, I hope, be remembered that if this book is to be a mirror to the centuries, it cannot but reflect a great deal that seems to us tangential, false, misleading or bizarre.

A&M	*Hymns Ancient and Modern*
AV	Authorized Version
DCB	*Dictionary of Christian Biography*
EE	*Elegant Extracts* (London, 1790)
HTR	*Harvard Theological Review*
JTS	*Journal of Theological Studies*
MCNT	*The Methodist Commentary on the New Testament* (London 1894, no pagination)
NEB	New English Bible
NEH	*New English Hymnal*
NIV	New International Version
NT	*Novum Testamentum*

NTA   *New Testament Apocrypha*, ed. W. Schneemelcher, tr. R. McL.
           Wilson, 2 vols (London, 1963–5)
NTS   *New Testament Studies*
RSV   Revised Standard Version

External Attestation of the Gospel

The subject of this commentary is the Fourth Gospel of our New Testament, ascribed by all tradition to the apostle John and symbolized in Christian iconography by the fourth cherub of Ezekiel and the Apocalypse, who wears the face of a man (Hamburger 2002). So much we learn from Bishop Irenaeus of Lyons between AD 180 and 190 (*Against Heresies* 3.11.8); around 170, Tatian of Edessa had already subsumed this narrative in his four- or five-fold *Harmony of the Gospels*. Before this time our Gospel is never named, but the disparity between this life of Jesus and the accounts of the Synoptic writers (Matthew, Mark and Luke) was perhaps already apparent to Papias (fl. 140), the earliest historian of the Gospels (Eusebius, *Church History* 3.39). What, if not a text that he believed to be an apostolic record, would have emboldened him to write, before 140, that Mark's narrative had preserved the reminiscences of Peter but without regard to order? (Cp. Eusebius, *Church History* 3.24 with C. E. Hill 1998: 586–7.) Those who reject this inference do not deny that a fragment of our Gospel has survived on a papyrus dating from about 130, and its contents must be at least a decade older if the quotation from 1:5 ascribed to the Alexandrian heretic Basilides is authentic (Hippolytus, *Refutation* 7.10/22). Two cardinal premisses of the Fourth Evangelist – that Christ is the Word or Logos of the Father and that the workings of his Spirit are inscrutable – were already commonplaces to Ignatius, bishop of Antioch, whose martyrdom took place in 107 or 112.

No earlier testimonies could be hoped for if the Gospel was composed, as the ancients tell us, in the last years of a long life by the youngest of the disciples – perhaps as late as 95, the era of Domitian's persecution. All ancient sources agree that the author was John the son of Zebedee; whether he was the John who wrote the Apocalypse (or book of Revelation) they were not so sure, and Papias records that the tomb of another John, the Elder, was also pointed out in Ephesus, the putative resting-place of the last apostle. Although in the second century of the Christian era no book was more canonical than the Apocalypse, Eusebius in the fourth century includes it among the 'controverted writings'. No such doubts touched the Gospel in this period. Hippolytus defends its authenticity in the third century, perhaps against an otherwise unknown Gaius (*DCB* 2.386); but it seems likely that the *Alogoi*, or Word-deniers, assailed by Epiphanius in 376 are a product of the heresiologist's tendency to transform a single man into a sect (*Panarion* 51). Those whom we now call orthodox could not renounce this testament of the Word made flesh, for it served as an emetic to two great blasphemies: docetism, which taught that the Saviour's body was a phantom, and adoptionism, which recognized a descent of the heavenly Christ on the earthly Jesus but refused to cement them by an incarnation. The case against docetism was strengthened by the opening words of the First Epistle attributed to John; against adoptionism Irenaeus quotes an anecdote told by Polycarp of Smyrna, that the apostle had once fled from the public baths rather than share them with Cerinthus, the nominal founder of this widespread heresy (*Against Heresies* 3.3.4).

The First Commentators

Polycrates of Ephesus (fl. 170), another Asiatic who claims knowledge of John's biography, declares that he 'wore the mitre', which implies that – like the Baptist with whom he shared the rare name 'John' – he came from a family of priests

(Eusebius, *Church History* 5.24). Polycrates also says that it was John who bequeathed to the Asiatic church its date for the celebration of Easter. Nevertheless, while Asia took possession of the body and reputation of the apostle (J. B. Lightfoot 1904), it was not here that the so-called gospel of John became the favourite study of commentators, but in the younger church of Alexandria, and among teachers who inclined to a docetic interpretation of its contents. The pioneers were heretics, or became so in later eyes. Heracleon (fl. 170) appears to have commented only on specimen passages, deriving from each a proof of Christ's antipathy to the flesh, of the divorce between creation and the spirit, or of the elect soul's duty to conspire with Wisdom in the consummation of her redemptive plan. Heracleon's critic Origen – though his evidence is disputed by Wücherpfennig (2002) – taught posterity to regard him as a proponent of the Valentinian myth, according to which the human soul is enslaved in matter as a result of the primordial fall of Wisdom from the Godhead; release comes when it imitates her repentance, and the appearance of the fullness, or *pleroma*, of the Godhead in its robe of flesh is designed not to redeem the body but to redeem us from it. Such tenets could be extracted from the Gospel only by allegory; but could the Church deny this trope to its adversaries when Clement of Alexandria, Heracleon's contemporary, resolved the contradictions between the Gospels by pronouncing the Fourth a 'spiritual' record which conveys high truths in symbols under the guise of history (Eusebius, *Church History* 6.14.7)?

The great commentary by Origen (c.185–254), conceived in opposition to Heracleon at the beginning of the third century, reached 32 books without progressing beyond the thirteenth chapter. Little survives after this, and more than half of the preceding text has perished; the 500 extant pages, however, show that he domesticated the allegorical method by submitting it to a statement of belief which he believed to be held by all churches, and by taking the undisputed sense of one text as the key to the latent meaning of another. While he endorsed a number of Heracleon's speculations, he avoided caprice, as a scholar of our own day would, by taking account of history and topography, by examining the general structure and tenor of each passage, and by comparing the Johannine narrative with that of the Synoptics. His Christ is divine, yet also a man in body, soul and spirit; he assumes that the temporal ministry of Christ is recounted accurately in all four Gospels, and only when the Fourth conflicts with the others does he resort to Clement's expedient of a spiritual reading. Origen subordinates the literal to the figurative in commentary, the visible to the invisible in cosmology, body to soul in anthropology, and the speaking flesh of Christ to his concealed divinity; nevertheless, the body is redeemed by the Incarnation, and the written text would not be patient of allegory at all if it were not the chosen vehicle of the Word.

The steadfast 'literalism' of the Antiochenes in the fourth century is frequently contrasted with the Alexandrian predilection for allegory. More accurately, we might say that the Alexandrians strove to bring the text home to the reader, the Antiochenes to recover the situation of the writer and the pattern of events behind his text. Theodore (d. 428) and John Chrysostom (d. 428), the Antiochene interpreters of this Gospel, show their acumen by repairing apparent breaches in the narrative and ascribing probable motives to the actors. This we may call 'historical criticism', but they also share with Cyril of Alexandria a desire to vindicate the impassibility of the Logos, which leads all three into subterfuge and anachronistic pedantry. For Cyril (d. 444) the application of the text to his contemporaries was not his own device, but the extension of a historic miracle, Christ's gift of the Paraclete, which itself completed the work that God began when he filled the nostrils of the first man with his spirit. A stronger concern with the sacraments is visible in his work than in that of Origen, but this concern – as his other works clearly show and his comment on 1:4 confirms – arises from his conviction that the incorporeal Logos has so joined himself to matter that if anything can be predicated of him in the course of his earthly ministry, and hence as man, we must also be ready to predicate the same thing of him eternally and as God.

The Middle Ages

Augustine (354–430) is perhaps the author most liberally represented in this volume, and with reason, since no other ancient critic – not even Chrysostom – has been quoted with such constant approbation during 1,500 years of biblical scholarship. That he owes his renown to his merits is apparent from his 124 *Homilies on John's Gospel*, the method of which is at once Antiochene and Alexandrian, for he sees the text as a narrative, veridical, linear, free of inconcinnity or conflict with other Gospels, and yet pregnant in every line with some divine truth or instruction for the soul. He always has an allegory at hand, and makes more use of numerology than any of his precursors in theological exposition. These instruments are laid aside, however, in his *Harmony of the Four Gospels*, which retained its authority during the Middle Ages, though the *Diatessaron* was not forgotten. Augustine was no stranger to historical criticism, and his advocacy ensured that all Western versions of the Gospel would include the acquittal of the woman taken in adultery (7:53–8:12); with the resurrection of Lazarus, the trial before the Jews, and the appearance to Mary Magdalene, this became a favourite subject for art and drama in the later Middle Ages, though in primitive iconography the shepherd and the fish predominate. Among scholars, Eriugena (c.810–77), the last of the Neoplatonists, followed Origen in his methods and in his praise of the Fourth Evangelist as the theologian *par excellence*. Others were more concerned with the harmonization of the Gospels or with filling the lacunae in their narratives: Bede (c.673–735) worked out the chronology of the festivals in this Gospel with his customary acumen, but for the most part he exemplifies the homiletic and moralistic tendency which dominates the early Middle Ages. Such practical men as Gregory the Great (pope from 590 to 604) were seldom trammelled by past readings or the probable intentions of the Evangelist when they chiselled the texts and images of the Gospel into sermons for the day. This is not to say that all sense of history was lacking, but they were interested not so much in the circumstances of composition as in the divine plan to which the Gospels testified. It is only in the later twentieth century that commentators have shown themselves so conscious that the Old Testament is the yeast of the New, even where it has not risen to the surface. On this and other matters, the observations of Theophylact (fl. 1100), which he wove into an erudite collation from his forebears, were repeated with esteem by commentators up to the early years of the twentieth century.

Preachers of the second millennium also could be eloquent and perceptive, as my excerpts from Radulphus (c.1040–c.1100) indicate. The Gospel now became the food of mystics and contemplatives, and to the Franciscan Joachim of Fiore (c.1135–1202) Jesus' promise of the Paraclete foreshadowed a consummation in which the rule of the Spirit would supersede the Law imposed on Israel by the Father and the Church inaugurated by the Son. Yet mystics can be pedants too: it is not so much his 'negative theology' as his credulous addiction to Aristotelian nomenclature that mars the famous commentary of Eckhart (fl. 1300) on the prologue (1958: 221–49). If I seem to have drawn rather more frugally on this period than on others, I suspect that I am exercising a preference which will coincide with that of the majority of my readers. One reason, no doubt, is that the medievals lacked the apparatus of modern criticism, another that they were frequently excelled in imagination by the lyricists, the mystery plays and above all by such allegorizing poets as Dante (1264–1321) and Langland (d. 1387). The latter's account of the Crucifixion and Christ's encounter with Satan in the underworld (1987: *Passus* 18) is among the most noble and tragic things in English literature.

Renaissance and Reformation

The invention of printing widened the reading public, and, when coupled with the exodus from Byzantium which restored Greek to the West in the fifteenth century, encouraged the diffusion of new translations, both in Latin and in the vernacular. Translation demands attention to the letter, and where this seemed to be ambiguous, the exegete might call upon the new disciplines to justify his choice of one equivalent or another. Erasmus (?1469–1536) showed what a distance there might be between the Greek and the Latin Vulgate derived from Jerome, not least in the rendering of the word *logos* in the prologue to this Gospel (1535: 218–20). The study of Hebrew literature, initiated by Reuchlin, culminated for English readers in J. Lightfoot's Talmudic commentary on the Gospels (1684) – an instrument of special value to readers of the Fourth Gospel because it gives evidence for the prohibitions attributed to the Pharisees and explains the significance of the Jewish festivals which punctuate the narrative. The Gospel itself was not, however, perceived as a text which stood apart from others in the canon, and might therefore require peculiar modes and tools of exegesis. Luther (1483–1546), for example, spoke of John and Paul as the two keys to the New Testament (1961: 18), but would not have been prepared to admit that one Gospel might be more spiritual than another. His sermons make it a tool of ecclesiastical reformation by transferring its reproaches to his enemies, and of moral reform by annexing an allegory to the literal exposition. Calvin (1509–64), who is less a man of the Middle Ages, follows him in the first respect, but scholarship consisted for him in rendering the Greek faithfully with an edifying paraphrase, or now and then a corroborative citation from Josephus. He shows himself conscious of the peculiar character of this Gospel by devoting a separate book to it in 1553 after digesting the other three into a harmony, but for him it was a true history like the others, and the same doctrine was contained in all the Scriptures. For a century after him, Protestant commentators held that the medicine of the soul was neither philology nor allegory, but devout exposition of the literal meaning, so that the Latin notes of J. A. Bengel's *Gnomon* (1740) were dwarfed by the orotund but largely uncritical *Exposition* of George Hutcheson. The late, and perhaps most popular, fruit of this tradition is Matthew Henry's *Commentary on the Whole Bible* (1706); but the spirit of evangelical simplicity (or 'puritanism') lives again, combined with scholarship of a much higher order, in the *Expository Thoughts* of Bishop John Ryle (1816–1900). Ryle, like not a few of his successors, found that he needed three volumes for John (1866, 1869, 1873) where one had sufficed for each of Matthew, Mark and Luke. As he can still be consulted with profit, I have cited more from him than from his predecessors of the Stuart period, though in the English eighteenth century I have taken account of the Wesleys and of the learned dissertations (Ibbot 1737, Kidder 1737, Berriman 1737) in which some of the most original exegesis was advanced.

In medieval and early modern times our Gospel was not the preserve of clerks, academic or ecclesiastical. The opening verse was used as an incantation in medieval times, while during the seventeenth century the devout bought copies of the whole text as a talisman against witchcraft (K. Thomas 1973: 34, 221, 296–7). The lance that pierced Christ's side at 19:34 was a regular concomitant of the Grail (Peebles 1911; Fisher 1917), which was supposed to be either the cup that caught his streaming blood or the chalice that he passed to his companions at the Last Supper (Matthews 1997: 174, 183). This chalice, of course, has no place in our Gospel, where the cup is a metaphor rather than a symbol, but the Johannine vocabulary of regeneration haunted the alchemist's crucible, in which the soul was figuratively dissolved and re-created through the baptism of sulphur in mercury. As mercury is the element of Hermes, the interpreter of divine mysteries, it coalesces readily with the Logos in the work of Jacob Boehme (1575–1624), perhaps the most widely read of Luther's followers before Kant. When astrology ousted alchemy as the key to all religions, Christ and his disciples were identified with the sun and the constellations of the zodiac. The Reverend Robert Taylor's erudite conjuring with the names of Thomas and Judas Iscariot (1831) illustrates the latitude of opinion that was reluctantly tolerated in the Hanoverian Church.

Beginnings of Modern Criticism

Among believers, the so-called Gospel of John was widely assumed to give the fullest account of Jesus' ministry, if only because it was easier to coax the 18 months of the Synoptics into its three-year span than it would have been to reverse the negotiation. Vivid scenes in the closing chapters lent themselves to the new techniques and interests of the painters – the flagellation, the *Ecce Homo*, Mary with the beloved disciple and, above all, the *noli me tangere*, which fed the prevailing taste for the erotic without transgressing the bounds of piety. Within the Roman Catholic Church, the Fathers remained the fountain-head of criticism, whether dogmatic, historical or moral; even those commentators whose works were thought to merit frequent republication – such as the Jesuits Cornelius a Lapide, Natalis Alexander and the so-called Maistre de Sacy – displayed their learning only in compilation and in the breaking of an occasional lance on a heresy put abroad by Protestant authors. Until the late eighteenth century, it was hardly necessary for the apologist to ward off an attack on the historical truth, antiquity or dogmatic authority of the sacred text. Even Reimarus, whose infamous fragments saw the light in 1774, did not contest the authorship of the Gospels, though he argued that they had falsified Christ's teaching. There were others who suspected that the Fourth was not the work of an apostle, but they were silenced for a time by Friedrich Schleiermacher, the father (or at least the unwitting progenitor) of liberal theology. Perhaps the first to state plainly that the Fourth Gospel was of less use to the historian than the other three was D. F. Strauss, the first edition of whose *Life of Jesus* shocked the faithful and perplexed the learned in 1835.

Noting that almost every deed and utterance attributed to Jesus in the Gospels marks the fulfilment of some Messianic prophecy, Strauss inferred that they ought to be handled not as forensic depositions but as pregnant myths. Myth, on this hypothesis, is false when it mimics history, but true when it embodies the ideals, and hence the future, of the race. Strauss intended his thesis to be fatal to the 'naturalistic' explanation of miracles as anomalous events whose causes escaped their first observers; he himself may not have seen what a grave wound he had dealt to the 'liberal' project of extracting a thread of fact from the skein of fable. In England, as in Germany, the liberals remained in the ascendant, and when Strauss's work was noticed, it was seldom perceived that he had destroyed in order to construct: 'Matthew and Mark and Luke and holy John, / Evanished all and gone' (Clough 1974: 163).

Worse came in 1844, when F. C. Baur, one of Strauss's tutors at Tübingen, drew up a catena of errors in topography and history to justify his dating of the Gospel to the mid-second century. Like Strauss, he inferred that if the narrative was not history, it was allegory, in which places stood for different truths, and persons for different factions in the Church. Clough's friend Matthew Arnold spoke for common sense and poetic intuition against the two professors (1889: 136–40), and the theologian F. D. Maurice (1857) turned aside from his war with the Unitarians in his lectures on the Gospel to denounce their sceptical treatment of its date and authorship. The readiness of other German scholars to endorse this scepticism betokened victory not for Strauss but for the Gospel of Mark, the priority of which was generally thought to have been proved by Weise in 1838. Renan (1861) despised the artificial speeches of the Fourth Gospel, yet its authorship and veracity were defended at the end of the nineteenth century by the conservative Bishop Westcott (1903) and by Adolf von Harnack, the last great spokesman of German liberalism. William Sanday applauded both (1905: 14, 42), but to many it now appeared that neither the Gospel nor the liberals could withstand the concerted labours of Johannes Weiss, Albert Schweitzer (1875–1965) and Alfred Loisy (1857–1940), all of whom maintained that Christ himself was a supernaturalist, the prophet of a kingdom which was to come in his own generation, suddenly and from on high (Schweitzer 1954: 222–68, 348–99). These are the pioneers of biblical criticism in the twentieth century, and if they seem to be neglected in this volume, it is because their intuitions have been refined in modern scholarship with the help of evidence hitherto unknown and with a hitherto unimaginable freedom of debate.

Twentieth-Century Trends

For Loisy at least, the Evangelist claims our interest in his own right, as a witness not to the life of Jesus but to the generous versatility with which the Church subsumed the pagan mysteries, thus transforming an erroneous prophecy into a lasting cult (1903). Yet authors of any kind, including John the putative apostle, were disenfranchised by the 'form-critics' of the early twentieth century, who maintained that almost every saying of Jesus in the Gospels was invented by the 'community' as a mandate for its own determination of some posthumous controversy. At the same time, the 'history of religions' school professed to have identified a community external to the Church which had inspired the Johannine prologue and left its traces in other portions of the Gospel even after the text had undergone a Christian redaction. The Mandaeans, who purport to be disciples of the Baptist, describe the descent of a man of light from the heavenly realms to the darkness of creation, where he opened a road to deliverance through baptism and abstinence from meat. Notwithstanding the lateness of the extant sources, Rudolph Bultmann treated them as relics of a widespread Gnostic movement which had preceded Christianity. The Gospel of John, he argued (1925, 1957), had inherited from this quarter its ascending and descending Son of Man, as well as its pervasive antitheses between light and darkness, vision and blindness, the aeon of God and the epoch of the devil. It was thus, as Strauss had divined, a tissue of symbols drawn from its own time and environment. The enterprise of 'demythologization' which he enjoined upon the interpreter entailed the removal of the ancient wrappings so that the substance of the Gospel – the kerygma, or proclamation – could be embalmed anew in the idiom of a scientific age. At the heart of the kerygma – and here is the contribution of Weiss – was eschatology, though in Bultmann's view the critical believer will not expect to survive his body or to witness the sudden inundation of earth by heaven on the latter day; instead, he will be aware at certain moments that he is faced by a vertiginous decision between the will of God and the counsels of the flesh. This decision takes the form of a world-view rather than a concrete action, and the Gnostics were therefore right to proclaim that knowledge is the criterion of salvation, while the Gospel of the Word is above all else the promulgation of a new, yet timeless and abiding truth.

Gnosticism (as Bultmann understood it, after the 'history of religions' school) was a synthesis of motifs familiar only to Indo-European races, while the home of the first Mandaeans was supposed to have been in Palestine. Students of the Fourth Gospel who followed Bultmann were relieved from an onerous choice between B. W. Bacon's notion of a 'Gospel of the Hellenists' (1933) and Hans Odeberg's attempt to trace its novelties to the native 'mysticism' of the Jews (1929). Yet Bultmann receives little mention in the great commentary of Hoskyns (1947), a conservative work which still attributes the text to the apostle; Hoskyns discerns an unremitting 'tension' between eternity and history in this 'restless' work, yet seldom hints that the work itself has a history outside the vocabulary of Roman government and the imagery of Scripture. More openly inimical to Bultmann is C. H. Dodd's *The Interpretation of the Fourth Gospel* (1953a), which dwells on the uncertain pedigree of the Mandaean sources; his strictures were confirmed in the authoritative study of the Mandaeans by Kurt Rudolph (1960), though the latter adhered to Bultmann's view of 'Gnosis' as a distinct religion, cousin rather than heir to Christianity. Dodd, though he doubted this, could not deny that there were elements in the Gospel which were foreign to the Old Testament and indigenous to Hellenistic culture. At the same time, he perceived that the Jews themselves had been instrumental in the formation of that culture, so that 'Jewish' and 'Hebrew' were not coterminous adjectives in late antiquity. By contrast, C. K. Barrett, in his magisterial commentary of 1955, applies the label 'Greek' to Hermetic authors and to Philo of Alexandria as though it were the antonym of 'Jew'.

The Origins of the Gospel

Whereas scholars such as Torrey (1923) and Black (1946) set out to exorcise harsh sayings and difficult syntax from the text by retranslation into Aramaic, Barrett found a warrant for the bad Greek of the Gospel in the bad Greek of the Septuagint and other aberrant texts. Nevertheless, the Dead Sea Scrolls, discovered at Qumran in 1947, could not be ignored in his or subsequent commentaries, as they showed that opposition to the Temple, Messianic expectation and a rigid bifurcation of the world into light and darkness had already come together in the teachings of a Jewish sect which flourished outside Jerusalem some decades before the ministry of Christ. Another document that invites comparison is the *Gospel of Thomas*, a Coptic version of which was unearthed in 1946, although it is thought by many scholars to have originated in Syria among speakers of Aramaic. Availing himself of the polarity between light and darkness, Thomas contrasts the saving knowledge secretly imparted to the inner man with the futile exercises that are publicly enjoined upon the Jews (see epilogue to chapter on John 14).

Raymond Brown sought clues to the intentions of the Evangelist at Qumran in his ample commentary, completed in 1970; the Scrolls and Gnostic parallels were freely cited in that of Barnabas Lindars (1972), perhaps the most judicious and comprehensive work on this Gospel to have appeared in a single volume. In his monograph of 1967 Wayne Meeks discovered that the 'prophet-king' of the Fourth Evangelist has no precursor in any Mandaean source that is likely to be ancient, but is perhaps anticipated in Samaritan and Jewish variations on the Pentateuchal history of Moses. During the 1970s a number of other scholars built on Odeberg's (1929) hint that the Gospel may be indebted to the Samaritans, whose heroes Dustan and Simon were reputed to have been pupils of the Baptist, while their prophesied Messiah, the Ta'eb, is expressly identified as Jesus at John 4:26 (see epilogue to chapter on John 4 below). This chapter, more than any other, lends itself to a feminist reading, while 4:9 contradicts the notion that the Gospel is antipathetic to the Jews as a nation, even if few scholars would be willing to restrict the pejorative usage of this term to the inhabitants of Judaea, as Lowe proposed (1976).

Most commentators agree that in its present form the text has undergone some dislocation. Chapters 5 and 6 are commonly transposed, though few would now presume to chop and splice the other chapters with the bold tenacity of Bultmann or Archbishop Bernard (1928). The frequent evocation of belief through signs or miracles seems to contradict the tenor of other Gospel which imply that faith cannot rest on demonstration. Since the Synoptics never speak of signs, and provide no analogues for the miracles at Bethany and Cana, it is generally supposed that the Fourth Evangelist made use of a primitive catalogue, now lost. This Gospel of Signs is almost always said to have contained just seven episodes, the Resurrection being excluded unless, as some opine, the walking on water in chapter 6 was not a miracle. Many were convinced by Lindars' study, *Behind the Fourth Gospel* (1971), that the philological evidence does not justify the extraction of the miracles from the main narrative; none the less, there is still a faction, led by R. T. Fortna (1970, 1988), which regards the reconstruction of this hypothetical text as the most important enterprise of criticism.

History and Tradition

One might think it a more feasible task to ascertain the relationship of the Fourth Gospel to the other three. In fact it is never easy to determine when it differs whether it does so of set purpose or from ignorance, and where its narrative coincides with any of them, one commentator argues for dependence and another maintains that the two are tributaries of the same tradition. Dodd holds the latter position throughout his *Historical Tradition in the Fourth Gospel* (1963), drawing the inference that matter which is common but not borrowed must be of some antiquity. Granting this, the least prodigal conjecture is that the common source is history, the acts and words of Christ himself, and the theory that the Gospel is what it claims to be – the memoir of a witness – is as tenable now as at any time during the last two centuries. John Robinson, conservative critic and radical theologian, maintains in *The Priority of John* (1985) that we can hear the *ipsissima verba* of the apostle in certain phrases. Hengel suggests that the reminiscences of the beloved disciple have coalesced with the second-hand reports of his companion John the Elder (1989). Among Classicists, who are apt to think the best of any writing that purports to be historical, it is possible to accept the claim to autopsy without accepting the miracles or the author's view of Christ (Lane Fox 1991).

Defenders of such conservative opinions are not forced to deny that a second generation may have had a hand in the editing and transmission of the Gospel; indeed, this is implied by 21:24, if not by 3:11. For J. L. Martyn (1979) and John Ashton (1991), the community consists of those for whom the work was intended, since (as Ashton says) the meaning of a text is determined more by its notional audience than by its genesis or even the identity of its author. Some would say that this assumption replaces one imponderable by another, and the interpreter's yoke is shifted rather than lightened if, as in Martyn's work, a new audience is envisaged for each new increment to the text. The same could be said of Raymond Brown's *The Community of the Beloved Disciple* (1979), except that where Martyn is chiefly concerned with the breach between the Johannine community and the synagogue, Brown postulates a series of collisions between insiders and outsiders, each resulting in a new layer of composition. The belief that Christ was God is held to have supervened upon a more modest estimate of him, resembling that still found in the Synoptics; the godless 'world', initially the preserve of Gentile pagans, comes to embrace the Jews, the followers of the Baptist and even Christians of a different stamp. Many scholars now hold that attention can be more profitably directed to objective and formal properties which enable us to classify the Gospel as an example of some recognized ancient genre. Once again, however, no two studies have arrived at the same conclusion. Richard Burridge (1992) holds that the four Evangelists set out to write biographies on the pagan model, Lawrence Wills (1997) that they drew on a variety of prose forms, and Mark Stibbe (1992) that classical tragedy was the template for the Johannine account of the trial and Passion. In some modern circles texts have more authority than the history that is supposed to underlie them, and the fissiparous methods of Bultmann, Dodd or Ashton are regarded as an evasion of the commentator's duty. No one has worked the vein of 'practical criticism' more assiduously than Thomas Brodie, who at every point in his commentary of 1993 acquits the Evangelist of error, inconsistency, hiatus or redundancy by methods that would once have been disparaged as allegorical. A. T. Hanson, in *The Prophetic Gospel* (1991), is another scholar whose diligence in the permutation of images and half-lines from the Old Testament would do honour to a Church Father – or, if you will, invites a repetition of Arnold's strictures on the school of Tübingen.

The poets too have not neglected the Gospel, though an attitude of wistful incredulity is now more common than the piety of Herbert or the ingenuous creativity of Blake. The prologue has supplied food for meditation to those who cannot believe in Jesus but would like to believe, with Coleridge, that a poet's imagination is 'a repetition in the finite mind of the eternal act of creation by the infinite I AM' (1983: 304; cf. John 1:1, 8:58). Lazarus and the Magdalen have lived on in art, if seldom without some prurient or ironic transfiguration. Esotericists have naturally been busy with this 'spiritual gospel', though only a taste of them can be given here, with my quotations from Swedenborg, 'Levi' and Michell. I have also included comments from Eisler on chapters 5 and 21, though no paraphrase that is less dense than his own reticulation of far-fetched data and adventurous deductions can explain how he came to hold that Jesus, John the Baptist and even the Evangelist were avatars of a speaking fish, once worshipped throughout the Near East (1923). Writers of fiction, hoping to penetrate the minds of Pilate, Judas or Christ himself have turned to the Evangelist whose report of the final days is at once the least invidious and the most circumstantial. It is this text, for example, which determines the chronology of *The Man Born to be King* (1943), a popular cycle of plays for radio by the novelist Dorothy Sayers. Scholars may object that verisimilitude can also be a property of good fiction, and occasionally of bad history; but when the learned differ irreconcilably, we should not be in too much haste to discount the answers that imagination gives to Pilate's question, 'What is truth?'

Note on the Form and Content of the Commentary

The present work, like most commentaries, is divided for ease of reference into chapters. These as a rule begin and end where chapters begin and end in printed editions and translations of the Fourth Gospel. Where, however, the author is more than usually repetitive, I have sometimes found it expedient to collect two or three of his chapters into a single chapter of commentary. Each of my chapters is prefaced by a brief summary of the principal themes and images, the chief difficulties that arise in exegesis, and the scholarly debates that they have engendered. An epilogue to each of my chapters takes a motif from the foregoing text and follows its metamorphoses in art and literature. Between these poles the commentary is a mosaic of opinions advanced by scholars and preachers for the elucidation of each portion of text and its application to life. The usual subject of each annotation is a verse or cluster of verses, but in almost every chapter I have also devoted an interlude of about a page, frequently coinciding with the traditional division between two chapters in the Gospel, to a text that has proved particularly seminal or obscure. My references to poetry – by which I mean primarily British poetry – are as catholic as my knowledge and the constraints of space permit; this matter I have inserted where it seemed to fall most naturally, fully conscious that at times I have omitted an exquisite meditation on the Gospel which is not expressly tied to any one verse or episode. One cannot do equal justice to every mode of criticism without adopting a wider variety of styles than can be accommodated in a single volume, and I have consequently been able to say very little about the Freudian, deconstructive and feminist readings which are apt to be most instructive when they draw the reader's attention to what the author leaves unsaid.

Prologue: The Doctrine of the Word

The function of a prologue, in antiquity as today, was to define the plan and character of the whole work, and it is generally agreed that, whatever the provenance of vv. 1–18, they find a commentary in the miracles and discourses of the Gospel. Verse 3 prefigures the living water of chapters 4 and 7, vv. 4–5 the symbolic light of 8:12, 9:5 and 11:9, and v. 13 the new birth of chapter 3. The most debated term is *logos* – 'word, discourse or reason' – which is otherwise attested as a Christological title only at 1 John 5:7 and Rev 19:13. Functioning as the counterpart to 'son of God' in the prefaces to Mark and Matthew, it intimates no doubt that Christ is the bearer of the words of eternal life, as at 6:68, the consummation of the 'word of God' as at 10:35 (cf. Loisy 1903: 98 and

Suggitt 1984). Since, however, *logos* also signifies a text, it may be surmised that an understanding of the word when used of Christ will be the key to the author's purpose in his book.

Apologists of the early Church distinguished the primordial state of the Logos as God's 'reason' from his emanation as creative 'speech'. Their Gnostic adversaries personified both Life and Logos as hypostases in an evolving Godhead. Origen maintains against both that the appellations *logos*, life and light are accorded to a single being, the second person or hypostasis of the Trinity, in his character as pilot of the *logikoi*, or beings equipped with reason (*Commentary* 1.24ff). He added that this reason is the true sense of the Scriptures, every word of which, when rightly construed, bears witness to the one truth. Mystics of his time affirmed that God had framed the world from a cosmic alphabet (*Commentary* 1.34/31); neglected by the orthodox, this conceit survives in the Saxon *Heliand*, where the Evangelists intone the secret runes of the Creator-Word (1992: 3–6) and in the imagination of Celtic poets:

> In the beginning was the word, the word
> That from the solid bases of the light
> Abstracted all the letters of the void
> (D. Thomas 1952: 20)

To Catholics of the fourth century Psalm 44:2 implied that Christ was an utterance from the heart of God (Socrates, *Church History* 1.6; cf. *Gospel of Truth* 23–4 in J. A. Robinson 1988: 43). Hence a Greek hymn declares him 'Of the Father's heart begotten' (*NEH* 33), while for the alchemist Jacob Boehme Christ is at once the eternal Word and the heart of God (1945: 248). In the West, the Vulgate's choice of *verbum* (word) in preference to *sermo* (speech) as equivalent to *logos* reinforced the association with the written letter. For Kathleen Raine it makes the whole world a text:

> Word that utters the world that turns the wind . . .
> Word traced in water of lakes and light on water . . .
> Grammar of five-fold rose and six-fold lily
> (1956: 76)

Erasmus rightly protests that *sermo* better represents the Greek original (1535: 218–19), and Calvin, who concurs with him, decides that the Word is wisdom in relation to God himself, and in relation to men the expression of his purpose (1959: 7). Hutcheson, perceiving that in Jewish thought the Torah itself is not a static instrument, asserts that Christ himself is 'the promise made and often repeated in the Old Testament' (1972: 10), though he does not go so far as to argue, with Servetus, that the ministry of the Word begins with Moses (Calvin 1959: 8). Karl Barth, the lodestar of Reformed theology in the twentieth century, states that the Word has a triple form as revelation, Scripture and preaching: in every case 'God's Word means that God speaks' (1975: 132, 136, 139).

Modern commentators have been at pains to trace the history of a term which was evidently not employed by Christ with reference to himself. The most familiar trail leads back to Philo of Alexandria (died AD c.50), whose Logos is at times the eternal plan in the mind of God, and sometimes his agent, priest or Son (Dodd 1953a: 67–9). This is not Platonism, for Platonists did not confer the name 'Logos' on the second god or Demiurge to whom they ascribed the origin of the world. Nor is it Stoicism, for the Stoic Logos, though a deity, is not a transcendent being but a subtle element permeating the body of the world. Dodd (1953a: 264–5) and Ashton (1991: 292–329) rightly point to the allegorical figure of Wisdom in Solomonic literature, who is almost always speaking (Prov 8:22–30; Wis 7:25–6) and is once equated with the Law (Sir 24:18). Other Jewish precedents include the personification of the word or Memra in rabbinic teaching (G. F. Moore 1922) and an encomium on the deeds of the Word in a paraphrase or Targum on the opening chapter of Genesis (Malina and Rohrbaugh 1998: 36–9). Perhaps Wesley concludes too hastily from this 'Chaldee paraphrase', together with Psalm 33:6, that the term was not borrowed from Philo (*MCNT* at I.1), but he was right to add 'or any heathen writer'. The concept of the Logos is indigenous both to Jewish and to Christian thought, because it serves to reconcile God's changelessness with his acts in space in time: 'For in the divine Idea this Eternity is compleat & the Word / is a making many more' (Smart 1954: 93).

The Jewish antecedents thus corroborate the dictum of Matthew Henry that Christ is called the Word because he reveals the Father's mind (1991: 1915, cols 2–3). Rēné Girard contrasts the universality of biblical discourse with the divisive rationality of Greek 'logic', which excludes what it cannot vanquish (1978: 484–9); notwithstanding 1:29 the Johannine Word is not the sacrificial beast or scapegoat of the man-made creeds, for these are merely pretexts for social violence, countermanded by his voluntary submission to the Cross. In Jürgen Moltmann's theology of hope the Creator knits himself to his suffering creation, in alogical but unanswerable defiance of the philosophies which purport to demonstrate the impassibility of God (1967). For Bultmann, on the other hand, the Word is itself divisive, as it forces an inexorable choice between flesh and spirit on the natural man who has hitherto acquiesced in his captivity to a universe defined by the natural sciences and the interests of the crowd. Revelation is the subject of the prologue and the leitmotif of the Gospel (1925), but, because it countermands all human law, it is inconsistent with the Old Testament, and the otiose repetitions of the prologue are best explained if we postulate a Gnostic source (1957: 1ff). In one of the first of many replies, Lamarche (1964) contends that the message of the first nine verses, couched in the vocabulary of the Gentiles, is recapitulated in Semitic terms in vv. 14–18, as though to foreshadow the reconciliation of the blind Jew with the more discerning but untutored Greek.

The Word as Creator

1:1a. Cf. Gen 1:1, Matt 1:1. Although this verse was used as an incantation in medieval exorcisms (Kieckhefer 1998: 251), Goethe's Faust, protesting that a word is a feeble instrument, wished to substitute 'in the beginning was the Deed' (1962: 40). Even had he been ignorant of Heb 4:12, Faust's master Jacob Boehme should have taught him that the Word of the Father's edict is accompanied by a 'sharpness', the Holy Spirit, which ensures its execution (1656: 121). Eckhart opines that the Word is said to be **in**, not 'from' **the beginning**, because it does not leave the Father in issuing from him (1958: 241).

1:1b. Abbott takes the preposition **with** in the second clause to mean that the Logos is 'devoted to' the Father, rather than conversant with him, as in Marcan usage (1906: 275–6). To Eckhart it connotes parity of honour because it signifies neither 'above' nor 'below' (1958: 224).

1:1c. In the NEB the third clause is rendered, 'What God was, the Word was'. Eckhart understands the verb to mean that Christ has been and so always is born (1958: 246). The word *theos* is not preceded in this clause by the definite article, and comparison with the second clause, where *theos* with the article clearly designates God the Father, suggests that the omission has a purpose. Origen surmised that the Son is God by derivation from the Father, who is *autotheos*, the Godhead in its fulness (*Commentary* 2.2); opponents of 'metaphysical' Christologies may appeal to Ex 7:1 in the Septuagint, where God commissions Moses with the promise 'I shall make thee god to Pharaoh', using *theos* again without the article. Natalis Alexander replies, however, that since the Word does not receive the title god by any discrete commission, it must belong to him eternally and by nature (1840: 22).

1:2–4a. Orthodoxy considers Christ a 'person' from the beginning: 'He with his *Word* commanded *All* to be, / And *All* obey'd him, for that *Word* was he' (Cowley, *Davideis* 1.365–6 in 1881: 48). An older doctrine taught that the eternal reason of God became his Son when it issued forth for the creation (Athenagoras, *Embassy* 10). Origen takes a middle way: although the Logos existed from the beginning, he was not light and life before the creation of humanity (*Commentary* 2.19/13). If, however, Logos in Wis 18 is no more than the personified plan of God (Ashton 1994: 22), can we be sure that the Logos of the prologue is a 'he' and not an 'it' at any point before verse 14? The verb *egeneto* is commonly rendered 'were made', but if we take it to mean 'were done', it appears that providence, rather than creation, is the subject of this verse (Ashton 1994: 19, citing *1QS* 11.11 in Vermes 1975: 93). Nor is it certain whether the verse should be punctuated: **without him not one thing has come into being. What has come into being in him was life;** or: **without him not one thing has come into being that has come into being. In him was life.** Because the second reading forestalls the inference that the Spirit belongs to the category of things that have been made or come into being, it was favoured by Catholics after the Nicene Council of 325; before that date all witnesses adopt the former reading (Metzger 1975: 196), though it allowed the Gnostic Heracleon to argue that the world is dead and hence not among the things that were made by Christ (Origen, *Commentary* 2.8). Nonnus adopts both readings, and his paraphrase at canto 1.9 suggests parallels with the philosopher-poets Cleanthes and Lucretius (2002: 86, 113). Medieval dualists, or Cathars, read 'without him was made the nothing', meaning by this the evil which they attributed to a power opposed to God (Nelli 1968: 193).

1:4b. Israel is styled a 'light to the Gentiles' at Isa 42:6 (cf. Luke 2:32); the mission of Christ implies that she has failed. Cyril of Alexandria expounds this verse in harmony with Acts 17:28, where being and motion are concomitants of life (1. 75, Pusey). This metaphor, in his view, is the nearest approach that human speech can make to the eternal nature of Christ; Theodore, however, held that the verse described him only in his economic function as illuminator of the human mind (Wiles 1960: 72). The phrase **light of all people** is wanting in the biblical personifications of wisdom, as in the parallel cited by Hanson (1991: 31) from a Jewish tragedy on the Exodus (Ezekiel, *Exagoge* 99 at 1983: 56). The author may be playing upon the fact that Greek possesses two words *phos*, one meaning 'light', the other 'man'. The man of light is, as Bultmann notes, a protagonist of both Mandaean and Manichaean myths, but the thanksgiving hymns of the Qumran sect, to which Lindars appeals, are older (1972: 87). The association of light with life in the theosophical writings called the *Hermetica* may betoken knowledge either of this Gospel or of its Jewish antecedents (Dodd 1935: 99–144); Sanday finds the 'ultimate source' in Ps 36:9 (1905: 195).

1:5. This verse, more congruent with 2 Cor 4:6 than with Gen 1:3, was quoted by the Gnostic Basilides (fl. 130) as a gloss upon his own parable in which Christ is the seed sown by the ineffable Father (Hippolytus, *Refutation* 7.10/22). Basilides was by repute a Zoroastrian, but Lindars finds a similar 'dualism' at Qumran (1972: 88). It is not clear whether the darkness has failed to capture or to comprehend the light. The first reading might be construed as an allusion to the pursuit of Jesus by the benighted Jews (Origen, *Commentary* 1.26), or to his emergence from the darkness of the tomb (Romanus, *Cantica* 27.5.3 at 1963: 203). In the allegorical cosmogony of the Manichees, the lord of darkness falls in love with the kingdom of light, and in trying to take possession of it ensnares the Primal Man (cf. Bultmann 1957: 26–8). In the alchemical scheme of Jacob Boehme, desire produces an involuntary contraction of the will, until the tension between centripetal and centrifugal forces erupts as the light of freedom, which 'governs within the darkness and is not comprehended by it' (1945: 92).

Interlude: The Baptist

The Tübingen scholars of the nineteenth century surmised that the Evangelist was engaged in a polemic against disciples of the Baptist, whose intrusion at v. 6 catches the reader by surprise (see Baldensperger 1898). This case was reinforced by the discovery of the Mandaeans, who traced their dualistic religion to the teachings of the Baptist. Rudolf Bultmann, noting many affinities between the Johannine prologue and the teachings of the early Christian sects that we call Gnostic, surmised that in these verses a Mandaean hymn has been clumsily adulterated by a Christian editor in the interests of his own creed (1925 and 1957: 5). Dodd in reply objected that the Mandaeans possessed no independent records of the Baptist, and that none of their writings antedates the ninth century (1953a: 115–30). After 1945, the gradual publication of a library of heterodox and esoteric texts from the Egyptian site of Nag Hammadi persuaded many scholars that if there had ever been such a thing as Gnosticism, its roots were in Judaism or at least in Jewish literature. Bultmann held that Primal Man, the archetype and redeemer of the spiritual elect in Gnostic myth, was also the literary ancestor of the Johannine Messiah; no variant of the myth, however, has yet been found to antedate John's prologue. Parallels to the imagery and vocabulary of the prologue are adduced from the Dead Sea Scrolls by modern commentators; Scobie, on the other hand, takes the absence of a heavenly redeemer in these documents as proof that the Mandaean myth did not originate in a Jewish cult (1964: 29–30).

Certainly the Evangelist subordinates John to the Christian Messiah, and to this end he denies us even the meagre information about the former that is vouchsafed in other Gospels. Why, then, are we allowed to mistake the Baptist temporarily for the subject of the eulogy? Ridderbos replies (1966) that he marks the crisis which is entailed by the appearance of the light. Lamarche (1964) sees John as the hinge between the two halves of the prologue – the light of the world to the Gentiles, the representative of Israel to the Jews, but superseded in both capacities by Christ. Brodie (1993) divides the prologue into three phases: first the creation, then the Old Covenant (represented by the Baptist), and finally the New Covenant, inaugurated by the Word made flesh. John's origins, the meaning of his baptism, and the date of his death are topics not even raised, let alone resolved, by the subsequent narrative. We are merely given to know that before his imprisonment the Baptist yielded his own disciples to the true Messiah.

John Proclaims the Unseen Light

1:6–8. As at Matt 11:12–13 the appearance of the Baptist marks an epoch in the work of providence, bringing with it a style reminiscent (to Borgen) of historical narrative in the Old Testament (1972: 120). Augustine, likening John to Moses, adds that Christ was so truly man that he needed a great man as his herald (*Homily* 2.2–5). All rivalry between Christians and the Baptist's sect is laid to rest in the mystery play *John the Baptist*, where these words are spoken by the man himself (Happé 1975: 382).

1:9. Cf. 6:14. The mind, according to Origen (*Commentary* 1.24–6), has its own objects of vision, and the true light of the world is to be contrasted with the radiance that beguiles our outward senses. Eckhart takes the light of every man to be the essence or ideal logos implanted by the One Logos (1958: 227); other contemplatives of the Middle Ages held that only the mystic truly beholds this light (Richard of St Victor 1979: 192, 240). The sentence can be read to mean that the light **was coming into the world**, or else that it is **in the world and coming** to everyone (Borgen 1972: 123), or even, as Cyril of Alexandria supposed, that it lightens **everyone who comes into the world** (1.110 Pusey). Baur construes the verse as a rebuttal of Jewish pretensions to the peculiar favour of God (1878: 154).

1:10. Käsemann (1969) refers vv. 5–13 to the incarnate Christ, but Chrysostom points out that he appeared to the patriarchs, unknown to the world, before the nativity (*Homily* 8.1). Barrett points out that in Bible usage to **know** is to enjoy communion rather than to exercise 'observation and objectivity', as in the Greek of classical authors (1955: 136).

1:11. Cf. Mark 6:1–6, which also fails to name 'his own country'. Here again the Logos assumes the functions that a Jewish writing might ascribe to Wisdom or the Spirit. In the first clause the neuter form *ta idia* means '**his own** property', while in the second the masculine *hoi idioi* means '**his own** people'. The Latin version, *sui non receperunt*, is said to have been felicitously misconstrued as 'swine did not receive him' (Chillingworth 1841: 342–3). The verse is as much a warning to petrified Christians as a pretext for invective against the Jews in the vein of Natalis Alexander (1840: 69–70).

Sons of God

1:12. The language may be intended to discriminate between Christ as Son of God and the 'children' (*tekna*) who enter the kingdom of God as his disciples. The Johannine writer addresses his congregation by a similar term at 1 John 5:21. Calvin, to refute the 'Papist' heresy of free will, translates the word *exousia* (generally rendered **power**) to mean "distinction" (1959: 17).

1:13. The reading **who were born** is better attested than the alternative, **who was born**, which would refer to Christ and therefore be a testimony to the Virgin Birth. Metzger notes that a number of ancient witnesses preferred the latter reading (1975: 198), and Henry More relates that it was usurped by the seventeenth-century fanatic David George (1662: 25).

1:14a. Augustine found the substance of the prologue in the writings of the Platonists, until he reached this verse (*Confessions* 7.9). Orthodox dogmatics, following Cyril of Alexandria, insists that the flesh which Christ assumes at 1:14 is the whole of human nature, and the Nicene Creed says 'he became man', not 'he became *a* man' – though no Church Father went so far as to hold with Swedenborg that 'God is man and man God' in the light of the Incarnation (1933: 134–5). Many theologians today doubt that any one man can be a compendium of humanity; and certainly the exclamation of Hopkins – 'I am all at once what Christ is, since he was what I am' (1970: 106) – is a more literal, if more egocentric, paraphrase of vv. 13–14 than the maxim of Athanasius, 'God became man that man might become God' (*On the Incarnation* 54.3).

1:14b. The Greek verb *eskênôsen* (**lived**, or properly 'tabernacled') was already applied to Wisdom at Wis 9:7, Sir 24:8, etc., and alludes, in both the Johannine and the Solomonic passages, to Yahweh's sojourn among his wandering people on their way to the promised land. Anna Wickham's couplet, 'God is woven in the mesh / Of my eternal flesh' (1984: 348), combines this verse with its predecessor. Erasmus notes that some took the words **among us** to mean 'within a body', others to mean 'in the company of men' (1535: 225).

1:14c. This is the first claim by the author to be a witness of the events that he describes. Knowing that his contemporaries referred it to the Transfiguration (of which John, son of Zebedee, was a witness), Erasmus replies that the glory of Christ consists in his life and teaching (1535: 225). Yet 12:28–33 supports Chrysostom's opinion that the glory is exhibited in his suffering – and in ours (*Homily* 12.3). As Temple observes (1961: 13), this glory was hidden from Caiaphas and Pilate. The word *monogenês* can signify 'only-begotten' or merely 'unique', and even after the Council of Nicaea in 325 had defined it to mean 'from the essence (*ousia*) of the Father', it was permissible to render it into Latin as *unicus* rather than *unigenitus* (Kelly 1972: 172–81). See v. 18.

1:15. Harvey demonstrates (1976: 23) that the verb *krazein* is associated in classical Greek with forensic testimony, and compares the phrase 'crying mysteries' (*mustêria kraugês*) in Ignatius, *Ephesians* 18. Origen (*Commentary* 2.35/29) enumerates six occasions on which John the Baptist witnesses to the mission and authority of Christ, in the following verses: 1:15–18, 1:19–23, 1:26, 1:29ff, 1:32ff, 1:35ff.

1:16. The word *pleroma* can designate the fulness of the Godhead (Col 2:9), of the ages (Gal 4:4), and of Christ in the Church (Eph 2:23). Among Valentinians of the second century, the emptiness of God becomes a *pleroma* for the purpose of creation, and Christ becomes its first-fruits on the Cross (Irenaeus, *Against Heresies* 1.1–2). Calvin, though uncertain whether the **all** who receive include the 'godly under the law', accepts in his exegesis of the following lines that God appeared in Christ to the patriarchs (1959: 23–5). Elsley takes **grace upon grace** to mean that the Gospel is given in place of the Law of Moses (1844: 411), while to Henry it signifies the communication of 'gracious habits for gracious acts' (1991: 1918, col. 3).

1:17. Is there an allusion to Ex 34:6, which follows the encounter of God and Moses? Hanson (1976–7) gives an affirmative reply, against the objection of De la Potterie (1975) that grace and revelation are not synonymous in Exodus. To Henry these verses illustrate the sufficiency of the Gospel and the bounty of Christ in sending it abroad (1991: 1919, cols 1–2).

1:18a. The author of 1 John 4:12 deduces that we must love our neighbour to prove our love of God. The Muslim *Gospel of Barnabas* quotes a cognate saying to prove that Christ, being visible, was not divine (1907: 63). The Fathers flung this verse at the Anthropomorphites, who reputedly held that God had a human shape before the Nativity. Their answer was that the Godhead may be partially visible to us, as at Ex 33:23, Matt 18:10 and 1 Cor 13:12 (Epiphanius, *Panarion* 70.8). Lodowick Muggleton held that the Father is visible to one who 'is of God' (Underwood 1999: 256); the Cathars, by contrast (see v. 30), inferred that the God who revealed himself to Israel was not the father of Christ (*Two Principles* 56 in Nelli 1968: 151). The Neminians, who worshipped Nemo (no one) because he had seen God, are most probably fictitious. More naturally construed, this verse explains the prohibition of image-worship in the Decalogue. Greek iconoclasm and Reformation logic deny that the human form of Christ can represent his deity; 'iconodules' reply that the man is not a discrete accomplice of the Word, but the Word enfleshed (Meyendorff 1975: 61–90).

1:18b. Only (-begotten) god or son? Fennema (1985), observing that the consensus of ancient witnesses favours *theos,* takes the phrase to mean 'the only-begotten, who is God'. Metzger (1975: 198) explains the alternative (*huios,* 'son') as the result of assimilation to John 3:16 and 18. Since **god** is the reading uniformly accepted by heretical authors, Burgon (1998: 96–7) concludes that **son** supplanted it only in texts designed to prove the orthodox claim that the Son on earth is the same eternal being as the Word. In the Septuagint the word *monogenês* is used of Wisdom (Wis 7:22); Temple (1961: 16) contrasts the 'aesthetic satisfaction' that it expressed when Plato applied it to the generated cosmos at *Timaeus* 92c.

1:18c. The assertion in the *Gospel of Truth* that the bosom is the Holy Spirit rests on the author's previous identification of the Spirit with Wisdom (24 in J. A. Robinson 1988: 43). Prudentius says explicitly that he who was once the wisdom of the Father has now descended from his lips (*Cathemerinon* 11.17–20). Yet Spenser meant one thing when he wrote of Heavenly Love that 'Out of the bosome of eternall blisse . . . He downe descended' (1970: 594), and another when he wrote of Heavenly Beauty, 'There in his bosome *Sapience* doth sit' (1970: 598).

Epilogue: The Silencing of the Word

Ignatius of Antioch caught only half the spirit of the Fourth Gospel when he spoke of the incarnate Christ as the Word who proceeds from silence (*Magnesians* 8.3). Origen seems to have understood it better when he argued that the flesh of the Incarnation has been retranslated into the word of Scripture (*Against Celsus* 4.15). But what becomes of the Logos if we lose our faith in Scripture? In the twentieth century, D. H. Lawrence's poem 'St John' is a sustained lampoon on the doctrine of the Logos (1972: 219–21), while Eliot's Gerontion, musing on 'the Word within a word, unable to speak a word', hints that the text has silenced Christ (1974: 39). No written sign is identical with the object that it signifies; but if our only access to the signified is through the signifier, what do we know except the sign? In Schoenberg's oratorio *Moses und Aaron,* the words are given to one man and the idea to another; while for Robert Graves the spoken word is the antonym of 'God' (1986: 220). Parodying 1:14, the clergyman R. S. Thomas complains that 'flesh is too heavy to wear' the God whose 'poetry dries on the rocks' (1993: 228, 224); and an elegant couplet by another Anglican – '*Christ is the language which we speak to God / And also God, so that we speak in truth*' (Sisson 1990: 67) – is marooned by the italics and the antiquated metre. For a world that has abandoned both the versification and the Christ of Milton, Hughes invents the anti-hero Crow, who, seeing Adam and Eve asleep and God distracted, 'bit the Word, God's only Son, / Into two writhing halves' (1972: 19).

Prologue: The Church and the Baptist Sect

Many scholars argue that this narrative has been severed from its roots at verses 5–6, and what we are told about the Baptist's ministry is not always reconcilable with the information given in the Synoptics. Whereas other Gospels hint that the Baptist is Elijah (Mark 9:13, Matt 11:14), he himself denies it here, as indeed (according to J. A. T. Robinson) any Jew would have done before Christianity began to teach that Elijah was the forerunner of the Messiah (1962: 36). Elsewhere the Baptist's followers have not changed their allegiance after his imprisonment, whereas here he himself connives at their defection before the termination of his ministry. Those who uphold the plenary inspiration of all four Gospels will no doubt agree with Origen that this narrative augments the other three by introducing superficial contradictions which oblige us to look for something deeper than factual inerrancy in the text.

Ashton (1991: 253) divides the passage into three acts: first, a series of questions and replies about the person of the Baptist, with no reference to the kingdom or the destiny of Israel; next, John's prophecy of Christ's coming and the fulfilment of that prophecy, but without the prediction of baptism by fire and the Holy Spirit or any actual immersion in the water; third, a novel account of the translation of disciples from the circle of the Baptist to that of Christ.

The Interrogation of John

1:19. Bultmann notes that in this and the following verses John is forced to deny the same three titles that are tacitly disowned by Christ at Mark 8:28 (1957: 58–9). To Meeks this series of questions tells against the view that the titles are synonymous (1967: 19). Luther praises John's indifference to these misplaced honours (1983: 118). Natalis Alexander, expounding the moral sense, asks the reader what he will answer when the question **Who art thou?** is put to him (1840: 74).

1:20–1a. Contrast Mark 9:13: 'Elijah is come.' Origen explains that he is not the same Elijah who was carried up to heaven in the body, but has received a portion of Elijah's spirit (*Commentary* 6.11–14). On the title **Christ** (Aramaic Messiah) see v. 42.

1:21b. Cf. Deut 18:15. Glasson notes that the prophet has acquired a more definite character in writings from Qumran (1963: 27–32), and J. A. T. Robinson observes that in the Qumran scrolls immersion is a synonym for entry into the covenant (1962: 18). Yet the evidence for a ritual lustration there is as scanty as the evidence for the baptism of proselytes before the second century (T. M. Taylor 1956).

1:22–3. Origen suggests that John is the 'voice' and Christ the rational substance (*logos*) of his proclamation (*Commentary* 2.31/26). The wilderness is Judaea, not the desert, as in Isa 40:3 and Mark 1:3; hence the mystery play *John the Baptist* makes him profess to be 'a voice that cryede / *Here* in deserte' (Happé 1975: 382). Eriugena, however, contends that the wilderness stands for the elevated, and therefore solitary, insight of the Baptist (p. 304 Migne). On **Messiah** see below, v. 42.

1:24–6. Cf. Matt 3:7. Noting that the Pharisees come after the priests and Levites, Origen brands them the most perverse of the inquirers (*Commentary*

6.13). By contrast, Chrysostom takes the words **among you** to betoken Christ's humility.

1:27. Cf. Mark 1:7–8, though only at 1:33 does our Evangelist make the Baptist say that Christ 'baptizes with the Holy Spirit'. With 3:29 in mind, Pope Gregory cites the custom in Hebrew law whereby a man may espouse a woman by unlatching the shoe of another man who has waived his right to the match (Aquinas 1997: 53).

The Descent of the Dove

1:28. Bethabara or **Bethany**? Origen (*Commentary* 6.24) preferred the former reading on the grounds that it was favoured by the manuscripts, that he knew a place with a similar name whose residents alleged that this had been the scene of the baptism, and that Bethany, the home of Lazarus, clearly lay elsewhere. Hastings objects that in fact the reading 'Bethany' is attested in the majority of Greek manuscripts, and that there may have been more than one site of that name (1906: 192).

1:29. Chrysostom suggests that Christ returned so that false notions which had arisen from his baptism might be corrected (*Homily* 17.1). In Lev 16 the **taking away** of Israel's sins was effected not by the sacrifice of a lamb but by the release of the scapegoat into the wilderness; none the less, Calvin insists that **takes away** here must mean not only 'absolves' but 'bears the penalty' (1959: 3). Hutcheson infers from the definite article that this Lamb supersedes all human sacrifices (1972: 24). Eriugena argues that the obliterated sin is that of Adam, which no personal oblation could have cancelled (p. 318 Migne). Verrochio, assisted by Leonardo, painted the episode according to the Synoptic accounts, but attached to the idle hand of the Baptist a pennant bearing the legend *Ecce Agnus* ('Behold the Lamb'). In the medieval pageant of Corpus Christi, the Baptist 'went before' the eucharist, showing 'the same to be **the Lambe that takes away our sinne**' (Fisher 1917: 99). Prayer to the Lamb of God who takes away the sin of the world is an indispensable part of the Gloria in sung liturgies, whether the setting be as slow and solemn as Vivaldi's or as jubilant as that of Beethoven in the *Missa Solemnis*. The Agnus Dei is also a characteristic element of the orchestral requiem, supplying the finale in those of Cherubini, Berlioz and Dvorak, though Fauré and Verdi make it the fifth of seven movements, Duruflé the sixth of nine, Victoria the seventh of ten and Cimarosa the eleventh of twelve. In the fifth of six movements in Benjamin Britten's *War Requiem*, the traditional formula, 'Lamb of

God, who takest away the sins of the world, have mercy on us' forms an antiphonal chorus to Wilfred Owen's lyric, 'There is one who hangs where shelled roads meet'. In Geoffrey Burgon's Requiem the Agnus Dei follows a funereal poem by John of the Cross, and alternates with a song of enamoured rapture from the same pen.

1:30–1. The words **after me** occur at Matt 3:11 and Mark 1:7, but only this Evangelist makes the Baptist speak of Christ as his precursor. Dodd argues that the phrase may indicate only that Christ is the recognized superior of the Baptist (1963: 274). Augustine interweaves the Johannine narrative with that of the Synoptics; thus at verse 31 he adduces Matt 1:14, where Jesus is baptized to fulfil all righteousness (*Homilies* 4.12).

1:32. At Mark 1:11 etc., it is Jesus who perceives the dove, and a voice from heaven proclaims him Son of God. Against the supposition that Christ is adopted here as the Son of God, Cyril of Alexandria infers from the perfect tense of the verb *memenēken* that the Spirit remains upon him from eternity. The descent of the dove is frequently depicted in early Christian and Byzantine iconography, as well as by such Western painters as Giotto, Verrochio, Poussin and El Greco. Since, however, every representation shows the Baptist pouring water over Jesus, it is not the Fourth Gospel that supplies the text. The theory that the dove was 'sacrosanct' in Jewish ritual is shown to be baseless in Hastings (1906: 491). Conybeare notes that in Philo, *On the Change of Names* 42, the turtle-dove is a emblem of prudent speech or *logos* (1910: 166), but the most celebrated dove in the Jewish Scriptures is the one released by Noah on the day when the Flood abated (Gen 8:10). Allegorists concluded that this dove was an emblem of the Holy Spirit, the deluge being clearly a return to the chaos preceding the creation. Marsh reports the opinion of G. F. Knight that, as the name Jonah signifies dove, this episode prefigures the dispensation to the Gentiles (1968: 125). This same dove, as an emblem of the true Church, is contrasted at Song of Songs 6:9 with the many heretical concubines of Christ (Aquinas 1997: 61–2).

1:33. Contrast the descent and ascent of the angels in v. 52. The descent of the dove, says Augustine, signifies peace, and is thus an admonition to those who divide the Church by pretending that only their sect administers a valid baptism (*Homilies* 5.12). J. A. T. Robinson (1962: 24) compares *1QS* 4.20, which perhaps foretells that God will sprinkle the 'spirit of truth' like water upon his human emissary. According to Calvin (1959: 33), Bucer compared the token given to Moses at Ex 3:12.

1:34. As Calvin notes (1959: 35) the Baptist knew the Messiah already at Matt 3:14. Augustine decides that he knew the Messiah, but not that he would baptize in the Holy Spirit (*Homilies* 5.2).

The First Disciples

1:35–7. See vv. 29 and 41. Hutcheson (1972: 26–7) notes with approval that John is taking the opportunity to say privately what he preached the day before. Augustine takes the opportunity here to say that we are all the sheep of Christ, sent into the midst of wolves (*Homilies* 7.5).

1:38. Cf. 18:4; Barrett (1955: 144) compares the words of Jacob at Gen 37:15. What, asks Vaughan, linking this question to verse 14, 'Was then thy dwelling?'; he concludes that it is in 'my sinful heart' (1914: 516).

1:39. Hutcheson observes that Christ speaks only to those who seek him (1972: 27). Augustine, noting that it was now the tenth hour (v. 40), infers that the title 'Rabbi' (or master) points to the Ten Commandments (*Homilies* 7.10). As William Ramsay comments (1994: 5), this Evangelist marks the hours with more exactitude than the other three, who mention only the third, the sixth and the ninth.

1:40–1. In Mark 1:16, etc. Simon/Peter and Andrew are called together. From the fact that Peter follows Andrew, Henry takes the opportunity to disparage papal claims (1991: 1922, cols 1–2). Natalis Alexander deduces only that one is called to be an evangelist as soon as one is called to be a Christian (1840: 78). The title **Messiah**, equivalent to the Greek *Christos*, means 'the anointed one', and may therefore denote a prophet, priest or king. Only in the Christian Redeemer are the three offices united, and in Jewish writing before the time of Christ the term is almost always used of the heir of David who is to rule in God's new kingdom. Seldom do we hear that the triumphs or sufferings of any man will inaugurate this kingdom (Schürer 1979: 503, 526, etc.), and accordingly the Messiah in the present Gospel is one who is to reveal all things and raise the dead (4:25, 11:27), but not a captain of armies, although Jesus himself is more than once suspected of coveting an earthly throne.

1:42. Even the Christian Sayers cannot imagine such compliance without much grumbling and false hopes of insurrection (1943: 84–5). Protestants exultantly quote this verse against the Roman claim that Peter was the first of the disciples (Elsley 1844: 414). Theissen suggests that **son of Jonah** (cf. Matt 16:17, John 21:17, though the NRSV here reads 'John') was a sobriquet bestowed on Peter because his mission resembled that of Jonah to Nineveh (1978: 11). For **Cephas** cf. 1 Cor 1:12, 9:5, 15:5; for **Petros** Matt 16:18; for Christ as a stone, 1 Cor 1:23, Matt 21:42, etc. Fitzmyer shows that Cephas was an Aramaic name before Christ, but Peter was not a Greek one (1981: 116–20).

More Disciples

1:43a. Martyn (1976) suggests that in the prototype it was Simon who came to Philip, saying 'We have found Elijah', so that all three of the appellatives disowned by John the Baptist were successively bestowed on the true Messiah. The Muslim *Gospel of Barnabas* concurs, with the proviso that the messenger springs from Isaac and the Messiah from Ishmael, the elder son of Abraham (1907: 238). Jesus surpasses Elijah when he raises the dead in chapter 11 and multiplies gifts of nature in chapter 6; alone of the four, however, our Evangelist sends neither John nor Jesus to the wilderness.

1:43b–4a. Murphy-O'Connor notes that while the town is condemned at Matthew 11:24, its sons are commended here (1998: 205). It lay about a mile north of the sea of Tiberias. The 'networking' that ensues, to use the term of Malina and Rohrbaugh, may be contrasted with the calling of the disciples in other Gospels (1998: 57). Eckhart, who combines the accounts, maintains that only detachment makes us receptive enough to **follow**, without presuming to outrun God or walk beside him (1958: 168–80).

1:45. Cf. Deut 18:15. Christ is never son of Mary in this Gospel or **son of Joseph** in Mark (cf. 6:3). G. Buchanan draws attention to the kingly role of Joseph, son of Jacob, in Samaritan literature (1968: 159–60), but Calvin accuses Philip of mistaking both Christ's place of birth and his ancestry (1959: 32). Chrysostom thinks that Nathanael's question reveals superior insight (*Homily* 20.1).

1:46a. Nathanael, whose name in Hebrew means 'God gave', is absent from other Gospels, but reappears at 21:2, where we hear that he comes from Cana, the scene of Christ's first miracle. These facts lend some weight to Catchpole's thesis (1998) that Nathanael is the disciple whom Jesus loved. He is probably not one of the twelve, as Augustine first admitted (*Homily* 7.17); to Brodie he personifies the spiritual progeny of Jacob (1993: 168–70).

The Son of Man

1:46b. The question foreshadows the false distinction drawn by the Jews between themselves and Jesus (Södering 2000). Nazareth is not mentioned in Josephus or the Talmud, though a new discovery proves that it appeared in the priestly calendar (O'Neill 1999: 135). Renan disparaged nineteenth-century Nazareth as 'a heap of huts built without style' (1927: 44), but Farrar compared the little town in its valley to 'a handful of pearls in a basket of emeralds' (1901:

39). According to the *Gospel of Philip*, Nazarene means 'revealer of things hidden' (J. A. Robinson 1988: 146).

1.47–8, See note on v 52 for the contrast between Nathanael and Jacob, already discerned by Barrett (1955: 154). Some think that Nathanael, like Jonah, had withdrawn under the fig-tree for some purpose (Westcott 1903: 27; Brown 1966: 83; Brodie 1993: 167). Barrett, however, finds that this tree is associated in Jewish thought with peace, prosperity and the study of Scripture (1955: 154). Moule (1954) notes that it recurs in other tales of Jewish sagacity; Nicklas (2000) speaks for the modern age by leaving the judgement to the reader.

1:49–51. Cf. 1:45. Dodd (1953a: 229) remarks that the title which is mockingly accorded to the crucified Jesus at Matt 27:42 and Mark 15:32 is here employed sincerely. 'Son of God' and 'King of Israel' appear to be synonymous: see Ps 2:7 and Lindars 1972: 119. Purvis notes that 'Israelite' was a term used by Samaritans to distinguish themselves from Jews (1975: 171). The term is of wider extension than 'king of the Jews' (Mark 15:32, etc.), but Calvin still regards it as a sign of immature faith (1959: 43).

1:52. Cf. Gen 28:12. Christ, as Theobald says (1988: 288), displaces Bethel, and we may add that Nathanael is worthier than Jacob: the latter, though he received the name 'Israel' when he looked on God (or rather his angel), was a liar and a coward, whereas Nathanael is an 'Israelite in whom there is no guile'. Consequently, he is shown not merely a ladder but the opened heaven, and sees that the Son of Man is no mere angel, but the captain of the host (cf. Abbott 1906: 595–6).

Son of Man is not a Greek locution; the Hebrew equivalent in the Psalms and Ezekiel denotes a human being in his weakness (Ezek 37:3; Ps 8:6; cf. Heb 2:7), while the phrase 'one like a son of man' is applied to angels in Daniel, and to Christ (with a reminiscence of Ezek 1:26) at Rev 1:13. As an appellation of Christ it occurs repeatedly in the Gospels, but almost always with the definite article; since this makes still more questionable Greek, and since there is only one verse in the New Testament (Acts 7:54) where the expression is used by someone other than Christ, it is widely held to be an echo of his own Aramaic speech. No speaker in the Synoptic Gospels doubts that it refers to Christ himself, and some scholars cite an Aramaic idiom (*hohu gabra* or *bar nasha*) which was current in Roman Palestine as a circumlocution for the pronoun 'I' (Vermes 1973: 160–91). If that is so, the Evangelists misconstrued it, for the prophecy that the Son of Man will sit at God's right hand is plainly modelled on Dan 7:13, where 'one like a son of man' is enthroned by God and given power to judge the nations (Manson 1943: 227–9). While this figure is a personification of Israel under the tyranny of strangers, there are texts of Jewish origin (2 Esdras and *2 Enoch*) which imply that the Son of Man is a personal being who will redeem his people at the end of time (Borsch 1967: 145–66). Bultmann supposed that Jesus saw himself as the precursor of this heavenly redeemer (1952: 9), and his theory finds an ally in the Fourth Gospel, where the Son of Man comes from heaven (6:62), and the onlookers are so far from equating him with Jesus that they once exclaim 'who is this Son of man?' (12:34).

Epilogue: The Lamb and his Wrath

The lamb divides with the fish the honour of being the most frequent symbol of Christ in the art of the Roman catacombs. Dodd (1963: 270–1) surmises that the title 'Lamb of God' (*amnos tou theou*) at v. 29 is traditional, though there is no documented precedent. Marsh (1968: 123–4) enumerates six recognized parallels or antecedents for the image of Christ as Lamb: the paschal lamb of Ex 12, the servant lamb of Isa 53:7, the scapegoat of Leviticus 16, the lamb that was offered daily in the Temple, the paschal lamb interpreted as a type of the Christian eucharist, and the wrathful Lamb in the book of Revelation. A reference to Isaac might be suspected if we were certain that the legend which reverses the substitution of the ram and makes his blood an oblation for Israel was already current in the first century (Spiegel 1969: 38–44, 80–5). But were all these lambs the same lamb, even in apostolic times? The modern Christian thinks, like Peter, of the suffering servant, who 'was led as a lamb to the slaughter' (Isa 53:7; cf. 1 Pet 2:22 with 1:19 and 2:25). This emblem of meek innocence has been cherished by hymnodists and poets of orthodox persuasion:

> I praise the loving Lord who maketh me
> His type by harmless sweet simplicity:
> Yet he the Lamb of lambs incomparably
> (Rossetti 1995: 404)

In Revelation, however, the Lamb is a seven-horned warrior, who tramples the nations in his holy ire (5:6, 6:15, 17:14, etc.). Although this lamb 'was slain' at 5:6, it is not, in Baur's opinion, the paschal lamb of our Evangelist (1878: 162). Jung concludes that the Lamb of the Apocalypse is the 'shadow' – the subconscious and half-assimilated complement – of the Christ preached in the Gospels (1968: 105–6). Ashton too opines that the 'decidedly ruthless' Lamb of Revelation has 'little in common with the human Jesus pointed to by John' (1991: 259). For all that, we should remember that the Baptist who proclaims the Lamb is also the only character who denounces the wrath of God on the unconverted (3:36), and that the Passover originates in the shedding of a lamb's blood to avert the angel of Death (Exodus 12:21–30). Ashton notes that the triumphs of the Lamb, as a representative of Israel, were recounted in the *Testament of Joseph* (19.8) and in the *Targum Neofiti* (1991: 259–60). Blake's question to the 'tyger', 'Did he who made the Lamb make thee?', is of a piece with his other animadversions on the cruelty that warps the love of the biblical creator (1969: 173). Another poem, 'Little Lamb, who made thee?', portrays Christ as he ought to be (in Blake's view), and not as he appears in the Johannine texts (1969: 115). Lewis juxtaposes the lamb with the lion of Judah (Rev 5:4–6) at the end of his *Voyage of the Dawn Treader*, where Aslan first appears as a lamb of brilliant whiteness and then in his leonine form (1997: 186–9).

Symbols of Purity:
John 2:1–22

Prologue: The First of the Signs

All harmonies of the Gospels, taking note of 2:11, have made this the earliest of Christ's miracles. It evidently reminded Christian artists of the miracles in the wilderness, for depictions of it on Christian sarcophagi furnish Christ with the wand of Moses (Trench 1904: 225). Augustine says that it ought to evoke our admiration more than our surprise, as it does not countermand but accelerates the processes of nature (*Homilies* 8.1). The statement in the Book of Common Prayer that Christ performed this work to hallow the institution of marriage would not, however, commend itself to Augustine, who maintains that the feast prefigures the believer's union with the heavenly Bridegroom (*Homilies* 8.5). Another celibate, Cyprian of Carthage, urged that we ourselves transform the water of revelation into wine when we divine the Christian sense of a Jewish scripture (Letter 63). Bede grants that the story does at least prove the legitimacy of marriage (Aquinas 1997: 80), but it was left to commentators of the later Middle Ages to apologize for Christ's indifference to the bond of motherhood. Notwithstanding Mary's co-operation in the miracle, modern feminists also feel that the mother of Christ is slighted in a Gospel which consistently refuses her a name.

The miracle at Cana is peculiar to the Fourth Gospel, and is described there as the **first of the signs** that awakened faith in his disciples. The word 'sign' (Greek *sêmeion*), which is used by the Fourth Evangelist where the others speak of *dunameis*, 'mighty works', implies that the feats reveal not merely the power but the authority of the thaumaturge and the purpose of his mission. In the twentieth century many commentators have surmised that our Evangelist based his narrative on an earlier collection of signs, and in Fortna's reconstruction (1988) the miraculous draught of chapter 21 is the third of these, to be followed by the healing at Bethesda, the feeding of the multitude, the opening of the blind man's eyes, and the resurrection of Lazarus. This theory, however, countermands the obvious sense of 21:14, does not explain why our Evangelist failed to complete the reckoning or to expunge all traces of it, and puts words into his mouth when it describes the other miracles as signs.

The Feast at Cana

2:1a. For Bede the **third day** signifies the dawning age of grace, which supersedes the ages of the patriarchs and the Law (Aquinas 1997: 80). Augustine (*On the Trinity* 8.4) contends that this marriage prefigures the heavenly nuptials in which Christ himself is the groom. Eusebius, *Onomasticon* identifies **Cana of Galilee** as the Cana that lies in the land of Asher at Josh 19:28, while Jerome (Letter 46.4) asserts that it was visible from Nazareth. The qualification **of Galilee** distinguishes this site from its namesakes at Matt 2:1 and Josephus, *Antiquities* 13.391.

2:1b. Neither here nor elsewhere does the Evangelist name the **mother of Jesus**, nor does he ever speak of a human father. Hoskyns (1947: 188) rejects and Brodie (1993: 174) endorses Loisy's claim that she is a type of Israel. Chrysostom suggests that the mother of Jesus and her family were invited because they were local celebrities (*Homily* 21.1) – all the more reason, no doubt, to suspect that Sayers was right to present the disciples as uninvited guests (1943: 94–5). Stanton remarks that Mary gives instructions like a relative of the groom (1985: 238); nevertheless, though the compliment at 2:10

should have been addressed to him, the inference that Christ himself was the bridegroom (Baigent et al. 1982: 302–3) is a fantasy, contradicted rather than supported by the metaphorical usage of the term at 3:29.

2:2–3. Codex Sinaiticus and other versions add 'for the wine of the marriage was exhausted'. If this was the first sign, why did Mary expect a miracle? Because, replies Romanus, she was conscious of a miracle at Christ's birth (*Cantica* 7.7 at 1963: 51). Cf. Chrysostom, *Homily* 21.1. Alcuin, however, argues that her unseasonable demand for a sign typifies the impatience of the Jews (Aquinas 1997: 81).

2:4a. The same construction **what have I to do with thee** (AV) is used by indignant demons at the approach of Christ (Mark 1:24), and all the Fathers followed Irenaeus (*Against Heresies* 3.16) in construing Christ's words as a reprimand to Mary. Hoskyns implies that Nonnus was the first Greek to deny this (1947: 188); Trench records the attempts of Bernard and Maldonatus to show that Christ did not mean to dishonour the Blessed Virgin, but to prove that he was acting from humanity rather than from personal affection (1904: 109). For Blake the commandment to 'obey thy parents' is annulled here (1969: 755); yet Wesley contends that Christ employs this 'constant appellation' here and at 19:26 because he 'regarded his Father above all' (*MCNT* II.4). The bourgeois Strauss maintains that both the acerbity of Jesus and his mother's nonchalance are incredible (1892: 524, 527). Giblin (1980) sees a pattern of self-revelation through apparent inconsistency that recurs in chapters 4, 7 and 11. Isaac of Stella's paraphrase is neat: 'I have power in common with my Father, weakness with my mother' (1979: 86). Protestants discover an admonition 'not to transfer to Mary the things that belong to God' (Calvin 1959: 47). 'What had she to do with you / but tempt you from your father?' asks Ted Hughes (2000: 134). Ancient commentators were more disturbed by the Gnostic marriage of this verse with Mark 3:33 to imply that Mary was not the true mother of Christ (Augustine, *On the Trinity* 8.5).

2:4b. Fortna sees the remnants of poor editing in the apparent contradiction between Christ's words and his subsequent action. Hutcheson assumes that there was some delay (1972: 33), but Romanus avers that Christ performs the miracle before his **hour** out of reverence to his mother (*Cantica* 7.11–12 at 1963: 52–3). Temple (1961: 36) and Hoskyns (1947: 188) are among those who argue that the **hour** to which Christ alludes is that of the Crucifixion, as at 12:23.

2:5. To one Victorian preacher 'Mary' exemplifies the spirit of pure womanhood which 'unsensualizes coarse and common things' by domestic service (Robertson 1906: 218). Chrysostom points out that the use of servitors rendered the miracle more conspicuous and more credible (*Homily* 21.2). Brodie, deploring Schnackenburg's neglect of the disciples, urges that the power to induce obedience is the true miracle (1993: 173). Ann Ridler concurs that 'the atoms did not change, but those who drank' (1994: 160).

The Miracle

2:6. Bede derides the **purification** as a Pharisaic rite like the washing of the hands at Mark 7:3 (Aquinas 1997: 83). Chrysostom (*Homily* 21.2) objects that wine would never have been stored in such a vessel. Isaac of Stella argues that, as the week contains the seventh day apart from the days of labour, so the six vessels represent the insufficiency of human striving; the two measures stand for the dual sense of Scripture, and the old wine for the wisdom of the Gentiles, which causes them to 'reel like drunken men' (1979: 87, 85, citing Ps 106:27).

2:7–8. On Hoskyns' computation (1947: 189), the entire capacity of the vessels was between 108 and 162 gallons. Strauss, without calculating, finds the quantity extravagant and dangerous (1892: 522). Hilary of Poitiers (*On the Trinity* 3.5) compares the wine of the eucharistic chalice, whose spiritual nature is known to the one who pours it in, but not to the one who pours it out. Hoskyns (1947: 189) follows Westcott in noting that the verb 'draw out' anticipates 4:11–16.

2:9. The title *architriclinios* is late and rare, and passed into the vernacular as the proper name Archetriclyn (Happé 1975: 513); Trench, however, quotes Sir 32:1–2 to demonstrate that the office at least was known among the Jews (1904: 113). Alcuin asserts that he reclined as guest in chief at the head of the couches, and perhaps held the office of priest among the Jews (Aquinas 1997: 84). Hoskyns suggests that his ignorance prefigures that of Nicodemus, the Samaritan woman and Pilate (1947: 189).

2:10. In the fifteenth-century *Gospel of Barnabas*, this compliment is addressed to Christ, not only because it was he who wrought the miracle, but because he is revealed at 3:29 to be the groom of the elect (1907: 15). Romanus avers that the transmutation of the water is foreshadowed by the parting of the Red Sea (*Cantica* 7.4 at 1963: 50), while Trench contrasts the conversion of the Nile to blood by Moses (1904: 121). To Radulphus the wine suggests the ardour of the converted soul (p. 1745 Migne); Grassi (1972) indeed suspects an allusion to Pentecost, since the Spirit is likened to water in the Gospel (7:39), and the Galilean apostles who receive it in Acts 2:12 are mistaken for drunkards.

2:11. The work of God, as Robertson says, took 30 years to ripen, or rather thousands (1906: 216). Even then the miracle is performed 'allusively', as Lindars comments (1972: 131), and it is only the disciples who are conscious of a sign. Sacy rejects the opinion that the text refers only to the first sign that Christ performed in Cana (1840: 87), yet it is true that all the numbered signs occur in Galilee.

Interlude: Christ and Dionysus

Incredulous readers have always been inclined to compare the miracles of Christ to those of wonder-workers, and since Dionysus was the god of wine, it was inevitable that the first of the signs should have been construed as an imitation of his mysteries. Even Justin Martyr could not deny that the cults had something in common (*First Apology* 54), and Vurtheim (1920) furnishes half a dozen references, which reveal that Dionysus was occasionally credited with the spontaneous creation of wine from water or from nothing; none of these, however, suggests that his worshippers (except in myth) could imitate the alchemy that is here ascribed to Christ. Nor, as Trench reminds us (1904: 119), does the narrative condone the incipient drunkenness of the *architriclinios*, let alone the intoxication that ancient texts associate with the Dionysian orgies. Scholars of the early twentieth century maintained that Dionysus and Christ were only two of the many 'dying and rising gods' who populated the ancient Mediterranean, but today it seems improbable that this hypothetical category will survive the criticisms of J. Z. Smith (1987).

It was commonly held in antiquity, however, that the Yahweh of the Jews was Dionysus, and that one of the latter's many names, Sabazius, was a variant of the Hebrew Yahweh Sabaoth, 'Lord of Hosts'. An early Byzantine tragedy, *Christus Patiens* (*Christ Suffering*), robs the *Bacchae* of Euripides for a third of its materials, preserving a number of verses from the Greek play that would otherwise have been lost. Another Byzantine poet, Nonnus, versified both the Johannine account of Christ and the myth of Dionysus, though without implying that the two were one. Yeats assimilates the Matthean story of the Nativity to a myth in which the infant Dionysus is torn to pieces in his cradle, and Athena, the maiden goddess of wisdom, stumbles on the traces of the crime:

> I saw a staring virgin stand
> Where holy Dionysus died
> And pluck the heart out of his side.
> (Yeats 1990: 258)

The first line recalls John 20:25, the third John 20:34. In Wole Soyinka's *The Bacchae of Euripides*, the god is represented by a sitting Christ, whose crown of thorns has given way to the 'ambiguous ivy-wreath' (1973: 286). Stibbe observes that the Dionysus of tragedy, like Christ, is a god who comes to his own and his own receive him not (1992: 134 47). In the *Bacchae*, however, Dionysus is a murderer – for Rēné Girard, the antitype of Christ (1972: 203–8).

Christ Expels the Traders

2:12. R. H. Lightfoot suggests that this topographical detail is a compliment to Capernaum, 'a kind of headquarters' to the Galilean mission which is omitted by the Fourth Evangelist (1956: 111).

2:13. The Evangelist's indication of the date is contradicted both by Burkitt (1915–16) and by Manson (1951), one arguing for the Feast of the Dedication and the other for the Feast of Tabernacles. J. A. T. Robinson replies that the 'specific provision for the tables to be set up prior to Passover makes this very arbitrary' (1984: 459).

El Greco, *Christ Driving the Traders from the Temple*. National Gallery, London.

2:14. Cf. Mark 11:15 etc. Jeremias (1969: 149) seeks evidence for the abuses which are narrated only here. The expulsion arrested the business of the Temple, as the money-changers supplied the Tyrian coin in which religious dues were paid (Barrett 1955: 164). Since these included a tax to finance the offerings, Neusner opines that the meaning of Christ's act became evident only when the eucharist supplanted the atoning sacrifices (1991: 101). Calvin, while admitting that the offences of the traders may have been small and that we might have expected Christ to begin by teaching them, concludes that 'something new and strange' was required to produce conviction (1959: 51).

2:15. 'In reformation, it is good to make thorough work' (Henry 1991: 1926, col. 2). As no weapon lay to hand in the sacred precinct, the whip must have been a makeshift, perhaps (as Wesley suggests) from rushes on the ground (*MCNT* at II.15). Perhaps it is because it is mentioned only in this Gospel that Heracleon makes it stand for the Holy Spirit (Origen, *Commentary* 10.33). Brandon's conjecture that Jesus was supported by an armed force relies on the testimony of Mark 11:18 that it was this riot which gave rise to the conspiracy against Christ (1968: 83). Hutcheson, by contrast, thinks it remarkable that 'one man had chased them all' (1972: 38), while Clarke suggests that the merchants were disabled by a sense of sin, like the guards at 18:6 (1740: 48).

2:16–17. The quotation conflates Jer 7:11 with Isa 56:7. Barrett (1955: 165) compares the vocabulary of Mark 11:17 and Luke 2:49. As Lindars comments (1972: 137), the episode and the appropriation of the prophetic verse are of a piece with Christ's rejection of the outward forms of Judaism in the Synoptic Gospels. Locke notes that Christ's disclosure of his Sonship seems to have passed 'without regard' (1790: 43).

2:18. Cf. 2:11. Harvey points out that demands for a sign, though discouraged by the rabbis, were excused by such texts as Ex 4:11 and Tob 5:2 (1976: 96–100).

The Saying about the Temple

2:19. This utterance is couched as a threat in the testimony of 'false witnesses' at Mark 14:58 and parallels; it is minatory in Christ's own mouth at *Gospel of Thomas* 71. A similar prediction is ascribed to the 'Lord of the sheep' at *1 Enoch* 90.29, and Natalis Alexander adduces Col 2:9: 'In him dwelleth all the fullness of the Godhead' (1840: 92). Others suggest that Christ is the prophesied messenger whom God will send to purify the temple at Mal 3:1–3 (Goguel 1928: 250). This conjecture illustrates Martyn's thesis (1976) that Christ is portrayed in the Gospel as Elijah, and explains why Handel set these verses from Malachi as a crescendo of three movements (recitative, then aria, then chorus) near the beginning of his *Messiah*. Henry, however, distinguishes Malachi's messenger, 'John Baptist', from the Lord who will visit the Temple in his prophecy (1991: 1926, col. 1). Berriman contends ingeniously that, but for this visit, the prophecy at Hag 2:9 that 'the glory of the latter house will excel that of the former' would have been proved false when the Temple was destroyed (1737: 178–83).

2:20. Work on Herod's Temple began in 20/19 BC (Josephus, *Antiquities* 15.38), and thus this conversation ought to have taken place after AD 27. This year did not, however, mark the conclusion of the project, which continued up to AD 63. It may be, as Marsh proposes (1968: 166), that the author, writing after the destruction of the new Temple, was mistaken in his chronology; or it may be that this dialogue takes place during an interim. The Septuagint version of Ezra 5:16 can be cited to prove that the aorist tense was used of work on buildings that had not yet been completed (Kidder 1737: 97). The *Gospel of Nicodemus* 4 applies the calculation to Solomon's temple, while Calvin quotes the prophecy of '49 weeks in Daniel 9.25', applying this to the Temple that was built by returning exiles in the fifth century BC (1959: 56). Augustine (*Homily* 10.11) entertains the conjecture that 46 is the number of Adam (A = 2, D = 4, M = 40), and the theory that the figure represents the age of Christ is not extinct (Kokkinos 1989). Theissen betrays the different interests of the modern scholar when he comments that the prophecy would have alienated those employed in the building, or in any trade that depended on the cult (1978: 56–7).

2:21. 'He that built the world can do much more', says Herbert in defence of the literal meaning (1974: 50). And, as an English laureate reminded his countrymen after the First World War, it was not Christ who wrought the destruction: 'We have destroyed the temple, and in three days / He hath rebuilt it – he hath made all things new' (Noyes 1920: 304).

2:22. Calvin writes that the Pharisees were unworthy of a clearer revelation (1959: 55), while Sacy observes that even the disciples failed to under-stand allusions to the rising of Christ at Mark 9:10 etc. (1840: 93). Some Protestants absolve Christ of deceit with the conjecture that he pointed to his own body (Henry 1991; 1927, col. 1). Giles Fletcher makes a conceit from the metaphor, likening the legs of Christ to 'marble pillars', veined with 'azure rivulets' (*Christ's Victory and Triumph*, 2.97–104, in Hunter 1977: 52). Eva Gore-Booth's couplet, 'To him shall be given a house more fair than the Temple he built for God, / The Glory of God itself is the Temple that manifests him' (1925: 14) interweaves Johannine with Pauline promises (cf. 2 Cor 3:18 and 5:1; Phil 3:21). The disciples are equally deaf to a forecast of the Resurrection at Mark 9:9–10.

Epilogue: The Fall of the Temple

We need not doubt that Christ foresaw the destruction of the Temple, for a prediction of this kind was uttered eight years before the Roman sack of Jerusalem (Josephus, *Jewish War* 6.5.3), and in any case, as a portion of the building survived the inadvertent fire of AD 70, the utterances ascribed to him lack the circumstantiality of hindsight (E. P. Sanders 1993: 257). It was plain to all that the Second Temple, built by returning exiles in the fifth century BC, was not the one ordained in the last eight chapters of Ezekiel. Speech or action against the Temple, as E. P. Sanders shows, could be thought to presage the inception of a new era in which the edifice of stone would be replaced by an incorporeal habitation (1985: 79–90); Christ appears to proclaim himself the corner-stone of this edifice at Mark 12:10 (cf. Ps 118:22). The Church – Christ's body in many Pauline passages – is a temple of living stones at Eph 2:14–21 and 1 Pet 2:4–5.

While the Fourth Evangelist implies that Christ anticipated the metaphorical application of the word 'temple' to the body (1 Cor 6:19), he indicates that the audience understood it as a reference to the building near at hand. Although the saying in this form is unique, the event that prompts it is recounted in all three Synoptic Gospels – unless we suppose that Jesus was allowed to cause the same disturbance on distinct occasions. Those who accept the historical priority of the Fourth Gospel are free to maintain that the others are mistaken in their chronology; otherwise one may speculate that the author has refashioned the order of previous accounts. Marsh (1968: 163), for example, seems to agree with Origen that the Gospels are for the most part true both literally and spiritually, but that they improve at times on the outward course of history for the edification of the inner man (*Commentary* 10.4/5 etc.).

Prologue: The Figure of Nicodemus

Nicodemus, known only from this Gospel, reappears to defend Christ at 7:50 and to bury him at 19:39. His name, if it is Greek, is derived from roots that signify 'victory' and 'people'; Strack-Billerbeck, however, suspected that it represents the Jewish appellative 'Niqdom', which was borne by at least three eminent contemporaries of Jesus. None of these three, says Bauckham (1996), could have been the nocturnal visitor, but he shares so many traits with a Niqdom of the Gurion family that, if both are real, it is hard to believe that they were not related. An Aramaic list of Christ's disciples includes one Naqqai, though his name, like the name Niqdom, is of uncertain derivation (Bauckham 1996: 17). Whatever his origins, exegetes have generally been censorious.

Augustine thinks his timidity a symptom of carnal-mindedness (*Homily* 11.5); Calvin sees an example of 'frail and transient faith', while Luther cites his obtuseness as a proof that only those who are called are able to believe (Rupp and Watson 1969: 322). Eriugena thinks him a specimen of faith perfected but not enriched by works (p. 314 Migne).

Poets and writers of fiction have served him better. In the *Gospel of Nicodemus*, a popular text in medieval times, the man who came to Christ by night is rewarded by a vision of his descent in to hell and deliverance of the dead. In the Muslim *Gospel of Barnabas*, he gives Jesus hospitality (1907: 258), provides the lamb for the supper (1907: 260) and is found in company with the 'seven disciples' (1907: 270; cf. John 21:2). In Henry Vaughan's poem 'Night' he 'sees the Sun at midnight', thereby imitating mystics who had passed the threshold of the nether world (1914: 522–3). In Andrew Young's verse drama *Nicodemus*, on the other hand, he is cut down by the Jews after he becomes the first witness scene of the Resurrection (1985: 252). The text itself suggests that he is more than a historical figure: at v. 13, the intimate pronouns 'I' and 'thou' give way to the collectives 'we' and 'you', while v. 19, though it passes over the head of Nicodemus, is answered at 12:34 by a crowd of Jews who could hardly have overheard the dialogue.

The New Birth

2:23–5. Brodie suggests that this passage prepares us for the ensuing dialogue, in which Jesus reads the heart of Nicodemus through a veil of flattery (1993: 195). The faith which awaits the evidence of miracles is pre-eminently the faith of Jews, as Barrett remarks (1955: 171). Cyril of Alexandria, however, maintains that Christ does not slight this faith but displays an exemplary caution in the acceptance of new converts for the edification of future ministers (1.213–14 Pusey).

3:1–2. A **leader of the Jews** must be a member of the Sanhedrin, or ruling council, of Jerusalem (Barrett 1955: 170); as Marsh observes, the title **rabbi** is one that he must also have claimed for himself (1968: 185). Santucci sneers that a 'petulant intellectual' was seeking a 'private interview', out of earshot of the rabble (1974: 125–6). The words **by night** encouraged the 'Nicodemians' of Calvin's day to cloak their Protestant sympathies (1970: 147). Where Hutcheson writes that Nicodemus' interest proves the efficacy of miracles (1972: 40), Chrysostom objects that in ascribing the works to God he fails to recognize the divinity of Christ (*Homily* 24.2). One Puritan was bold enough to reason that if God alone does wonders, there is no such thing as witchcraft (Scot 1972: 89).

3:3. Very truly (Greek *Amen, amen*) is a typically Johannine construction, thought by Lindars to indicate a saying 'found in sources' (1972: 120). Chrysostom points out that the Greek may mean 'born from above or born again' (*Homily* 24.2); the former is more compatible with 1:13, but Hoskyns notes that the meaning 'again' is attested at Wis 19:6 and Gal 4:9 (1947: 211, with further possibilities). A variant, which refers without ambiguity to a second birth, is applied to Christian baptism in Justin, *1 Apology* 61. The *Gospel of Barnabas* fuses this pronouncement with another verily, verily saying at Matt 18:3, making Christ's interlocutor ask how a man of 40 can become a little child (1907: 229).

The expression **kingdom of God**, employed only here and at v. 5 by the Evangelist, proves to J. A. T. Robinson that the saying is authentic (1962: 274). The 'vast Jewish background' posited by Hoskyns (1947: 212) disappears on scrutiny, since the cognates speak of kingship rather than kingdom and make Israel the sole inheritor of the promise. The kingdom here is the one of which Christ says that it will not be of this world (18:36). Rebirth and the infusion of the spirit are associated, as M. Smith notes, in a magical papyrus of unknown date and provenance (1985: 102–3); water and spirit are synonyms in the preaching of the Naassenes (Hippolytus, *Refutation* 5.2–4/7–9) and in alchemical symbols of regeneration (Jung 1967).

3:4. Nicodemus takes *anôthen* to mean 'again'. The phrase **having grown old** may be hyperbolical, though some take it as an index of his age (cf. Marsh 1968: 185). Augustine contrasts the womb of an earthly mother, through which we receive a temporal inheritance, with that of the Church, through which we receive a portion in the Kingdom (*Homily* 12.5). Nevertheless, Traherne dared to pray that his manhood might be perfected by returning to the womb, his 'early tutor' (1980: 47).

3:5. To Cyril of Alexandria, the gift of the Spirit distinguishes the sonship of the new covenant from that of the Israelites (1.216–20 Pusey). The *Gospel of Philip* explains that the baptized have their salvation on loan until the Spirit imparts it as a gift (J. A. Robinson 1988: 148). In view of 4:2, however, it is safer to see, with Temple, an allusion to the baptism of John (1961: 45). Brodie (1993: 197) takes it as a metaphor for inward purification, but Calvin takes the water to signify nothing more than spirit (1959: 65), and for Chrysostom it is the principle of all life (*Homily* 26.1). Since the Spirit is later identified as the Spirit of truth (14:17), it might not be absurd to take 'born of water' as a reference to Moses, who is called Hydrogenes (or 'water-born') in some Hellenistic texts because of the etymology offered for his name at Ex 2:10.

3:6. Calvin reports but does not endorse the inference of the 'traducianists' that souls are born from souls (1959: 66). As Westcott sees, the dichotomy between body and soul was of no interest to the Fourth Evangelist; for him there is spirit, 'by which our complex natures are united to heaven', and flesh, which binds it 'to earth' (1903: 50). Bultmann holds that the terms are borrowed from Gnostic anthropology, and reveal two 'possibilities of being', one 'hither-manly', one 'thither-godly' (1957: 100).

3:7. As types of the new birth Chrysostom cites the passage of the Red Sea, the purification of Naaman the leper, and the birth of Isaac from the dead womb of Sarah (*Homily* 26.2). Wesley admonishes us that it consists not in having been once baptized, but in continuing evidence of faith, hope, peace and love (1944: 162–73). The Anabaptist Dirk Phillips contends that infants cannot be baptized because they are incapable of the sinlessness which those who have been reborn in Christ are expected to attain through co-operation with the Spirit (Liechty 1994: 216–17).

Witness in the Spirit

3:8. This verse was already famous at the turn of the second century to Ignatius (*Philadelphians* 7.1), who is thus an early witness to the currency of the Gospel, or at least of its prototype. The subject may be either wind or spirit, but even the Latin Fathers who accepted the reading *spiritus* were aware of a simile, as Erasmus notes (1535: 233). Matthew Arnold preserves the Latin reading in his coda, 'The spirit bloweth and is still' (1950: 241). Yet the play on *pnein* and *pneuma* ('blow' and 'wind' in many versions) is better reproduced in Edwin Hatch's hymn 'Breathe on me, Breath of God' (*A & M* 236). After all, neither *pneuma* nor *spiritus* connotes a rushing gale (Maurice 1857: 93), and in this Gospel the Spirit is imparted by a quiet insufflation (20:22), not the rushing blast of Acts 2:2–3. To Mozley the simile intimates that 'what is truly spiritual in man is . . . in a certain sense most natural' (1876: 242). For Luther it implies, in anticipation of 4:24, that Spirit is not confined by place and time (1983: 416). H. Drummond (1953: 151) applies the same words to the ascended Christ, who said of himself on earth 'I know whence I came and whither I go' (8:14).

3:9–10. Nicodemus is called a teacher for the first time; as Marsh observes, the Greek is in fact 'the teacher', as though he were the most eminent of the rabbis (1968: 186). Barrett compares the locution 'teacher of Asia' at *Martyrdom of Polycarp* 12.2 (1955: 176). Coleridge thinks that his fault lies in his ignorance of a truth that was ubiquitously taught in the pagan mysteries (1972: 188); Calvin, on the other hand, maintains that it was Nicodemus himself who misconstrued the new birth as a 'Pythagorean *palingenesis*' (1959: 65).

3:11–12. The plural pronoun is adopted, as at 1 John 1, when a Johannine author speaks as the mouthpiece of the community (cf. North 2001: 31–3). Meeks (1972) argues that the 'Johannine sectarians' here pass sentence on the ignorance of their worldly minded critics. Alcuin suggests that Jesus speaks for himself together with 'all who are born of the Spirit'; other medieval commentators took the plural verb to betoken the compresence of all three members of the Trinity (Aquinas 1997: 111).

The Son of Man

3:13. Cf. 6:62 and 20:17 with Luke 24:51, Acts 1:9 and Eph 4:9–10. The Fathers explain that, while the human flesh of Christ did not antedate his incarnation on earth, he is said to have been the Son of Man in heaven because the attributes of divinity and humanity apply equally to his undivided person (Chrysostom, *Homily* 27.1, etc.). Talbert (1975/6) assembles figures from Jewish and Classical literature who performed an ascent, a descent or both for the good of humankind. Few, as Ashton remarks, descended bodily and ascended in the same guise (1991: 351). Odeberg discovers here a polemic against merkabah mysticism, with its visions of ascent in the heavenly chariot of Ezek 1 (1929: 73). When modern esotericists identify Christ with Enoch ('Levi' 1964: 15), it is no doubt because in the *First Book of Enoch* the patriarch is snatched up into heaven and revealed as the Son of Man.

3:14. When the Israelites in the wilderness suffered snake bites, they were healed by gazing on a brazen serpent which was fashioned by Moses at the behest of God (Num 21:9). In this verse, as at 8:28, 12:32 and 12:34, the term 'lifted up' is purposely ambiguous, not merely, as Chrysostom argues, honorific (*Homily* 27.2). Theophylact (Aquinas 1997: 114) suggests that he was lifted up to sanctify the air, and insists that, just as the serpent was not venomous, so Christ assumes not sin but the likeness of our sinful flesh (Rom 8:3). The brazen serpent itself became an idol (1 Kings 18:4), and in the light of the present verse, it is not hard to understand how a Gnostic group who were known to outsiders as Naassenes or Serpentines could also be said to venerate none but Man and the Son of Man, regarding the latter as the visible portrait of the invisible Logos (Hippolytus, *Refutation* 5.2/7).

3:15. This is the first occurrence in the Gospel of the phrase 'eternal life'. Theophylact contrasts the promise of long life and prosperity under the covenant with Israel (Aquinas 1997: 116).

3:16. 'Given, not lent', writes Meynell (1923: 68); the word **gave** is unusual in this Gospel, and suggests to Lindars a sacrifice like that of Isaac at Gen 22:12

(1972: 159, also citing Rom 8:32). Erasmus allots the verse to the Evangelist (1535: 234), and it frequently stands alone, as in the most moving anthem of Stainer's *Crucifixion*, and in the sermons of many a modern evangelist. Conceding that the wrath of God is more frequently attested in Scripture, Calvin replies that his love precedes all things, but is made apparent through the Son (1959: 73).

3:17–21. Barrett compares Cornutus, *Epidrome* 16, where it is said to be characteristic of the (Stoic) Logos not to punish, but to preserve (1955: 181). Chrysostom, however, warns the reprobate that Christ will return as judge (*Homily* 28.1). The criterion of salvation in v. 18 is reaffirmed in 1 John 4:3 and 15; Pope Gregory inferred that some who do not even pretend to faith will perish before the Last Judgement, (Aquinas 1997: 118). Worse still, whether the verb in v. 20 means 'reproved' or 'exposed', it is still true, as Chrysostom says, that many Christians are convicted by these verses (*Homily* 27.2). Crashaw dovetails v. 19 with 1:5 and 9:5: 'The world's Light shines; shine as it will, / The world will love its darkness still' (1927: 97).

In Longfellow's *Divine Tragedy* (1925: 651), it is at this point that Nicodemus finds his own heart exposed and pronounces Christ a prophet rather than (as before) a fascinating 'dreamer of dreams'.

3:22. If the expression 'born of water' in v. 5 alludes to baptism, the transition of thought in the present verse is not so abrupt as the geographical movement. The Baptist's speech is, as Dodd says (1963: 311), an 'explanatory appendix' to the foregoing dialogue with Nicodemus; at the same time, its references to purification and marriage suggest a deeper interpretation of the wedding feast at Cana.

The Baptist's Testimony

3:23. Schnackenburg places Aenon, with Eusebius, west of the Jordan in ancient Bethan (1968: 412–13), Brown in Ainun of Samaria (1966: 151). Bultmann notes the word Aina in Mandaean texts (1957: 124); Brodie applauds the conjecture that the name was chosen because it was thought to signify 'Springs of Peace' (1993: 201–2). Eusebius, however, translates it as 'eye' or 'their spring' in the *Onomasticon*.

3:24. Cf. Matt 4:12–17, Mark 1:14. Westcott surmises that these events were 'preparatory' to the mission which follows John's imprisonment in the Synoptic accounts (1903: 58). Yet the Evangelist makes John resign his mission voluntarily, and, in contrast to Josephus, Mark and Matthew, does not care to name his gaoler, Herod Antipas, or take notice of his death.

3:25–8. Eriugena guesses that the conversions wrought by Christ had awakened envy among the disciples of the Baptist (p. 324 Migne); the discourse might be a pendant either to the miracle at Cana or, as Lindars remarks, to the midnight colloquy with Nicodemus (1972: 167). From the application of the term **rabbi** to the Baptist, Barrett infers that it was 'not appropriate' to Jesus in v. 2; in the Baptist's reiteration of his own disclaimer, Calvin detects a note of expostulation (1959: 80). Chrysostom holds that the purpose of this speech is to show that Christ is not diminished but exalted by the Baptist's testimony (*Homily* 29.2).

3:29. At 2:9 the master of ceremonies paid unwitting tribute to the power of Christ. Brodie (1993: 191) contends that the bride is all humanity, represented in the next chapter by the official and the Samaritan at the well. Lindars, comparing Mark 2:19, proposes that this is the answer of Christ himself to a question raised by John's disciples (1972: 168). Christ is represented as the Bridegroom of his saints at Mark 2:19 and Eph 5:25–7; perhaps the conjunction of this symbol with a nocturnal interview in the present chapter emboldened poets and commentators to turn the Song of Songs into an allegory of the hymeneal love between the Redeemer and the soul:

> Oh night that joined the lover
> To the beloved bride
> Transfiguring them each into the other
> (John of the Cross 1979: 13)

3:30. Hutcheson finds occasion here for a sermon against emulation (1972: 53–4), while Calvin implies that the warning is addressed above all to ministers of religion (1959: 80–1).

Testimony from Above

3:31–3. Cf. 5:30–7. The Baptist seems to have eavesdropped on Christ's words to Nicodemus at 3:11–12, which were spoken in the character of the Church. He goes on to echo 3:13, 6:33, Matt 11:3. Eriugena takes v. 32 to mean that Christ has heard the words pronounced at Ps 2:7 and now proclaims himself to be the Son (p. 328 Migne). Chrysostom takes **no man** in this verse to signify 'only the disciples' (*Homily* 30.1); Augustine applies v. 32 to the reprobate and v. 33 to the elect (*Homily* 14.8).

3:34–5. Cf. Deut 18:18. Augustine refers the phrase **not by measure** uniquely to Christ (*Homily* 14.10), while Calvin thinks that it may include all believers. This parable, as Dodd styles it (1963: 385–7), proclaims the inferiority of the Baptist (Augustine, *Homily* 14.8). Augustine contends that it also proves the Son equal to the Father (*Homily* 14.11), and that any notion of increase in Christ pertains only to his human form (*Homily* 14.4). Chrysostom, however, notes that Christ does not proclaim his own divinity, while assuming that his audience is acquainted with the Father and the Spirit (*Homily* 30.2).

3:36. Cf. 1 John 5:5 etc. **Whoever believes**, says Wesley, has eternal life already, 'for he loves God; and love is the essence of heaven' (*MCNT* at III.36). Liddon, on the other hand, implies that one must master the Athanasian Creed to make this simple confession (1880: 119–43). Temple comments that if we eliminate **wrath** from our notion of God, we eliminate the consciousness of sinfulness and impurity in ourselves (1961: 55–6). Calvin follows Augustine (*Homily* 14.13) in maintaining that we bring it upon ourselves through our disobedience in Adam (1959: 86).

4:1. Apollos is the only known disciple of John (Acts 18:25), unless, with *Clementine Homilies* 2.23 and *Recognitions* 2.8, we reckon the Hemerobaptists, Simon Magus, Dositheus the Samaritan and Luna (Scobie 1964: 192).

4:2. Augustine resolves the apparent contradiction by saying that Christ did not perform the act of immersion, but baptized the inner man (*Homily* 15.3). Theissen sees the refusal to baptize as a salient difference between the ministry of Jesus and that of the Baptist (1978: 104–5).

Epilogue: Baptism and Rebirth

Whatever we make of the preposition *anôthen* in v. 5, this chapter plainly inculcates a second birth and associates it with the promise of eternal, or sometimes everlasting, life. A reading which denies that length of days is implied would be false to the intention of the Evangelist, who speaks elsewhere of bodily resurrection; yet, as Dodd and others have demonstrated, the word 'eternal' (*aiônios*) connotes not merely the abrogation of death but a profound change in the quality of life. The Fourth Gospel tempts us to presume that we can 'Keep the new birth for that far day / When in the grave your bones you lay' (Clough 1974: 278); but to the empirical student of religions the 'twice-born' constitute only one psychological type, and not the commonest except perhaps among the great saints and pioneers of faith (James 1960: 94, etc.). Inward regeneration is supposed to result from baptism in Roman Catholic teaching; Protestant usage often limits it to the blotting out of sins. Hutcheson, however, affirms that spiritual regeneration, like any birth, is painful and entails not only a 'visible relation' to the parent but mutual affection between the offspring (1972: 41).

The notion of a return to the womb was familiar in the mysteries of Bacchus (Harrison 1963: 34–5), and the secret of the Eleusinian mysteries was 'a grain of wheat sown in silence' long before the same commonplace was adopted as a symbol of resurrection at 12:24 (Hippolytus, *Refutation* 5.4/9). Hoskyns is wrong, however, to suppose that a mechanical or magical operation is always presupposed when pagans adopt the symbol of rebirth. The thirteenth tract in the theosophical corpus called the *Hermetica*, for example, proclaims that regeneration is the knowledge of what is true and most enduring; those who attain this knowledge are declared to have been begotten by the will of God, and as soon as the postulant understands this doctrine, he experiences renewal. The influence of the Fourth Gospel has been suspected (since the Hermetic text is later), but having compiled two pages of 'remarkable' correspondences, Dodd found no proof that either had been a quarry for the other (1953a: 51–4). There is at least no doubt that Christian alchemy is indebted to this Gospel for its imagery of regeneration, as when Boehme writes that 'the second Adam brought the soul again into . . . the fountain of wrath, and ignited again the light in death' (1945: 248).

Prologue: The Significance of this Episode

Early Christian readers turned to allegory to reconcile this chapter with Matt 10:5, where Christ forbids his ambassadors to visit the Samaritans. Since both the race and the sex of the interlocutor exposed her to contempt, the Gnostic Heracleon makes her a symbol of Sophia, or fallen wisdom: she is in turn a paradigm of the soul who thirsts for the fullness of knowledge, and therefore of the spiritual elect. Origen's reply – perhaps the first extended criticism of one New Testament scholar by another – rejects not the use of allegory, but the arrogance of Heracleon's conclusion. Modern exegesis is more hospitable to Eriugena's notion that the excursion to Samaria foreshadows the Church's mission to the Gentiles (p. 333 Migne); it can also be maintained that the

Samaritan is merely a figure of history or a clue to the antecedents of the Gospel (see epilogue). In modern appropriations of the episode, she may serve as a type of all who would appear to have been excluded from the kingdom by the accidents of gender, race or caste.

Above all, she may stand for all women. Scott, who believes that there is a role in this Gospel for Heracleon's Sophia, writes: 'Contrary, then, to the conclusions of later rabbinic writers . . . this woman is seen to know something, and to be prepared to discuss it openly, with a *male Jew*' (1992: 188). Kraemer indeed contests the widespread claim that every Jewish male of Jesus' time regarded women as evil company (1999: 36–7), yet some correction, at least of the reader's prejudice, is intended at 4:27. Heracleon himself is not a feminist, for his Wisdom is as passive in enlightenment as she is passible in error; nevertheless, this scene may have inspired other Gnostic texts where a female character – usually a sinner, like the Magdalen – is the recipient of Christ's esoteric teaching. Haskins reports that the woman of Samaria has frequently been confounded with the Magdalen and the adulteress of chapter 8 because of her own confession of promiscuity (1994: 26–8). Eva Gore-Booth imagines that the Gospel was first carried by the Samaritan to Mary and John, to be followed by Mary of Bethany, Martha, Mary Magdalene and 'the one so nearly stoned' (1925: 64–5). Schüssler Fiorenza concludes too readily that this female apostle vindicates a woman's right to leadership (1983: 138), but her assertion that invidious distinctions between the sexes are abolished by worship 'in spirit and in truth' is indisputable. At the same time, Schneiders (1991) is right to point out that the woman represents the whole people, indeed all possible brides of Jesus, and hence it seems impertinent to dwell on her 'coy' femininity in the manner of Raymond Brown (1966: 175).

The Woman at the Well

4:3–5. Barrett (1955: 193) cites Josephus, *Antiquities* 20.118 to prove the necessity of the journey. Cf. Luke 17:11, though at Matt 10:5 the missionaries are commanded to shun the cities of the Samaritans. Sychar, now thought to be the modern Askra, is identified by Chrysostom with Shechem, which the sons of Jacob had defiled by bloodshed and the Samaritans by idolatry (*Homily* 31.5–6).

4:6–8. Christ's **thirst** here (which does not fulfil a prophecy, as at 19:14) is a symptom of his humanity for Tertullian (*Flesh of Christ* 9). Origen (*Commentary* 13.29) juxtaposes the subsequent dialogue with Gen 24:43–54, where Isaac's servant solicits a drink of water from Rebecca. The parallel is amplified by Eslinger (1987), and is certainly no less apposite than the legend about the Buddha which Bultmann cites (1957: 131). According to *Gospel of Thomas* 28 ('I appeared in flesh . . . none was thirsty'), thirst is the proper condition of the soul.

4:9. Farrar records that a nineteenth-century Samaritan put a similar question to a Jewish academic (1901: 149n). Daube (1956: 375–9) is generally agreed to have proved the Greek to mean that the Jews would not share vessels with their neighbours. *Mishnah Niddah* 4.1 implies that the woman is as unclean as if she were menstruous. The final sentence, absent from many reputable codices, may be the Evangelist's note.

Living Water

4:10–11. If **gift of God** was already a rabbinic appellation for the Torah (Marsh 1968: 213), Jesus appears to be saying to his own countrymen, here as at 4:22, that the text is dead to those who lack the Spirit. Bultmann finds a parallel at

Giovanni Lanfranco, *Christ and the Samaritan Woman*. Ashmolean Museum, Oxford.

Hermetica 4.5 and notes the frequency of the expression **living water** in the Odes of Solomon (1957: 132n, 135–6); yet Hoskyns shows, with references to Isa 44:3, Zech 13:1, Sir 15:3 and Philo, *On Flight* 97, that the Jews were already familiar with 'the parabolic character of water' (1947: 241).

4:12. The well is now described as a cistern rather than a spring. Sanday observes that, though it was 75 feet deep, an allegorical reading of this text is not precluded (1905: 130). Chrysostom deduces that 4:20 refers to Abraham and his family (*Homily* 32.2); R. H. Lightfoot compares 'our father Abraham' at 8:53 (1956: 132). Lindars suggests that 'Samaritan pride', affronted by the claims of Jesus, betrays itself in the allusion to Jacob's cattle (1972: 182).

4:13–15. Verse 13 is enrolled by Guyenot (2002) in a polemic against the followers of the Baptist. For the phrase **living water** cf. Jer 2:3, Zech 14:8, John 7:38 with the gloss at 7:39. Craveri notes that the term was used in Palestine to distinguish running springs from hoarded water (1967: 255). The metaphorical transformation of the term 'water' is compared by Dodd to the literal but symbolic conversion of water into wine in chapter 2 (1953a: 314). Cf. *Gospel of Thomas* 13: 'you have become intoxicated from the bubbling stream that I have measured out' (J. A. Robinson 1988: 127). As Marsh points out (1968: 219) against Dodd (1953a: 13) we cannot assume that the woman's reply betrays a 'crass' misunderstanding of the metaphor.

4:16–18. Augustine thinks that the purpose of this exchange is to reveal Christ as the true spouse of the soul (*Homily* 15.19). Carmichael too interprets the scene as the 'Johannine symbolical equivalent of a marriage' (1979–80: 335). Five husbands is at least two more than rabbinic custom sanctioned (Barrett 1955: 197); Heracleon defends her by appeal to the Valentinian myth in which a penitent wisdom sows the seeds of spirit by fornicating with the cosmic powers (Origen, *Commentary* 13.25). The frequent association of promiscuity with idolatry (Ezek 16:51, etc.) lends some weight to the conjecture, endorsed by Hoskyns, that these husbands are the five cults which the Assyrians are said to have installed in Samaria (1947: 242, citing 1 Kings 17:24–9).

Spiritual Worship

4:19–20. As Samaritans did not acknowledge the prophets of the canon, Farrar quotes Gen 49:10, Num 24:17, Deut 18:15 (1901: 152n). Strauss finds the ensuing question abrupt, and too portentous for the woman's limited intellect (1892: 305). The shrine at Gerizim is said at Neh 13:28 to have been founded by one Manasseh, whom the Jews expelled because he had married the daughter of the Samaritan governor in Palestine; the cult at Shechem is denounced at Sir 50:25–6. Marsh, who assumes that Sychar is Askra, argues that the reference to Gerizim is symbolic (1968: 220). For 'place' as a synonym for 'temple' see Deut 12:5 and 11:48. Lindars adds that the temple of Gerizim may have stood on the site now occupied by Hellenistic ruins (1972: 188).

4:21. Believe me appears, as Lindars says, to be a unique equivalent for *Amen, amen* (1972: 188). In Cullmann's view, the Evangelist aligns himself in this verse with the Hellenists of Jerusalem (1976: 53) – though we should note that it is the sanctity of the Temple, not of Zion, that is denied by Stephen at Acts 7:48. Both Sacy (1840: 158) and Natalis Alexander (1840: 160) observe that only religions which are delivered from particular localities can aspire to universal dissemination.

4:22. Cf. 3:11. Christ 'draws her thoughts', says Maurice (1857: 123) from the place to the object of worship; prophecy, as Hoskyns remarks, 'is critical' (1947: 243). The Samaritans may be ignorant because they read the Pentateuch without the Jewish commentary (Marsh 1968: 220), but Jews who cling to the Temple have also misunderstood their own God. Christ's use of the pronoun **we** implies, as Antiochene commentators of the fourth century perceived, that he regards himself as a Jew (De la Potterie 1983: 79). R. H. Lightfoot (1956: 134) aptly quotes Athanasius: 'Israel was the school of the knowledge of God to all the nations' (*Incarnation* 12.5). Yet the saying, as Augustine saw, cannot be true of all Jews (*Homily* 15.26), and in the mouth of the Evangelist can only mean 'we Christians'. Eriugena decides that Christ associates himself only with the patriarchs and prophets (p. 338 Migne). Origen's conclusion that it refers to the Jews historically, but to Christ and his Church allegorically (*Commentary* 13.57), will appear obvious to most; De la Potterie (1983) traces a 'movement' from the Jews in v. 21 to Christ in v. 22 and thence in v. 23 to the whole community of believers. Farrar cites Isa 2:2 and a saying ascribed to Tacitus that Christians 'sprang from Jews' (1901: 151n). Neusner observes that Judaism aims not at the **salvation** of humanity, but at the sanctification of a single people (1991: 5–6, 94); Loewe (1981) agrees that in Jewish expectation the Messiah does not bring deliverance, but deliverance the Messiah.

4:23. Spirit and truth are associated at 15:26, while Jesus styles himself the truth at 14:6. Against Dodd (1953a: 170–7), De la Potterie (1963) contends that in this Gospel truth is 'heard and listened to' rather than contemplated, as in Gnostic and theosophical texts of the period, and concludes that truth is Christ himself, as the Word of God. Truth is the characteristic of the *logos* of God the Father at 17:17, and the content of Christ's teachings at 8:40. Bengel detects an allusion to the Trinity, the Father being adored in the Holy Spirit and in the truth that comes through Christ (1850: 384).

4:24. 'The most fundamental proposition in theology' (Temple 1961: 63). Most readers agree with Origen that spirit is not a body, even a body of the most rarefied material (*Commentary* 13.21). The opinion of Tertullian that spirit is a 'body of its own kind' remains eccentric (*Against Praxeas* 7.8), as is the implied equation of spirit with the Holy Spirit in Gregory Nazianzen, *Oration* 32.12. According to Dodd, this verse hints at a 'materialistic' tenet of Stoic cosmology, which had been 'transcended' in Hellenistic thought and 'after Hebraic antecedents' had come to signify 'absolute reality' – not as static essence, but as the ebullient power which gives life to its antonyms, flesh and matter (1953a: 225–6). The verse is easily turned against the Jews (Kidder 1737: 86), and whereas Bunyan seems to take Gerizim for his pulpit (1868: 737–43), Newman admonishes Protestants that if this verse is pressed too far, all order in the Church will be dissolved (1838: 7–8). Braced in Robert Bridges' lines by 3:6 and 2:19–21, it threatens to overthrow the edifice of dogma:

> Reason builded her maze, wherefrom none should escape . . .
> Chanting their clerkly creed to the high-echoing stones
> Of their hand-fashioned temple; but the Wind of heav'n
> Bloweth where it listeth, and Christ still walketh the earth
>
> (Bridges 1953: 697)

Sacy, however, argues that so long as we are of flesh and blood we must have religious forms, though they will not be efficacious without the presence of the Spirit (1840: 160). Natalis Alexander equates this spiritual worship with the Church catholic because of its universality (1840: 178).

4:25–6. On Samaritan expectation of the Ta'eb see Macdonald 1964: 362. Origen, remarking that the Samaritans acknowledged only the Pentateuch, concludes that the woman's insight justifies Christ's appeal to the testimony of Moses at 5:45–6 (*Commentary* 13.26). Christ's answer **I am he** – in Greek 'I am' – may well contain an allusion to the name of God at Ex 3:14 (see further Brown 1970: 533–8).

4:27. For the diffidence of the disciples cf. 21:12. Origen suggests that the disciples are scandalized not because Jesus is a male or a Jew but because of the 'magnitude of his divinity' (*Commentary* 13.28).

4:28. Did the woman leave the pot behind in her excitement (Chrysostom, *Homily* 34.1), or on purpose, either to expedite her journey (Hoskyns 1947: 246), or in order that Christ could drink (Barrett 1955: 201)? Temple, who infers that she intended to return, quotes Scott Holland's dictum: 'You cannot allegorise that water pot' (1961: 68). Both overlooked Heracleon's conjecture that the waterpot signifies the receptive intellect (Origen, *Commentary* 13.31), and Augustine's interpretation of it as a symbol of human greed (*Homily* 15.30).

4:29–30. As Marsh suggests (1968: 220), the woman perceives her interlocutor's knowledge as a sign that he is the Christ who will 'tell us everything'

(v. 25). Christ having told her a few things, says Wesley, her conscience taught her the rest (*MCNT* at IV.29). Henry pronounces her a true disciple who 'left all' to bear testimony (1991: 1938, col. 2).

Labourers for the Harvest

4:31–4. The **work** consists, says Temple, in the awakening of the Samaritan and her subsequent proclamation (1961: 69). Origen takes bread to mean the knowledge of God, and adds that the majority receive it from the disciples, they from Christ and the holy angels, Christ himself from the Father alone (*Commentary* 13.34).

4:35–6. Cf. Mark 9:37. Notwithstanding the scepticism of Hoskyns (1947: 246), Lindars finds the remnants of a proverb here, and argues that the syntox betrays a Semitic antecedent (1972: 195, citing Jon 3:4). Observing that the harvest was later in Galilee than in Judaea, Bengel enumerates the four months as Nisan, Ijaz, Sivan and Thammuz (1850: 385). Farrar writes that v. 35 suggests December and v. 36 May (1901: 149); J. B. Lightfoot asserts that only local knowledge could have prompted the Evangelist to describe this spectacle, much less common in Palestine than in England (1904: 33–6). Origen, by contrast, while disputing Heracleon's judgement that the harvest is in the souls of the disciples, agrees with him that **lift your eyes** is a summons to meditate on the unseen world (*Commentary* 13.40–1).

4:37–8. Bengel suspects a Greek proverb in v. 37 (1850: 386). Carmichael elicits an allegory of childbirth, with allusion to the sixth day of creation (1979–80: 345–6). Readers may identify the **others** as (a) the prophets of the Old Covenant (Augustine, *Homily* 15.32; Chrysostom, *Homily* 34.2); (b) the Baptist and his followers as evangelists of Samaria (J. A. T. Robinson 1962: 61–6); (c) the disciples of Christ, as seen from the point of view of the Evangelist; (d) the Evangelist's own contemporaries (Lindars 1972: 197–8); and even (e) the Samaritan (Schüssler Fiorenza 1983: 327). Edith Sitwell marries eschatology to Johannine symbolism when she prophesies that humanity, after ripening 'under an Abraham-bearded Sun', will hear the Seraphim intoning the 'universal language of the Bread' (1952: 24–6).

Conversion in Samaria

4:39–43. Strauss cites *Clementine Homilies* 2.6 to show that a prophet was expected to know all things (1892: 306). Verses 40–3 persuaded Bengel that the

Samaritans are the crops that await the harvest (1850: 386). Augustine, struck by the readiness of the Samaritans to believe a woman, argues that she represents the Church (*Homily* 15.33). Romanus makes her a type of both the Church and Mary, exclaiming that she left her city bearing water and came back bearing God (9.5.5ff in 1963: 66). Scott, who compares the calling of the woman with that of Philip, contrasts the ready faith of the villagers with the doubts of Nathanael at 1:46 (1992: 194–5).

4:44. The saying was proverbial: see Hoskyns (1947: 260). The *Gospel of Thomas* 31 conflates it with a variant of Mark 2:17: 'No prophet is accepted in his own village; no physician heals those who know him' (J. A. Robinson 1988: 130). The historian Toynbee counts this rejection among the 'Socratic' elements in the gospels (1938: 509). Chrysostom understands the country of Christ to be Capernaum, which is denounced at Matt 11:23 and is the scene of his most conspicuous works in Mark (*Homily* 35.1); but Jerusalem, as Origen says, is the true home of the prophets, and their grave (*Commentary* 17.54).

4:45. Chrysostom has no doubt that it is laudable to base one's faith on signs (*Homily* 35.2), while Origen submits that unless the sign were also a wonder, the Galileans would not have believed (*Commentary* 13.55). Yet, though Deut 24:11, Rom 15:19 and other biblical texts appeal to 'signs and wonders' (a phrase used only here in John), they are mentioned in the other Gospels only as concomitants of false prophecy (Mark 13:22, Matt 24:24). Hoskyns observes that *Rabbah Exodus* 16 praises those who 'believe by hearing and not at the beholding of signs' (1947: 261).

Epilogue: The Gospel and Samaria

Jews despised Samaritans as a mongrel breed of native Israelites and Assyrian settlers after the fall of the northern kingdom. Their chronicles relate that they were the tribe of Joseph, settled in that territory by Joshua, and only temporarily displaced by the Assyrian conquest of the northern kingdom (Macdonald 1964: 15–21). They opposed the restoration of the Temple in the fifth century BC, and cherished a sanctuary on Mount Gerizim, near Israel's ancient capital at Shechem (Neh 13; 1 Kings 16:24; Josephus, *Antiquities* 11.297–347). Subordinating Yahweh, the tribal deity of Judah, to the ubiquitous Elohim (Gaster 1923: 66–8), they personified such attributes of the latter as the ineffable name, or Shema (Macdonald 1964: 95–7). Because they regarded only the Pentateuch, or at most the Hexateuch, as authoritative (Gaster 1923: 96–110), some Christians confused them with the Sadducees

(Hippolytus, *Refutation* 9.29); at the same time, they shared with the Pharisees the anticipation of a Messiah, sometimes known as the Ta'eb.

It has not escaped modern scholars that Christianity too purported to fulfil the Law while abolishing the ceremonies of Jerusalem; that it preached the Father as God (Hebrew Elohim) and the Son as Lord (Hebrew YHWH); and that 'Wisdom', 'Power' and even 'Name' of God were among the early salutations that the Church bestowed on Christ (Purvis 1975). G. Buchanan (1968) even discovers a Samaritan Messiah in the Fourth Gospel. Yet Jesus accepts the whole canon, refuses to determine the true location of the Temple, and is content to be called a Jew in Samaria, just as he submits to the term Samaritan in Judaea (8:48). If it was the aim of the Evangelist to seduce the admirers of Simon and Dositheus, the most recent Samaritan claimants to Messiahship (Freed 1970), or to make a covert attack on John the Baptist (the putative master of Dositheus), we may wonder why he employs this subterfuge, when he is not afraid to make the Baptist foretell his own eclipse in chapter 3.

Prologue: Miracles as Parables

Harmonies and synopses sometimes recognize in the healing of the nobleman's son the same miracle that is rehearsed at Matt 8:5–13 and Luke 7:1–10. The miracle at Bethesda is unparalleled, and Irenaeus' remark that it manifests Christ in his role as Creator is in keeping with the spirit of this Gospel (*Against Heresies* 5.15.2). Chrysostom makes it a baptism for sin and a consolation to all whose faith is tried by sickness or adversity (*Homily* 36.1). Dodd observes that in the plan of the Gospel it looks back to the water of life in chapter 4 and forward to the resurrection announced at 5:29 (1953a: 218–29). Coincidences in imagery and language between this episode and the healing of the paralytic in Mark 2 have prompted modern commentators to ask whether one is derived from the other, or both from a common original. The latter view has prevailed, although where Dodd postulates an oral or diffuse tradition (1963: 177), Buse adduces the parallel to support his case that Mark and our Evangelist have both drawn on a 'Petrine' source (1954–5).

The Nobleman (Official)'s Son

4:46. The first miracle, says Origen, brought exhilaration, the second release from death (*Commentary* 13.57). Dodd agrees, except that he describes the effect of the first as 'enhancement of life' (1953a: 319).

4:47. According to Heracleon, Sophia is now succeeded in the allegory by the Demiurge, her offspring (Origen, *Commentary* 13.60). Origen reports that early tradition made the supplicant an official of either Herod Antipas or Augustus Caesar (*Commentary* 13.57). He is often identified with the centurion of Matt 8:5, though, as Chrysostom observes, both the location of the miracle and the conduct of the petitioner are differently reported (*Homily* 35.2). In Sayers' dramatization of the episode, he is a Jew who was also present at the wedding feast in Cana and had heard of the tumult in Jerusalem (1943: 106–10).

4:48. Signs are refused to inquirers at Mark 8:12 and Matt 12:39. Here, however, no sign is solicited, and a miracle is performed. To Fortna, this is the ugliest of the scars left by incompetent redaction (1988: 5–6); the integrity of the text can be defended if we suppose that Christ is upbraiding the counterfeit faith which seeks material consolation at the expense of higher goods (Hutcheson 1972: 71).

4:49–50. The submission of the nobleman to this tart command is for Sayers a pre-condition of the miracle. Hoskyns notes that similar words are employed at 1 Kings 17:23 when Elijah has raised the widow's son (1947: 261).

4:51–2. The word used of the invalid is *pais*, as at Matt 8:13, where it means not 'son' but 'servant'. The event is said in v. 52 to have happened **yesterday** either because the centurion arrived home in the evening (when a new day would commence by Jewish reckoning) or because he was retarded by his entourage (Marsh 1968: 241). Luther, who notes that the nobleman is also said to believe when Christ first speaks to him at 4:50, concludes that he had an inchoate faith, which is now made perfect (1983: 253, 260).

4:53–4. The Evangelist says clearly enough what some modern scholars have rediscovered with labour, that his list of signs is limited to those done outside Judaea (cf. Bengel 1850: 388). A later report ascribed a similar healing to another Galilean, Hanina ben Dosa (Vermes 1973: 74–5).

The Healing at Bethesda

5:1. Bengel lists the Fathers who maintained that the feast was Pentecost (1850: 388); Trench records, however, that Kepler had identified it as Purim, and Theodoret (*Against Heresies* 2.28) as the first Passover of three (1904: 263–4). If we subscribe to Bultmann's transposition of chapters 5 and 6 – an expedient to curtail the oscillations of the narrative between Judaea and Galilee – it will be the same Passover as the **festival of the Jews** at 6:4 (1957: 177–9). To Hutcheson the feast is **of the Jews** because the law that established it has been annulled (1972: 72).

5:2. The AV has 'by the sheep-market', the RSV 'by the sheep gate'; Bengel speculates that the water served as a dip for fleeces (1850: 386). Its name appears in manuscripts as Bethesda, Bethzatha, Betzetha and Bethsaida; Eusebius read the second in his *Onomasticon*, Tertullian the fourth in his treatise *On Baptism*. Erasmus surmised that Bethesda was the name in Greek and

Hogarth, *Christ at the Pool of Bethesda*. St Bartholomew's Hospital, London.

Bethsaida in Hebrew (1535: 237). Wieand, who contends that archaeology has located the site, suggests that the reading Bethsaida was introduced by the author of chapter 21 (1965–6). Even if the excavations indicate that there were indeed five porches at Bethesda, we are not compelled, as Barrett thinks (1955: 211), to deny that the Evangelist intends them to represent the five books of Moses (cf. Augustine, *Homily* 17.2). Since he employs the present tense in describing the porches, H. E. Edwards infers that he wrote before the Roman sack of Jerusalem and concomitant destruction of the pool in AD 70 (1953: 126–7).

5:3–4. A sentence excised from all modern translations states that at certain times an angel troubled the pool, and that if the sick were immersed in the turbid waters they would be healed. For Tertullian this act prefigures the descent of the Holy Spirit into the font (*On Baptism* 6); Eisler, however, can cite no ancient authority for his suggestion that the **pool of sheep** (his rendering in v. 2) was so called because the neophyte becomes a new lamb in baptism – let alone for his equation of the angel with the Phoenician fish-god Sid, from whom he derives the name Bethsaida (1923: 67 and n.1). Ginzberg sees a likeness to Miriam's well, which followed the wandering Israelites (1998: 22). Contemporaries of Bengel, however, argued that such periodic turbulence was more likely to be a natural phenomenon (1850: 389). Harris suggests that the current flowed, as the currents of the soul should do, from an 'inner cavern' (1893: 37).

5:5. To Barrett the 38 years are merely an index of the 'gravity of his illness' (1955: 212). Brodie detects an allusion to Israel's bondage (1993: 239), though to 'Levi' the healing proves that in the economy of heaven none has better opportunities than another (1964: 134). Augustine suggests that, as 38 is two short of the sacred number 40, so the paralysis illustrates the sickness that we incur by the violation of the two cardinal imperatives, love of neighbour and love of God (*Homily* 17.3).

5:6. In Hogarth's painting *The Pool at Bethesda*, the cripple is not even looking at the waters (St Bartholomew's Hospital, London). Marsh observes that Jesus takes the initiative, like Yahweh in the Old Testament (1968: 253); Cyril of Jerusalem remarks that he appears uninvited, as he came from heaven (2000: 72). Sacy explains that he is not so much canvassing the man's wishes as making him aware that he is now at a critical juncture (1840: 190). Clough's vision of Bethesda, however, dwells on the patient and includes no healing (1974: 191).

5:7–9. The man's reply is identical with that of the Samaritan at 4:17, except that she says *andra* (male) where his word is *anthrôpon* (human being). Christ's reply is identical with his command to the paralytic at Mark 2:11.

Breaching the Sabbath?

5:10–12. *Mishnah Shabbat* 7.2 and Jer 17:21 forbid the carrying of burdens on the Sabbath from house to house. Harvey maintains that the question is not malicious, as its object is to save the offender from punishment by apprising him of his sin (1976: 50).

5:13–14. We recognize Jesus better in the Temple than in the crowd, observes Augustine (*Homily* 17.11). For **sin no more** (AV) cf. Matt 9:2 and John 8:11. Chrysostom remarks that the body is punished for the sins of the soul, but adds that Christ spoke not to condemn the man but to admonish him; the allusion to his sins was none the less a proof of divine omniscience (*Homily* 37.1). Hartley Coleridge seems to assume a cure by immersion, as in chapter 9, when he extols prayer as the sinner's Bethesda and his river Lethe (1908: 94). Henry King, in similar spirit, likens the pool to the flowing wound of Christ (1921: 238).

5:15–16. Fortna perceives a 'sharpening of theological conflict' (1988: 278–9); Harvey, however, renders the verb *diôkein* in v. 16 as 'prosecute' rather than 'persecute' (1976: 51).

Christ the Son of God

5:17. Barrett cites a number of rabbinic comments on Gen 2:2 to prove that the second half of this saying would have given no offence (1955: 212), and Archbishop Temple assures us that Christ did not enjoin neglect of the Fourth Commandment but a deeper understanding of its import (1961: 107). Dodd quotes Philo's comment (*Cherubim* 96–100) that because God does not change he is never weary (1953a: 321). Augustine writes that the Father works on the Sabbath, as on all days, to administer and sustain the created order (*Genesis Read Literally* 4.23); Christ does likewise because the day of rest was instituted as a type of his resurrection (*Homily* 17.15).

5:18. The title 'Son of God', as Milton's Satan perceives, 'admits no certain sense'. God is the father of Israel at Hos 11:2 and of the king at Ps 2:7; at Gen 6:1, Job 1:6 and 39:7 the sons of God are angels; the locution 'son of (a) god' occurs in Aramaic at Dan 3:25. The title may confer on Jesus the role of a plenipotentiary, but not complete equality in nature (Ashton 1991: 292–329). Dodd remarks that the adjective *isotheos* ('peer of a god') could be applied without offence to human beings among the Greeks, who allowed gradations of divinity, though it could only be a blasphemy to the monotheistic Jews

(1953a: 324–7). Odeberg (1929) asserts that in rabbinic thought a rebellious son was one who made himself equal to his father, but even if the reference could be verified, it hardly covers the present case, in which any kind of sonship is assumed (by Christ) to presuppose obedience and (by his critics) to entail equality (see McGrath 1998). Augustine, while endorsing the Jewish inference (*Homily* 38.3), adds the rider that, since Christ was begotten equal to the Father, he could not properly be said to have *made* himself so (*Homily* 17.16).

5:19. Augustine, like all the orthodox Fathers, insists that this verse implies no inferiority in the Son, but declines to follow Hilary of Poitiers (*On the Trinity* 7.17) in restricting it to the humanity of Christ. Rather, he says, it amplifies the statement in 1:2 that the Word was with God in the beginning (*Homily* 18.3–5), and reveals that every act of God is performed in concert by the whole Trinity (*Homily* 20.9–10). Natalis Alexander adds that the Son can do no otherwise because his nature, being divine, is immune to change (1840: 197).

5:20. The verb is *philein*, surely intimating that the bond between Father and Son resembles that between Jesus and his *philoi*, or 'friends' (11:5, 13:23). According to Augustine, the eternal generation of the Son consists in his seeing what is shown to him by the Father (*Homily* 21.2); by contrast, Hilary understands the 'showing' as the nativity on earth (*On the Trinity* 7.19).

5:21. Augustine, fearing the inference that some are raised by the Father and others by the Son, protests that they work together in the raising of Lazarus and of Jairus' daughter (*Homily* 21.10–11). The rabbinic sayings amassed by modern scholars to show that only God was supposed to raise the dead would prove to ancient minds that Christ was God, and not, as Hoskyns states, that he possesses only a 'delegated authority' (1947: 269).

5:22–3. Cf. Rom 2:16. Augustine explains that judgement on the day of resurrection will be dispensed in the form of the Son of Man, but not in the form of God (*On the Trinity* 13.30). Eusebius of Caesarea declares that we owe the same honour to the Son as to the Father whose image he is (Col 1:15), just as we owe the same honour to a statue as to the king whom it represents. The Nicene Council of 325 determined that this parity of esteem is founded in unity of nature, if not equality of power: see note to 5:18.

Eternal Life and Judgement

5:24. Christ makes his own the Baptist's saying at 3:36. Hoskyns remarks that the greatest work of Christ is the communication of inward life and not, as might be inferred from previous verses, the corporeal resurrection of the dead (1947: 269).

5:25. The final resurrection, explains Augustine, is still to come; the one that 'now is' we experience through faith (*Homily* 19.9–10). Donne says that we shall be raised with power by the Son of God, but judged with clemency by the Son of Man at v. 27 (1958: 161). Calvin too opines that dead means 'dead in sin' (1959: 130–1). For Brodie, however, the unexpected phrase **in their graves** (v. 28) marks a 'leap' from the healing of infirmity to the conquest of death, to be clarified at 6:30 by a reference to 'the last day' (1993: 249).

5:26–7. The Son, says Brodie, assumes the characteristics of the Creator (1993: 248–51); yet v. 27 reads '[a] **son of** [a] **man**' – not even, as Erasmus notes, the titular designation '*The* Son of Man' (1535: 239). He therefore accepts Augustine's view that judgement is conferred on Christ in his human nature (*Homily* 19.16), though Chrysostom re-punctuates to avoid this 'heresy' (*Homily* 39.3). The apotheosis of the human Christ is represented in Michelangelo's *Last Judgement* (Vatican, Sistine Chapel), yet this great fresco merely conceals the paradox which Cowper brings out by substituting 'though' for **because**: 'Tho' once a man of grief and shame, / Yet now he fills a throne' (1905: 454). Elsley suggests that Christ adopts this lowly appellation in contempt of the Jews, who styled their coming Messiah the Son of David (1844: 432). Comparison with Dan 7:13–14 ('one like a son of man') suggests that Christ, as an innocent sufferer, will be given the right to judge his persecutors; or else we may surmise, from the words of Paul at Phil 2:6–11, that God has 'highly exalted him' because of his obedience in the flesh.

5:28–30. A recapitulation of 5:21–5, embellished by an allusion to Dan 12:2. Unity with the Father, as elsewhere, is the fruit of obedience, and thus the verse, as Dodd remarks, rebuts the charge of blasphemy at 5:18 (1953a: 327).

Witnesses to Christ

5:31. As Dodd observes, Christ 'passes somewhat lightly over the biblical *testimonia*' with the 'self-evidencing power of the "Word of God"' (1953a: 331); thus he is bearing witness of himself after all, as at 8:14.

5:32. Most modern commentators hold against Chrysostom that **another** is not the Baptist but the Father (cf. Hoskyns 1947: 271). Bengel, however, draws a parallel with v. 39 to suggest that Jesus' hearers were mistaken in their estimate of both John and the Scriptures (1850: 392). Barrett cites *Aboth* 4.22 on God as witness (1955: 220), but in this Gospel Christ is the only witness to the Father's testimony.

5:33–5. Cf. Gal 1:1 and Kierkegaard's contention that a man is no apostle if he relies on external witnesses (1962: 104–27). Luther infers from v. 35 that the Jews sought John for their own aggrandizement (1983: 119); they were drawn to the external beacon, but lacked, as Natalis Alexander says, the light within (1840: 208–9). Lindars sees a precedent for the praise of John at Sir 48:1 on Elijah (1972: 228); as to his disappearance from the story, Theodore comments that no lamp is needed when the sun is risen (Wiles 1960: 38).

5:36–7. Cf. Deut 18:18–22 and contrast 1:8 on the Baptist's testimony to the light. These verses appear to confirm that the Father, rather than John, is adduced as a witness to Christ at v. 32. Borgen concludes that Christ is the form that the Israelites failed to apprehend at Deut 4:2 (1976b: 72). John 1:18 and Acts 9:7 also imply that God is better known through his word than through our perceptions. In the Old Testament it is sometimes said that God displayed himself to such favourites as Abraham, Jacob and Moses (Gen 18:1; 32:30; Ex 33:11); the Evangelist may believe, as Hanson argues, that the theophanies of the Old Covenant were Christophanies (1991: 73–83), though we cannot exclude the opinion of Lindars that he took them to be appearances of angels (1972: 229).

5:38. For the **word abiding in you** cf. 1 John 2:17. Does this mean that failure to receive the word of life is a cause of ignorance or a proof of it? It may not be an evasion to say, with Barrett, that both are true (1955: 222).

Christ in Scripture

5:39. The majority of modern scholars understand the Greek verb as an indicative, 'You search', rather than an imperative, 'Search'. Bengel notes that this was the view of Athanasius, Cyril and Nonnus the poet (1850: 393). A fragment of an unknown gospel (*Papyrus Egerton* 2) contains a similar admonition in which the mood of the verb is certainly imperative, but few scholars have endorsed Black's reconstruction of an Aramaic prototype for both versions of the saying (1946: 54). The Syriac version too is 'unequivocally imperative' (Dodd 1953a: 330). In this form the saying can be adduced to vindicate the use of reason in theological matters (Ibbot 1737: 94).

5:40–2. Chrysostom glosses this as 'I need no honour' (*Homily* 41.1). The Greek word for love is *agape* (cf. v. 20). It is not clear whether it signifies the love of God for his creatures or theirs for God, but of course the Jews lack both (Barrett 1955: 224).

5:43–5. Cf. 10:12. Chrysostom understands **another** to mean the Antichrist (*Homily* 4.2, citing 2 Thess 2:11–12). Bengel asserts that by his time as many as 64 false Christs had imposed upon the Jews (1850: 394). In v. 45 even Moses, the *paraclete* or defender of the Jews, is turned against them, as Deut 31–2 foretells (Meeks 1967: 294). Barrett notes a parallel in the *Egerton Papyrus* (1955: 225). Chrysostom (who reads the verb in v. 39 as imperative) submits that throughout this passage Christ does not adduce any concrete testimony from the Scriptures because he wishes to provoke interrogation (*Homily* 41.2).

5:46–7. Barrett takes these verses as a slight on the oral Law (1955: 226), though they rather seem to upbraid the Jews for their blindness in the interpretation of written testimony. Lest this appeal to Moses should be taken as a sign of Christ's inferiority, Calvin pleads that his argument is suited to the prejudice of his audience (1959: 143).

Epilogue: Jews and Jewry

In Galilee a miracle causes wonder, in Jerusalem hostility. Jesus avoids Judaea at 7:1 'for fear of the Jews', yet he attends the feasts of the Jews at 5:1 and 6:4, and does not disown the name 'Jew' at 4:9. Northern Palestine is his asylum, yet even there the 'Jews', when he meets them, are his foes (Meeks 1966). Who, then, are the Jews of the present Gospel? Lowe (1976) submits that, but for a handful of exceptions, the name *Ioudaios* in all four Gospels denotes 'Judaeans, either with reference to the population in general or . . . to the Judean authorities'. Malina and Rohrbaugh therefore adopt the rendering 'Judaeans', and advance this as the antonym to 'Israel' in the anti-language of the Evangelist (1998: 135–6). Such verses as 6:52, however, would be more intelligible if the word *Ioudaios* occasionally signified a person outside the province of Judaea who elected to keep the Mosaic Law and frequent the Temple during festivals. Judaea may be the centre from which all senses of the word *Ioudaios* radiate, but, as Ashton (1994) sees, the province may at times expand to accommodate all opponents of the spirit or contract to leave room for none but the advance guard of rabbinic legalism.

The frequency with which this Gospel employs the word *Ioudaios* – 'not Sadducee, Pharisee or Scribe but Jew Jew Jew' (Smith 1978: 153) – is a proof that it conceives of the people of Christ as a sect distinct from, not as a sect of, Judaism. This divorce cannot be laid at the door of 'Gnosticism' (Heer 1970: 23–4) until it is shown that Gnosticism antedates the Gospel. Nor can we be certain that the author's view of the Jews was hardened by the expulsion of Christians from the Palestinian synagogue, as scholars are now divided as to the date of the so-called Blessing of the Minim (see 9:22). What is certain is that the Johannine usage, together with 1 Thess 14–15 and Matt 27:25, has tempted Christians to blame Christ's death on the whole Jewish people, even when they do not acquit themselves:

Spit on my face you Jewes and pierce my side . . .
But by my death cannot be satisfied
My sinnes, which passe the Jewes impietie
                                    (Donne 1929: 284)

Prologue: One Miracle, Four Gospels

Chrysostom contends that, with the walking on the water, the feeding of the
multitude reveals the love of Christ for his people in presence and in absence
(*Homily* 42.1). In the tradition of Origen, Eriugena declares that the same
divine abundance flows for any Christian who can fathom the many meanings
of the Scripture (pp. 345–6 Migne). To Luther it assures us of the daily bread
for which we ask in the Lord's Prayer (1983: 168–9). Modern scholars remark
that Christ has taken the place of Moses – to whom we must no doubt add
Elijah and Elisha, other prophetic ministers of fertility (Glasson 1963: 27–59).
Whatever the walking signifies, the feeding may be safely reckoned among the

'nature miracles' which exemplify the power to impart new life (Hastings 1913: 189–90). Since the feeding occurs in all four Gospels, and the purpose of Christ's mission is so clearly expounded in the Johannine sequel, it is often urged that there must be a fact behind the story, even if it was not a miracle. The theory that Christ merely persuaded those with food to share with those who had none will not explain the prodigious surplus (cf. Strauss 1892: 513, quoting Paulus). There is at least an eighteenth-century logic in the proposal of the 'Illuminati' that Christ stood at the entrance to a cave from which new loaves were passed to him by his adjutants (Schweitzer 1954: 41). J. A. T. Robinson (1985: 203–4) would argue that the narrative in this Gospel is the most informative because it is only the abortive coronation of 6:15 that accounts for Pilate's question to Christ in all four texts, 'Art thou the king of the Jews?'

Only here and in Mark is the feeding followed by the walking on the water. This coincidence is the chief exhibit in any case for making one of these texts dependent on the other; yet the parallels observed by numerous scholars, and recorded in the notes below, suggest rather that the Fourth Evangelist tacked and veered between all three Synoptics, or (what is even more incredible) that they each drew independently from him. The question is not made simpler if, with Bultmann (1957), Dodd (1963) and Fortna (1988), we surmise that the Fourth Evangelist relied on an autonomous Gospel of Signs, for we have still to discover whether Mark read this document or its author read Mark, and in either case why so much and no more was taken up in the later text. It is probable enough, as Wills maintains, that the two Evangelists (or their sources) have drawn separately on itinerant traditions (1997: 90); those who limit the number of signs in the Fourth Gospel to seven generally find no place for the walking on the water, which may be treated either as part of the foregoing miracle or as a discrete but natural event.

The Miraculous Feeding

6:1–4. At the outset the narrative is closer to Matthew than to Mark. Luke 9:10 locates the miracle at Bethsaida, and as Philip was a native of this town (1:44), his appearance at 6:5 may imply that Jesus alighted there, perhaps setting out, as Lindars suggests, from Capernaum (1972: 239). Dodd contends that readers could not fail to remember that Passover was also the Easter season (1953a: 333).

6:5–10. The purpose of Christ's question, according to Sacy, is to make his disciples conscious of their poverty (1840: 236). No other account of the feeding mentions the youth (*paidarion*); Barrett divines a reference to the servant of Elisha at 2 Kings 4:42–4 (1955: 229). The seating of the multitude in v. 10 affords an exiguous parallel to Mark 6:39.

6:11. The verb is *eucharistêsas*, but two typical features of the primitive eucharist – the breaking of the bread and the prayer to heaven – are omitted, although we find them at Luke 9:16 etc. Temple suggests that the author did not wish to dwell on the physical institution of the sacrament, lest attention be distracted from the inward communion that it signifies (1961: 78–80).

6:12–13. Daube, who observes that the injunction is rabbinic (1956: 42–3), agrees with Bultmann that the number of baskets indicates the magnitude of the feast (1957: 157). Trench, who cites as parallels Ruth 2:14 and 2 Kings 4:43–4, approves the comment of Guilliand that the remnants proved the reality of the miracle (1904: 291). Hoskyns, while rejecting the ancient view that these words inculcate a special care for the remnants of the eucharist (*Apostolic Constitutions* 8.3), accepts that the baskets stand for the twelve apostles (1947: 289–90). Eriugena likens the broken loaves to texts of multiple sense in Scripture, and the undivided fish to those that admit of only a spiritual construction (p. 346 Migne). Luther equates the five loaves with the senses and the two fish with the patriarchs and prophets (1983: 169–70).

Walking on Water

6:14. Cf. the disclaimer of the Baptist at 1:21 and the Samaritan's confession at 4:19. Meeks (1967) observes that the kingly and prophetic roles are seldom fused in Jewish literature. Hoskyns suggests that this misunderstanding was inspired by prophetic movements such as Josephus commemorates at *Jewish War* 3.42–3, etc. (1947: 290). For **to come into the world** cf. 1:9.

6:15. Jesus flees, as at Mark 6:47, but only here, as Hoskyns notes, is the crowd's response to the miracle recorded (1947: 290). J. A. T. Robinson compares the insurrection of the Sicarii at Josephus, *Jewish War* 2.261 (1985: 203–4), though it is Mark, with his citation of 1 Kings 22:17 at 6:33 and his seating of the multitude in companies of 50 and 100 at 6:40 who provides the clearest evidence of political intent (cf. Montefiore 1962). Natalis Alexander, on the other hand, interprets Christ's withdrawal as a mark of contempt for the world (1840: 272).

6:16–17. Marsh writes that the darkness symbolizes the 'universal condition' of those who live without Christ (1968: 291), while Natalis Alexander takes the stormy waves as symbols of temptation (1840: 273). Sacy agrees: whenever Christ is absent, even his followers must toil (1840: 272).

6:18–19a. R. H. Lightfoot (1956: 165) observes that if the lake is six or seven miles across at its widest, this phrase corresponds to 'in the midst of the sea' at Mark 6:47. The Greek in fact says 25 or 30 furlongs; Hoskyns contrasts the inaccuracy of Josephus' estimate of 40 furlongs (1947: 291).

6:19b. The fear of the disciples and comparison with Mark 6:49 suggest that this is a miracle, though, as Bernard observes, the same words at 21:1 are translated not as 'on' but as 'by' the sea (1928: 1.185). Rodgers imagines this episode as a perilous trial of love (1952: 42–3), but the 'towering' Jesus of Glyn Jones is 'vestured in torrid purple, like creation' (1996: 68).

6:20. Whatever the words *ego eimi* ('I am . . .') may signify at Mark 6:50, the echo of Isa 43:5 ('fear not') corroborates Ball's appeal to Isa 43:10 ('I am') in his exegesis of this saying and its cognates at 8:24, 28 and 58 (1996: 181–5).

6:21. Lindars suspects that this landfall symbolizes the 'attainment of eternal life through faith in Jesus' (1972: 248). Jesus' navigation of the storm-tossed vessel, drawn to the attention of modern exegetes by Kiefer (1980: 11), has not escaped the poets. 'He doth steer / Ev'n when the boat most seems to reel' writes Herbert (1974: 159), importing the storm from Mark 4:27–8. Jesus is surely Milton's unnamed 'pilot of the Galilean lake' (1966: 145), and the one whom Tennyson hopes to meet after 'Crossing the Bar' (1952: 831).

The People Seek a Sign

6:22–3. According to Augustine (*Homily* 25.8) and Chrysostom (*Homily* 43.2), these observations should have informed the crowd that Jesus had walked across the sea. Whereas Brown finds v. 23 so difficult as to necessitate a rewriting of the sentence (1966: 258–90), Brodie replies that the sudden multiplication of the boats is a variation on the miracle of the loaves (1993: 77).

6:24–5. Many commentators see a reference to the ceremonial eucharist in the verb *eucharistein* ('to give thanks') in v. 24 (e.g. Barrett 1955: 237); Chrysostom adds that in v. 25 the disciples ask not how but **when** Christ arrived, because the feeding had already prepared them for a miracle (*Homily* 43.1). Astonishment would be justified, however, for if the miracle took place at Bethsaida (Luke 9:10), the statement that Capernaum lay opposite is imprecise at best (Calvin 1959: 152). Radulphus veils the error in an allegory: Christ's passage of the sea prefigures his victory, through death and resurrection, over the sorrows of the world (p. 1819 Migne).

6:26–7. Natalis Alexander, commenting that 'seldom is Jesus sought for Jesus, sake', construes v. 27 to mean: labour not for the body but for the soul (1840: 273–4). Pope Gregory and Bede apply this reprimand to Christians who seek office in the Church with worldly motives (Aquinas 1997: 225). Chrysostom cites Eph 4:28 to pre-empt the inference that v. 27 excuses Christians from physical labour (*Homily* 44.1).

6:28–9. Cf. 3:34 and Mark 10:17. Although the answer is wasted on the inquirer, Theophylact suggests that Christ replied for the good of others (Aquinas 1997: 226). Augustine reminds us that to **believe** is to obey his will (*Homily* 25.11).

6:30. Chrysostom blames the questioners for seeking another miracle (*Homily* 45.1); Augustine comments that while they beheld the mighty works, they failed to see that they pointed to Christ himself as the goal of faith (*Homily* 25.31). The *Gospel of Thomas* 91 (quoted by Lindars 1972: 256) makes this question the overture to a variant of Matt 16:3.

The Bread of Life

6:31. In Ex 16:15 and Ps 68:24 Moses was not the donor, and the bread was not from heaven (Temple 1961: 84). Hymnody styles Christ the bread of wayfarers (*A&M* 389) or 'bread of heaven' for pilgrims in the wilderness (*A&M* 296). Germanus of Constantinople applies the word 'manna' directly to the eucharistic bread (1984: 58).

6:32. This, as Augustine notices, is the first passage in which Christ declares himself to be greater than Moses (*Homily* 25.12). Barrett cites rabbinic texts to show that the Jews expected a second redeemer to bring a second gift of manna (1955: 239–40). The passage from 2 Bar 39:8 adduced by Dodd has the advantage of being contemporary with the Evangelist (1953a: 335). Likening the body of Christ to the tabernacle which housed the manna at Ex 16:33, Cyril of Alexandria concludes that the indwelling of Christ through Scripture and the eucharist has superseded obedience to Moses (1.461–73 Pusey).

6:33. Lindars upholds the rendering **that which comes down** (i.e. the bread) against **he who came down** as in the AV (1972: 258); Barrett, however, finds a 'characteristic ambiguity' (1982: 47). Theophylact explains that as bread gives life to the body, so Christ gives life to the soul through the operation of the Spirit (Aquinas 1997: 228). Messiaen's 'The Manna and the Bread of Life' (the sixth piece in his *Book of the Holy Sacrament*) tries to imitate the polyphony of the desert.

6:34–5. The disciples are guilty either of unbelief (Calvin 1959: 158) or of the literalism conventionally imputed to the Samaritan at 4:15. Christ's answer, with its allusion to the description of the manna as the 'bread of angels' in Ps 78:25, supplies the first words of the eucharistic anthem *Panis angelicus* (best known, perhaps, in the setting by J.-B. Fauré). Origen invokes the present verse as a gloss on Ps 34:8: 'taste and see that the Lord is good' (*Commentary* 20.43). Calvin observes that the reference to **thirst** attributes more to Christ than is true of common bread, and that Christ proves his superiority by imparting life as well as sustaining it (1959: 159–60). R. H. Lightfoot (1956: 167) reckons this as the first in a series of seven 'I am' sayings, to be followed by light (8:12, 9:5), the door (10:7, 9), the good shepherd (10:11, 14), the resurrection and the life (11:25), the way, the truth and the life (14:6), and the vine (15:1). This reckoning overlooks the absolute use of *ego eimi* at 6:20 and 8:2; Freed (1982) would also attach importance to 'I am not the Christ' at 1:19.

6:36–8. Apollinarius, a bishop of the fourth century, was denounced as a heretic when he called Christ the man from heaven, as he was thought to have implied that the flesh of Christ was not from Mary (Gregory of Nazianzus, Letter 102). It is orthodox, however, to assert that what is true of the God who is Christ is also true of the man who is Christ; thus the carol 'Once in royal David's city' can declare that a child 'came down to earth from heaven' (*A&M* 432), and Wesley was right to say that he 'left his Father's throne' and 'bled' (Wesley 1876: 201). On the evidence of Psalm 2:8, Elsley takes those **whom the Father gives me** to include the Gentiles (1844: 436).

6:39–40. This charge (cf. 6:29) is said to have been fulfilled at 17:12. The reference to the latter day (a phrase unique to this Gospel) echoes Job 19:25 (Septuagint) and anticipates Martha's confession at 11:24. Barrett cites it to prove that the eucharistic bread cannot confer immortality by itself (1982: 45). Origen cites v. 40 to corroborate his argument that Matt 6:11 is a petition for supersubstantial (*epiousios*) bread and not for the daily bread that perishes (*On Prayer* 27.7–9).

The Jews Doubt Christ

6:41. Barrett refers to the **murmuring** of the Israelites at Ex 16:2 (1955: 244); the presence of these Jews corroborates Fortna's remark that the miracle is more at home in Jerusalem than in Galilee (1988: 84). For Hutcheson what follows is a sermon against the 'covenant of works' (1972: 122).

6:42–6. In contrast to Mark 6:3, the mother of Jesus is not named. Hoskyns compares the reply to Hos 11:4 and Mark 4:11 (1947: 296). Barrett notes that the verb 'to draw' is employed in a similar sense at Jer 38:3, as well as at John 12:32 (1955: 245). Wesley avers that at first we are drawn by 'good desires' and never by the coercion of the will (*MCNT* at VI.44). The saying **all shall be taught of God** (AV, perhaps from Isa 54:13) is quoted by Spenser satirically as a charter for idle priests (1970: 499).

Eating the Son Of Man

6:47–51. Nothing is new but the last phrase, which according to R. H. Lightfoot intimates, more clearly than any previous verse, that the Incarnation entails the Crucifixion (1956: 162, 169). Barrett observes that Jesus now assumes responsibility for the gift (1955: 246). Though Christ does not speak openly of his death, comparison with 10:11, 15:13 and 17:19 shows that the preposition *huper* ('**for**') in the final clause implies a sacrifice. Gottfried von Strassburg playfully reunites this alimentary symbol with the georgic imagery of 12:24 when he declares that the death of Tristan and Iseult is the bread of the living (*Tristan* 238 at 1977: 5).

6:52. Hoskyns compares the obtuseness of Nicodemus at 3:4 (1947: 298). Brodie suggests that the subsequent discourse comes 'down-to-earth', and thereby mirrors the (unreported) descent from the mountain after 6:15 (1993: 285). It has been suggested frequently that the following discourse is a polemic against the docetics, who denied that God was truly come in the flesh (see Lindars 1972: 271–2).

6:53–6. Hoskyns comments that Christ has rendered his doctrine 'more objectionable' by adding words that slight the prohibition on eating blood at Lev 17:10–14 and Acts 15:29 (1947: 296). Natalis Alexander sees an answer to Job's question at 31:31: 'Who will give us his flesh that we may be filled?' (1840: 281). Ignatius of Antioch understands the flesh as faith and the blood as love, discovering the first in the bread and the second in the wine of the eucharist (*Trallians* 8) The *Gospel of Philip* states that the flesh is the word and the blood the spirit, associating the latter in particular with the hidden name of Jesus, whom it declares identical with the eucharist (J. A. Robinson 1988: 144 and 148).

6:57–8. Erasmus paraphrases: 'As the living Father sent me and I live by the Father, so he who eats me will live because of me' (1535: 242). Although v. 58 may seem repetitive, Calvin argues that the gifts of Christ are now traced for the first time to the Father (1959: 171–2).

True and False Disciples

6:59–60. Chrysostom notes that Capernaum is the 'place where most of his miracles had been done' in other Gospels (*Homily* 47.1). Even at this point, the *Gospel of Barnabas* leaves him 72 disciples, no doubt his future emissaries to the cities of Galilee at Luke 10:1 (1907: 125).

6:61–2. R. H. Lightfoot observes that the ascent must be preceded by the Cross (1956: 169), while Hoskyns deduces that the Resurrection and the Ascension reveal the meaning of the eucharist (1947: 301). Dodd assumes that the eating of Christ's flesh would have been particularly offensive to a 'Hellenistic public' (1953a: 341). Yet another theory, not quite out of fashion, holds that the eucharist was pre-empted by the Dionysiac rite of eating the god (Dodds 1951: 277–8).

6:63. Hoskyns observes that Spirit and life are conjoined at 2 Macc 14:6 and refers us back to John 4:24 (1947: 301), while R. H. Lightfoot adduces Gen 2:7 and Ezek 37:5 (1956: 169). Dodd, rejecting the view that the Greek word *rhêma* is a Semitism, concludes that it means, like *logos* in the prologue, a word 'instinct with the energies of God's creative thought' (1953a: 342n). Chrysostom supports him with a quotation of Rom 10:6–7 (*Homily* 47.3).

6:64–6. Hoskyns argues that the false disciples are identified in 1 John as those who deny that Christ is God come in the flesh (1947: 302). Calvin draws the lesson that a preacher must have the courage, though not the intention, to offend (1959: 177).

6:67–8. To Chrysostom the words of Christ are a proof of self-sufficiency (*Homily* 47.3), to Hutcheson an expression of solicitude for his flock (1972: 130). Marsh suggests that Peter echoes 'the great *I am* of his master' in reply (1968: 313).

6:69–70. Cf. Luke 6:13 on choosing. Lindars cites John 1:49 for 'Holy One of God', but the reply will be more trenchant if we imagine that the Evangelist was aware of the demon's exclamation at Mark 1:24.

6:71. Only here is the number of the disciples fixed at 12 in the present Gospel. In contrast to Hastings (1906: 909), Marsh contends that the treachery of Judas is not merely predicted but inevitable (1968: 316). Erasmus suggests that the word *diabolos* (not used of Satan elsewhere in the New Testament) means 'slanderer' or 'accuser' rather than 'devil' (1535: 242). Calvin contrasts the use of 'angel' to signify a good teacher in Mal 2:7 (1959: 179).

Epilogue: Bread and Sacrament

In a structuralist analysis of this chapter, Crossan (1980) argues that a polarity between bread and Christ gives way to a metaphorical equation of the two. To some it is more than a metaphor, and no controversy has so divided Christendom as the one that turns on the presence of the Lord Jesus at his own Supper. He himself said of the bread 'this is my body', and of the wine 'this is my blood'. Transubstantiation – the doctrine that the substance of the elements is transmuted into the flesh and blood of the Crucified, while the accidents of bread and wine remain – was defined for the Western Church in 1215 by the Fourth Lateran Council (Tanner and Alberigo 1990: 230). The Council of Trent assumed that John 6:53–4 confirmed this teaching, yet denied that the text entailed the administration of both bread and wine to the laity (Tanner and Alberigo 1990: 726). The Reformed tradition urges, on the contrary, that the body of Christ abides with God in heaven, while his flesh and blood are received below in a 'heavenly and spiritual sense'. One interpretation of Luther argues that the resurrected body acquires the attribute of ubiquity and mingles imperceptibly with the elements of the eucharist.

Might it not be enough to say, with Origen, that to feed on Christ is to nourish faith by contemplating his image in the Gospel? Zwingli maintains that the flesh of Christ is consolation (Bromiley 1953: 206), Luther that it is faith (1961: 235). Such interpretations gain some colour from the rabbinic belief that the manna in the wilderness was an emblem of the Torah (Glasson 1963: 47). Nevertheless, the carnal mind seeks miracles, and the second-century heretic Mark the Mage was accused of counterfeiting the change of wine to blood for his congregation (Irenaeus, *Against Heresies* 1.13), while in alchemical literature we meet a figure who comes to life again after swallowing his own flesh or dismembering it and cooking it in a vat (Jung 1967: 70–6). Such a vessel, according to Loomis (1963), was the original Grail, while Geoffrey Ashe connects John 6:53 with the first French version of the legend, where the Grail is a platter carrying the host (1967: 188–9). In the British romance of Joseph of Arimathea, it is the chalice of the holy blood, and accompanied by another edible symbol of Christ, the fish. To modern minds this may be only, as Emily Dickinson whispered, 'loved philology' and 'tremblingly partook' at best (1970: 676); yet the Anglican cleric Andrew Young can still extol the Word 'from whom the light of day as daily bread is broken' (1985: 186), while David Jones can trace the barley of Wales to one who 'said / I am your bread' (1952: 82).

Prologue: Coherence and Purpose of the Narrative

From chapter 7 to chapter 17 there is barely a trace of the sayings and miracles that punctuate the Synoptic accounts of the ministry in Jerusalem; conversely, the Synoptics make no reference to the healing of the man born blind, the discourse on the shepherd, the resurrection of Lazarus, the foot washing, the promise of the Paraclete, or the valedictory prayer. Even the triumphal entry of Jesus into Jerusalem and his agony in Gethsemane are pared down to a few phrases. It is therefore begging the question to say, with J. A. T. Robinson, that only the Fourth Evangelist gives a date to the final journey when the others hardly report the same event (1985: 142).

At 7:14 the controversy ignited by the healing in chapter 5 is resumed as though there had been no interval. The transposition of chapters 5 and 6 will not suffice to restore a continuous text unless we also move or eliminate verses 1–13 of chapter 7. In Bultmann's commentary, segments of chapters 7 and 8 are interspliced to produce a coherent narrative; the same principle would oblige us to append 12:34 to 8:28, and both perhaps to the conversation of Christ with Nicodemus in chapter 3. The train of events in verses 1–13 is difficult to interpret, as Jesus says one thing and does another, with a subterfuge that is at once ineffectual and untypical of this Gospel. Augustine felt obliged to acquit him of lying; Bultmann, who attributes verses 11–13 to the ubiquitous redactor, perceives that the principal object of the passage is to show that Christ remains hidden from the multitude even where he is revealed.

A Secret Journey to Jerusalem

7:1. Augustine finds here a justification of flight under persecution (*Homily* 28.2). Theophylact suggests that Christ withdrew because his hour was not yet come (Aquinas 1997: 254). The word **Jews** is often understood to signify the leaders of Jewry, as by Natalis Alexander (1840: 289). Hutcheson cites Luke 23:7 in support of his conjecture that the festal crowd included Herod Antipas, who conspires against the life of Jesus at Luke 13:31 (1972: 93).

7:2. Ryle suggests that the Feast of Tabernacles, a season of mirth which followed the harvest and ended the Jewish year, anticipates the Second Coming (1869: 7–8). It is of course a fit setting for the Word who 'tabernacled among us' at 1:14.

7:3. Chrysostom praises the candour of the Evangelist (*Homily* 48.1–2). Augustine upholds the perpetual virginity of Mary by translating **brethren** as 'kindred' (*Homily* 28.3), and Calvin too accepts this rendering. Bede surmises that Christ went to Jerusalem to rejoin the followers whom he had left behind there (Aquinas 1997: 254–5); Barrett, however, argues that the apostasy of the Galilean disciples at 6:66 prompts the request that Christ should show himself in Jerusalem (1955: 256–7).

7:4–7. Hoskyns compares the provocative intervention of the mother of Jesus at 2:1–11 (1947: 311). Action in secret signified humility to the rabbis (Hoskyns 1947: 311), and also to Jesus at Matt 6:4. Chrysostom construes **my hour** as the hour of crucifixion (*Homily* 47.2), Augustine as the Day of Judgement: he adds that the **brethren** stand for those who go by the clock of the world and not by God's (*Homily* 28.5). For Bultmann the journey brings about the crisis, which divides the human race into believers and unbelievers.

7:8. Porphyry censured Christ for his inconsistency (Jerome, *Against Pelagius* 2.17), and some manuscripts respond by making him say 'I go not *yet* up to Jerusalem'. Giblin (1980) numbers this among the passages in which Jesus declines to act and then appears to change his mind. One lenitive, adopted by Epiphanius, is to construe the phrase 'go up' to mean 'ascend' (*Panarion* 51.25).

7:9–10. Augustine suggests that Christ **went in secret** because his purpose was to instruct his disciples, not to parade his glory (*Homily* 28.8); Chrysostom argues that had he gone up openly, the Jews would have forced him into a premature disclosure of his divinity (*Homily* 48.2). Bede takes the **brothers** as symbols of the carnally minded, for whom Christ remains in Galilee and is not yet manifest in his royal city (Aquinas 1997: 258). Hoskyns likens the epiphany in Jerusalem to the advent of the Lord's messenger at Mal 3:1 (1947: 313).

7:11. Here as elsewhere the seeking is 'probably hostile', according to Barrett (1955: 259). Chrysostom notes it as a sign of hatred that the Jews do not even use the name of Jesus (*Homily* 49.1). For Augustine his concealment represents the perpetual state of pilgrimage in which Christians live (*Homily* 28.9).

7:12–13. Cf. 7:32 and 6:41 for the **murmuring**; Justin Martyr, *Trypho* 69, for the accusation. The first opinion is that of the people, the second that of their rulers, according to Chrysostom (*Homily* 49.1). Augustine sees the failure of the Jews to apprehend Jesus as a token of his power (*Homily* 29.1), while even their wonder at v. 15 does not persuade Chrysostom that they admired him for the right reason (*Homily* 49.1).

Moses, the Sabbath and the True Law

7:14–15. The **middle of the festival** is the fourth day, since according to Neh 8:18 one day had been added to the seven of Lev 23:34–6 (Hoskyns 1947: 314). Since the ensuing discourse presupposes knowledge of the miracle at Bethesda, many follow Bultmann (1957: 205) in annexing either 7:15–24 or 7:21–4 to 5:47, the first allusion to Moses (cf. Barrett 1955: 263).

7:16–18. The authority of the Father replaces that of rabbinic succession, according to Barrett (1955: 262). Hoskyns cites Philo, *Special Laws* 1.65: 'the prophet [in Deut 18:15] will act simply as the organ of divine revelation' (1947: 314). Whereas Ryle explains **not mine** as 'not mine only' (1869: 21), Augustine decides that the doctrine does belong to Christ as Word, but not as man (*Homily* 29.3). Lindars reads v. 18 as an attack on the 'ambition of the rabbis' (1972: 289), though Westcott quotes a rabbinic exhortation to 'do his will as if it were thine' (1903: 118).

7:19–20. No Evangelist need despair, says Natalis Alexander, when even Moses failed to move this stubborn populace (1840: 321). Chrysostom thinks that the Jews are charged with breaching the commandment not to kill (*Homily* 49.2), Augustine that they sin by failing to recognize Christ's fulfilment of the Law (*Homily* 30.2). Meeks maintains that they prove themselves false prophets by failing to recognize the 'prophet like Moses' at Deut 18:18–22 (1967: 45–57).

7:21–4. Augustine notes that to make a man whole on the Sabbath (as in chapter 5) is nothing compared to creation in six days (*Homily* 30.3). Barrett quotes *Shabbath* 18.3 and *Nedarim* 3.11 to confirm that circumcision was permitted on the Sabbath and thus to demonstrate that Christ's action was a fulfilment, not a suspension, of the Law (1955: 264). Certainly, as Natalis Alexander asseverates, miraculous healing is not the 'servile work' forbidden in the commandment (1840: 300).

7:25–6. Cf. Mark 1:15 for the Greek **Jerusalemites**. Augustine suggests that, failing to grasp the power of Christ, the people wrongly supposed that he had been spared by the will of the rulers (*Homily* 31.1).

7:27. Augustine notes that the prophets named both Nazareth and Bethlehem as the birthplace of the Messiah (Matt 2:6, 23), while Isa 53:8 says, 'who can declare his generation?' (*Homily* 31.2). Hoskyns cites Justin Martyr, *Trypho* 8, and rabbinic sayings on the obscurity of the Messiah (1947: 317). Seventeenth-century radicals turned the text against academic theologians: 'What is thy birth and where can divines tell / Yea but not such as in Cambridge dwell' (Underwood 1999: 225).

7:28. The word **cried** (*ekraxen*) is also used at 1:15, 7:37, 12:44. Bengel hears the voice of ardour (1850: 407), R. H. Lightfoot of inspiration (1956: 186). Chrysostom suggests that the Jews do not know **whence Christ is** because they lack knowledge of the Father (*Homily* 50.1), Augustine that they knew of his youth in Nazareth, but not of his virgin birth (*Homily* 31.2). Bultmann remarks that Gnostic sources insist on the obscurity of the Messiah (1957: 223), though he also proves from Lucian, *Alexander* 11 (and anyone else can prove from Mark 6:3), that a prophet's claims are least credible to those who know his parents.

7:29–31. Every prophet purports to be the messenger of Yahweh (see Ross 1962), but Augustine adds that this one is **from** the Father by nature, but is voluntarily **sent** from him in the flesh (*Homily* 31.4). Chrysostom's proposal that the escape of Christ is a miracle (*Homily* 50.2) accounts for the question of the **many** in v. 31. Augustine identifies them as the poor and humble, in contrast to Christ's accusers (*Homily* 31.7).

The Promise of the Spirit

7:32. Barrett finds it improbable that the priests and Pharisees should act in concert (1955: 268); Martyn makes the opposite complaint – that they should not be segregated, as a Pharisee might also be a priest (1979: 84).

7:33–6. Cf. 8:14, 13:3, 14:4, 16:5 for the verb *hupagein*, 'to depart'. Chrysostom interprets this to mean that the Jews will call on him belatedly after the sack of Jerusalem (*Homily* 50.2). Marsh discovers another 'I am' saying, though he grants that *ego eimi* may mean simply 'I am going' (1968: 339). As Augustine saw, Christ is predicting his resurrection and departure (*Homily* 31.9), but Temple suggests that vv. 35–6 anticipate the mission to the Gentiles which succeeded these events (1961: 125–6). Calvin, however, cites Jas 1:1 to show that the Jews are more likely to be thinking of a mission to other Jews of the Diaspora (1959: 196).

7:37. Chrysostom suggests that Christ postponed this call until the other distractions of the festival were forgotten (*Homily* 51.1). If, as J. Lightfoot opines, the water came from the pool of Siloam, this verse foreshadows the miracle at 9:7 (1859: 324). In fact, we possess no evidence that water was drawn on the eighth day of the feast; Ryle contends, however, that the performance of this rite on the previous seven days sufficed to prepare the audience for Christ's sermon (1869: 49). Bunyan exhorts the Christian to make his doctrine as pure and his life as clean as the water of life that wells from the Lamb at Rev 22:1, prefigured as this is by the river Jordan and the waters of creation on which the Spirit broods at Gen 1:2 (1868: 550–5). Housman insinuates that the stream has now been dammed by the greed of ecclesiastics:

> Ho, everyone that thirsteth
> And hath the price to give,
> Come to the stolen waters,
> Drink and your soul shall live
> (1939: 123, alluding to Isa 55:1)

7:38. Theodore of Mopsuestia took **as the scripture says** with the previous clause, to yield the sense 'He who believes in me according to scripture' (Barrett 1955: 270–1). In Henry's gloss the same construction refers to those who 'entertain him as he is offered to us in the gospel' (1991: 1962, col. 1). If we assume instead that it introduces a quotation in the following clause, the source remains obscure. Jerome adduces Prov 5:16 in his prologue to Genesis; Hoskyns, who infers from the use of the singular that 'the author has a particular passage in mind', prefers Deut 8:16 (1947: 322). Lindars refers to Prov 18:4, Isa 58:11 and Sir 24:30–4 (1972: 299). While many recent commentators assume that it is God from whom the Spirit flows, and J. A. T. Robinson suggests that it is the Evangelist who is saying this of Jesus (1985: 306; cf. Eusebius, *Church History* 5.1), the majority of the Fathers agreed with Origen (*Commentary*, Fr. 36) that the subject is the believer. Augustine construes the waters as love and the belly as conscience (*Homily* 32.40), while Gregory the Great finds an image of preaching (Aquinas 1997: 273–4).

7:39. Was the Spirit not given before? Yes, says Augustine, quoting Luke 1:15, but not hitherto with the gift of tongues (*On the Trinity* 4.20). Chrysostom equates the glorification with the Cross (*Homily* 51.2). Cyril of Alexandria explains that Christ brings a plenary infusion of the spirit that was breathed into Adam at Gen 2:7 but dissipated by the Fall (1.690–8 Pusey). Goodenough, at the end of his account of the Feast of Tabernacles, cites this verse as an instance of the Christian appropriation of Jewish 'mysticism' (1953: 156).

The Jews Divided

7:40–2. Cf. 1:20–1 and 4:19, 25. Marsh compares the confession of Jesus as **Christ** with that of Peter at Mark 8:29 (1968: 345). The objection derives from Mic 5:2, which foretells that the Messiah will be born in Bethlehem. Alcuin remarks that the multitude knew the prophecies, but not that they were now fulfilled in Jesus (Aquinas 1997: 276–7). Chrysostom contrasts the secret chattering of the doubters with the frankness of Nathanael at 1:46. (*Homily* 51.1).

7:43–5. The **division**, in Theophylact's view, was not among the rulers, but between them and the people. Chrysostom blames the Pharisees for their antipathy to truth (*Homily* 51.2), while Augustine remarks that their emissaries returned empty-handed and full of admiration (*Homily* 33.1). Yet schism, which recurs at 9:16 and 10:19, is an 'inevitable effect' of the proclamation in Barrett's view (1955: 273).

7:46–9. Ashton considers the argument of the soldiers a clear advance on the naïve argument from miracles at 7:31 (1991: 302). Theophylact says that the Pharisees made a courteous reply for fear that their interlocutors might desert to Jesus (Aquinas 1997: 278). The statement that the people are **accursed** is not supported in rabbinic texts, though the laity are stigmatized as 'people of the land' (Hoskyns 1947: 325–6; Barrett 1955: 274).

7:50–1. Once again the Jews are accused of treason against their own law (Chrysostom, *Homily* 51.1). In the film *The Greatest Story Ever Told* Nicodemus remonstrates in like terms at the trial of Jesus, and Justin Martyr makes a Gentile use the same words in objecting, at the cost of his life, to illegal proceedings against a Christian officer (*2 Apology* 1). Calvin, however, finds Nicodemus still too pusillanimous (1959: 204).

7:52. The assertion that no prophet can arise from Galilee, though fore-shadowed in Nathanael's sneer at 1:46, is unparalleled in Jewish literature, according to Barrett (1955: 274). Chrysostom (*Homily* 52.1) glosses 'search' as 'search the scriptures' (cf. 5:39), but Brodie suggests that, since they omit the word 'scripture', the Pharisees have misconceived the essence of their own religion (1993: 322). Since the Pharisees should have known that Jonah came from Gath-Hepher, a few miles north of Nazareth (2 Kings 14:25), Lindars suggests that the reference is to 'the prophet' of Deut 18:18 and John 1:21 (1972: 303). Augustine comments that Jesus was 'no prophet, but the Lord of all the prophets' (*Homily* 33.11), while Fortna suggests that this verse was written in irony when Galilee had become the 'place of discipleship' and consequently the '*terra Christiana*' (1988: 309–10).

Bruegel, *Christ and the Woman Taken in Adultery.* Witt Library, Courtauld Institute of Art, London.

Interlude: The Woman Taken in Adultery

First the mother of Jesus, then the Samaritan – now another nameless female, in a Gospel that even gives a name to Malchus. In Maeterlinck's *Mary Magdalene* (1910) and the film *The Greatest Story Ever Told*, this temptress calls herself Mary Magdalene, and the two were confused in medi-eval art (Haskins 1994: 28–31). Farrar (1901: 382n) proposes instead that the Evangelist, or a scribe of an early period, has taken over the story of 'the woman of many sins' who spoke with Jesus in the *Gospel to the Hebrews* (Papias, in Eusebius, *Church History* 3.39). The episode was lacking in the codices of Origen and Chrysostom, yet Jerome found it in 'many Greek and Latin codices' (*Against the Pelagians* 2.6), and Augustine argued that it had been excised as a matter of policy, lest wives should claim the pardon and forget the condemnation of the offence (*On Adulterous Liaisons* 2.7). Erasmus did not excise it, and the Puritans were loth to give up the one episode in the Gospel which implies that the kingdom is open to those who sin. In many recent commentaries, however, it appears as an appendix, as it does in certain manuscripts; others, which Temple prefers to follow, attribute it to Luke (1961: 128). For all that, it is well placed in its present location, following as it does on Nicodemus' question whether the Law condemns a man unheard (7:51), and coming shortly before a sermon in the Court of the Women (8:20), from which the adulteress, if convicted, would have been expelled (J. Lightfoot 1859: 329).

Even many feminists who deplore the anonymity of women in the New Testament have neglected this one in deference to the scruples of the modern commentator. Some of her advocates allege with Derrett (1963–4:5) that under Jewish law it was hardly possible to provide the required two witnesses unless they had been privy to the offence. The absence of the adulterer gives rise to the suspicion that he connived at her entrapment (Scott 2000); and even if such forensic pleadings fail, she was a victim of unequal laws, which made her the husband's chattel while denying her any claim on his fidelity (Rooke 2000). Those who maintain her guilt can point to the silence of the Evangelist and the injunction **sin no more**. Artists have almost always painted her with sympathy. In Bruegel's painting *Christ and the Woman Taken in Adultery*, she stands in the middle looking down at Christ as he squats to write between the apostles and the Pharisees (Courtauld Institute, London). In Poussin's work of this title, Christ protects the kneeling woman while haranguing her accusers, two of whom attempt to decode the writing as the others flee or silently abscond (Louvre Museum, Paris). She cowers behind Christ's left hand in an engraving by Doré (1995: 221), but in the Codex Egberti (Haskins 1994: 29) and a water-colour by Blake she stands erect while her accusers turn their backs (Museum of Fine Arts, Boston).

The Adulteress Brought to Jesus

7:53–8:2. On **every man to his own house** (AV) cf. 1:11, 16:32, 19:27b. For Alcuin the Mount of Olives denotes the pity of Christ, the dawn his mercy, the sitting his humility (Aquinas 1997: 281). Craveri yokes this episode and the cursing of the fig-tree (Mark 11:13, etc.) as illustrations of the barrenness of Israel (1967: 286–7).

8:3–5. Lev 20:10 condemns both parties to execution; stoning was a traditional penalty, seldom if ever enforced upon adulterers, though often threatened by the accusers of Jesus in this Gospel. In the North-Town mystery play the scribes and Pharisees plot to surprise the lovers, but the man escapes at sword-point (Cawley 1974: 137). The conspirators add that if Christ condemns the woman, he will falsify his own teaching on forgiveness, and if he pardons her, he will be her accomplice and subject to capital penalty. Charles Wesley seizes upon the words **she was taken** (AV) as an admission that the act was sinful in their eyes only because it was detected (2001: 243).

The Woman Acquitted

8:6. Bengel observes that, as God inscribed the Decalogue only once, so Christ wrote once in the whole New Testament (1850: 411). But why did he write? It is difficult to improve on the supplementary italics of the AV, '*as though he heard them not*'. Alcuin sees a parabolic injunction to search our own hearts before passing judgement (Aquinas 1997: 282). Seeley won immortal notoriety by suggesting that the virgin Messiah stooped to hide his blushes (1895: 119). 'Cease', cries Blake to the finger of God that inscribed the Law at Deut 9:10 (1969: 754); God's finger is the instrument of exorcism at Luke 11:20, and if Satan is above all the accuser, we see an exorcism here. In a medieval mystery play, however, the accusers discover a record of their own sins (Cawley 1974: 141). In the *Gospel of Barnabas* (which seems to follow this play) Jesus shapes a mirror in the dust (1907: 249).

8:7–9. Cf. Rom 3:23, 1 Kings 8:46. Augustine comments that Jesus gave no judgement lest he appear to infringe the Law (*Homily* 33.5). J. Lightfoot observes that his challenge to the accusers is justified by the rabbinic rule that the husband who denounces his wife must himself be free of guilt (1859: 329). In Hutcheson's view the **eldest** are the **first to** go away because they are conscious of the greatest burden of sin (1972: 159). Daniel's refutation of the elders who accused Susanna may also be compared: *Christ and the Adulteress* and *Daniel and Susannah* are alternative titles of the same painting from the school of Titian.

8:10–11. Some maintain that the words **go and sin no more** (AV) do not incriminate the woman any more than they incriminate the paralytic at 5:14; Brown, however, thinks it a salient difference that in the present case a crime has been alleged (1966: 340). Augustine cites the closing words to prove that Christ does not encourage sin (*Homily* 33.6). Wolfe condenses vv. 9–11 to imply that the Pharisees are not only partners in the woman's sin but the causes of it: 'Then God call off the hounds and bid the whore, / And all who made her, go and sin no more!' (1927: 38).

Jesus the Light and Judge of the World

8:12. The image of light recurs at 1:4, 9:5, 1 John 1:5, with *Gospel of Thomas* 24 and 77. Hoskyns adopts Strack-Billerbeck's suggestion that the metaphor is inspired by the display of the candelabra on the first day of the Feast of Tabernacles, but he finds more elucidation in Isa 43:8–13 which associates the 'divine I am' with the duty of bearing witness to the blind (1947: 330). Dodd contends that, since the Jews do not accuse Christ of blasphemy, they fail to grasp the magnitude of his claim (1953a: 204–8).

8:13–14. These verses are antithetical to 5:37. Alcuin reminds the Pharisees that the prophets had borne witness to Christ (Aquinas 1997: 286). Chrysostom writes that, though Christ condescends to their low estimation of him, it is God who bears witness to God here (*Homily* 52.2). Augustine takes the words **where I am going** as a reference to the Father (*Homily* 35.6).

8:15–16. Judgement is passed from the Father to Christ at 5:22, from Christ to Moses at 5:45, and back to the Father here. Theophylact takes the first clause to mean that the Pharisees misjudge Christ as a mere man (Aquinas 1997: 286). To Augustine the second clause means either 'I do not judge now' or 'I do not judge according to the flesh'. Chrysostom infers from v. 16 that Christ does judge, but not alone (*Homily* 52.2). Dodd concludes persuasively that Christ is the judge in so far as he exposes the self-condemning deeds of others, as at 3:19–21 (1953a: 210). Hoskyns, remarking that judgement here denotes condemnation, squares this verse with the promises of salvation (3:17 etc.) by denying that one can be given without the other (1947: 331).

8:17–18. The law on testimony is cited from Deut 17:6; cf. Matt 18:16. Lindars reckons this among the 'I am' (*ego eimi*) sayings (1972: 318). Alluding to the indictment of Susanna, Augustine finds that the only 'two or three witnesses' whose testimony is infallible are the persons of the Trinity (*Homily* 36.10). Chrysostom adds that God is the only subject who is allowed to bear testimony to himself (*Homily* 52.3). Bede suggests that the Father bears witness to Christ at Psalm 2:7 (Aquinas 1997: 288).

8:19. Origen contends, against the heretics who infer that the God of the Jews is not the Father of Christ, that to know God means to have fellowship with him, not merely to be aware of his existence (*Commentary* 19.3–4). As Calvin explains, such fellowship or saving knowledge is given only in Christ (1959: 213). Theophylact turns this verse against the Arians, who maintain that Christ is a creature, for then we could not know God by knowing him (Aquinas 1997: 290).

8:20. The treasury was in the Court of the Women, where, according to Bengel, the greatest crowds were gathered (1850: 413). The Fathers had some right to construe the treasury allegorically, since, as Brown (1966: 342) and Lindars (1972: 319) both protest, we cannot suppose that Jesus preached in the strong-room of the Temple. Origen suggests that Jesus' words are his gifts to the treasury (*Commentary* 19.1); Bede's statement that in teaching heavenly things to his disciples he was opening his own treasury mingles reminiscences of 3:12 and Matt 13:52 (Aquinas 1997: 292). **His hour** means evidently the hour of death, as Augustine (*Homily* 37.8) points out.

Whence and Who is Christ?

8:21. Cf. 14:3–4, where Jesus prepares the place for the disciples. Ashton compares the departure and return of Wisdom at *1 Enoch* 42 (1991: 539). Origen contrasts the 'seeking' of truth by the believer with the 'seeking' of his death by his adversaries (*Commentary* 19.3). In Christ's prediction Hoskyns sees an illustration of the prophetic rule (Deut 24:16, Ezek 18:24–8) that each shall be punished for his own sin (1947: 333), while Bede comments that all are held accountable for one **sin** rather than for their several 'sins' (Aquinas 1997: 294).

8:22–3. Suicide is condemned by Josephus at *Jewish War* 3.375. Origen finds a scurrilous intimation of the truth that Jesus will lay down his own life (*Commentary* 19.4, citing 10:18). Despite the precedents at 3:12–13 and 7:27–8, some Fathers take the reply of Jesus to intimate simply that he is without sin (Aquinas 1997: 295–6); Calvinists can persuade themselves that **from below** means justly predestined to hell (J. Edwards 1830: 165). Barrett, while he cites rabbinic parallels, surmises that the thought is coloured by 'popular Platonism' (1955: 282), though there was little of this in the time of our Evangelist.

8:24. Hoskyns hears an echo of Ex 3:14 (1947: 334); Daube, however, traces the Messianic *ego eimi* to a midrash on Ex 12:12, 'I am the Lord' (1956: 326). Behind this verse and 8:24 Ball hears the voice of Yahweh at Isa 43:10 (1996: 188–94). Bultmann objects that the Jews perceive no blasphemy (1957: 265n), but Temple holds that the saying can be understood in three senses: 'I am what I say', 'I am He (the Messiah)', and nakedly 'I am' (1961: 134). Jesus now says 'sins', not 'sin' as in v. 21; perhaps, as Brodie surmises, he is speaking of the 'specific deviations' which proceed from the one great sin, the refusal of life (1993: 326).

8:25. On the difficulties of the Greek adverbial phrase *tên arkhên* see Schnackenburg (1980: 200–1). Chrysostom's gloss, 'as I told you *from the beginning*' (*Homily* 53.1) is widely accepted, and Westcott won little support for his two alternatives: 'Altogether I am that which I speak to you' and 'How is it that I even speak to you at all?' (1903: 131). As Barrett remarks, the Evangelist knew less Greek than his modern commentators (1955: 284).

8:26–8. He refrains from condemnation, argues Chrysostom, and speaks only of salvation (*Homily* 53.1); Augustine, however, sees a premonition of future judgement (*Homily* 29.5). The **lifting up** is prophesied at 12:32 and 3:14, though, as Brodie comments, threat has supervened on promise since the visit of Nicodemus (1993: 325). Chrysostom interprets v. 28 to mean that the Jews will at last perceive Christ's unanimity and equality with the Father, both of which are proved by the following verse (*Homily* 53.2).

8:29–30. For the **sending** cf. 9:4. Temple explains the belief of the **many** in v. 30 with the comment that obedience is a form of apologetic (1961: 335).

Truth is Freedom

8:31. Lindars follows Dodd and Bultmann in pronouncing the words **who believed in him** to be an interpolation (1972: 323–4). If retained, they confirm Augustine's principle that knowledge depends on faith (*Homily* 41.1).

8:32. Calvin understands freedom as a 'voluntary righteousness' which does not come of our own will (1959: 222). Barrett compares rabbinic sayings on freedom under the yoke of the Law and the Stoic position that liberty is life in accord with reason (1955: 285). Tolstoy imports a modern notion of freedom when he makes this one of three rubrics to his argument that Christ forbade both political and military coercion (1936: 1).

8:33. As at Isa 41:8, Matt 3:9 and Rom 4:16, the Jews appeal to Abraham. Origen's reply (with a glance at the parable of the sower) is that theirs was a seed that perished because it was strangled by their pride. Augustine convicts the Jews of error, since Joseph and the prophets went into captivity (*Homily* 41.2). Hoskyns, however, quotes Cyril of Alexandria's dictum that Joseph was free even in his bonds (1947: 339). Dodd suggests that these diehards represent Judaizing Christians in the time of the Evangelist (1955: 5–7).

8:34. The untranslated word **Amen** added gravity to this saying for Augustine (*Homily* 41.3). Barrett strangely purports to show that this is a Greek and not a Jewish sentiment by citing the proem to Philo's treatise *That Every Good Man is Free*, together with another text that may spring from a Jewish milieu, *Corpus Hermeticum* 10.8 (1955: 286).

8:35–6. Cf. 1 John 3:8 on the bondage of sin; Chrysostom adds that Christ's sonship is the source of his power to forgive (*Homily* 54.2). As Natalis Alexander observes, they had endured conquest, though not domestic service (1840: 340–1); his conjecture that they were alluding to the story of Hagar and Sarah is taken up at length by Ryle (1869: 120). Paul's version of this at Gal 4:21–31 lends weight to Marsh's suggestion that the freedom bestowed by Christ is prefigured by that of Isaac in Abraham's household at Gen 17:21 (1968: 364). This freedom is shown, according to Augustine, not in sinning but in abstinence from sin (*Homily* 41.8).

Son of God, Son of Abraham

8:37–40. Chrysostom cites the words **ye seek to kill me** (AV) as evidence of sin (*Homily* 54.2). Augustine writes that, if truly received, the word of the Lord is like a hook to a fish (*Homily* 42.1). Origen understands v. 40b to mean that Abraham did not try to kill Melchizedek, and accounts for Christ's description of himself as a man by saying that he sometimes speaks as man, sometimes as God (*Commentary* 20.12).

8:41. Origen understands the word **illegitimate** as a reference to the story that Christ himself was born of adultery (*Commentary* 20.14). Hoskyns cites 1:13–14, 7:27–8 and 8:19 as other intimations of 'a peculiarity in the birth of Jesus' (1947: 342). Hutcheson, with sound precedent in the Jewish Scriptures, applies it to idolatry (1972: 175), though other Reformed theologians have supposed that the Jews are contrasting the children of Sarah with those of Hagar (Ryle 1869: 129).

8:42–3. Hilary takes the procession to be the incorporeal birth of Christ in heaven, and the coming forth as the prototype and ground of our own sonship (*On the Trinity* 6.30). R. H. Lightfoot distinguishes **speech**, the audible utterance, from **word**, its 'content and import' (1956: 196).

8:44. The words **from the beginning** are applied with contrasting force to Christ at 8:25. Lindars notes a similar antithesis between the spirit of truth and the spirit of falsehood in documents from Qumran (1972: 330). Against those who deduce that vice and virtue are congenital, Augustine says that the Jews were the devil's children by imitation not by birth (*Homily* 42.11), and that the devil fell at the instant of his creation but was not created evil (*City of God* 11.13). Ignatius no doubt agreed when he borrowed the phrase **sons of the devil** at *Magnesians* 3.3. Origen takes Adam to be the victim (*Commentary* 20.21), but Augustine compares the devil with Cain (*Questions on the Two Testaments* 2.90) because at 1 John 3:12 he is made responsible for the murder of Abel. According to Theophylact, the devil lied first to Eve (Aquinas 1997: 315).

8:45–7. Origen sees a rebuke to Jews who admire Christ's miracles but not his words (*Commentary* 20.24). According to Theophylact, they betray their own sinfulness by hating one whom they cannot convict of sin (Aquinas 1997: 316). Augustine, once again pre-empting a Manichaean inference from v. 47, asserts they they receive their nature from God but not their faults (*Homily* 42.16).

Has he a Devil?

8:48–50. On the Samaritan Christ see chapter on 4:8–45. The mildness of his rejoinder is admired by Augustine, Chrysostom and Pope Gregory (Aquinas 1997: 317–18). Origen thinks that he failed to disown the name because he wished to be all things to all men (*Commentary* 20.16/28); Luther applauds his preaching of the truth without concern for his own reputation (1983: 175–6). Westcott, however, understands **I honour my father** as a retort to the insult (1903: 138), which Theophylact construes to mean that Christ transgressed the Law (Aquinas 1997: 317). The source of **glory** becomes apparent at 17:45, the price at 12:33.

8:51–3. Origen holds that only those who undergo the death of the spirit are said to **see** it, though all the prophets **tasted** physical death. Abbott draws a similar distinction (1906: 430–1). For misplaced pride in ancestry, cf. 'our father Jacob' at 4:12, and for the imputation of being a demoniac Mark 3:22–30, etc.

8:54–5. Calvin admits that Christ glorifies himself, but 'by the direction and authority of God' (1959: 233). Hence, as Theophylact notes, the proof of his knowledge is his obedience (Aquinas 1997: 322–3). The lie, according to Origen, consists in the accusation of Christ and in the false opinion of Abraham's death, which is rebutted by Matt 22:32 (*Commentary* 20.33).

How Abraham saw Christ

8:56. Pope Gregory thinks that Abraham saw Christ's **day** when he encountered the Blessed Trinity at Gen 18:2 (Aquinas 1997: 323); Chrysostom identifies the day with that of the Crucifixion, foreshadowed in the offering of Isaac at Gen 22:9–11 (*Homily* 54.2); Luther too refers to the blessing on Abraham's seed at Gen 22:11 (1983: 180). Hoskyns, comparing Heb 11:13, notes that rabbinic sources attribute prescience to Abraham (1947: 347–8); Ignatius claims that the patriarchs 'lived according to the Lord's day', not the Sabbath (*Magnesians* 9.1). The saying of Lancelot Andrewes, that the day of Christ was Abraham's jubilee (1887: 131), is corroborated by Grélot's appeal to the *Book of Jubilees* (1988/9). Noting an apparent contradiction of Luke 10:24, Calvin explains that there are degrees of seeing (1959: 234).

8:57. Irenaeus was the first to deduce that Christ was more than 40 years old; Kokkinos (1989) awards him 46 years to match those of the Temple in Jerusalem. The variant 'has Abraham seen thee?' does not remove the problem (Schnackenburg 1980: 223). Chrysostom observes that some corrected the text to read 'forty', in the light of Luke 3:23 (cf. Brown 1966: 360). Hoskyns infers from Num 4:3 that 50 was a round figure (1947: 348). The conjecture that Christ was prematurely worn with toil, rejected by Erasmus, is revived by Hutcheson (1972: 183). Theophylact sees a reference to the jubilees which were sometimes used to measure the age of the world since Abraham (Aquinas 1997: 324). Bammel reports that Christ survives Tiberius in a number of Jewish legends, some placing his death in AD 46 (1984: 207).

8:58. Bultmann calls this the 'I' of the eternal Logos, divorcing this from the other 'recognition sayings' in which there is no other predicate than the pronoun (1957: 248–9); Ball, however, traces it once again to Isa 43:10 (1996: 195–8). Gregory the Great opines that the paradoxical juxtaposition of tenses is intended to draw their minds from time to eternity (Aquinas 1997: 324). Bengel vindicates the natural reading of this verse against the Socinians, who denied that Christ was God and proposed that he antedates not Abraham but the blessing on Abraham's children (1850: 420–1). Natalis Alexander, imputing to Grotius the view that Christ preceded Abraham only in the foreknowledge of God, asks why the Jews would have stoned him if he meant no more than this (1840: 364).

8:59. Pope Gregory regards it as a mark of Christ's forbearance that he did not preserve his safety by a miracle (Aquinas 1997: 325); Calvin, however, argues that he escaped by 'secret power' (1959: 236). Daube compares Luke 4:29, since casting an offender over a precipice was a recognized alternative to stoning (1956: 303–8). Noyes in *Drake* implies that a lofty spirit is the 'great prophet' who eludes the ignorant crowd (1920: 2).

Epilogue: History and Dogma

Three times in chapter 8 the words 'I am' are used without a grammatical predicate. At 8:58 at least, the locution is plausibly understood as a declaration of Christ's divinity; it must be remembered, however, that in Greek and Aramaic one could always say 'I am' without being thought to pronounce the name of God. The name derived from Exodus 3:14 in Philo is not *ego eimi* ('I am'), but *ho ôn* ('he who is'). But if there is no manifest disclosure of Christ's divinity in these chapters, there is even less material for a historical biography, or even a verification of his status as a prophet. Christ vouchsafes no evidence of his Messianic pedigree, and does not reply to an imputation on his (name-less) mother. A Jew to the Samaritan in chapter 4, a Samaritan to Jews in chapter 8, he eludes his brothers in chapter 7, and seems to be a stranger in Jerusalem. Early readers of John, the Valentinians, concluded that during his earthly ministry Christ already wore the pneumatic or spiritual flesh of the res-urrection, which, according to this Evangelist, could pass through doors and escape recognition even among his chosen followers.

Modern theology bristles with invective against the 'docetic' Christ – a superhuman fantasy who merely 'seems' to be made of flesh and blood. Some assert that this is the Christ of the Fourth Evangelist – fleshly indeed, but already almost 'a foot above the ground' as in the Fathers (Goulder 1977: 81). Even if the Johannine Son of Man does not have a Gnostic prototype as Borsch (1967) and others argue, he belongs to heaven and, unlike men of common mould, returns to it at will. Yet Bultmann, who believed in the Gnostic Son of Man, believed also that the Jesus of history is a mirage, and that true faith con-sists not in taking fiction as fact but in grasping the dangerous liberty that is offered to us by the proclamation (*logos*, *kerygma*) of the first Easter Sunday. The ancestor of Bultmann's view (though not of his scepticism) is the ancient tenet that Christ as the Word or Logos has abolished the Law or Nomos (Rordorf 1979) – that is to say, he supersedes not only the code of works with its useless sacrifices, but the literal exegesis of the Gospel. Himself the walking Word, he has the right to misquote the Scriptures, to invoke the name of Moses without quotation, to enlarge the deposit either by free invention or (as Hanson (1991) prefers to argue) by the bold collation of heterogeneous fragments. Thus 7:37–8 is perhaps not only a saying about the Spirit, but a saying of the Spirit, who is able to educe the living Gospel from the Law.

Prologue: Light and Shepherd as Symbols

The opening of a man's eyes in Mark – with spittle and by stages once again –
is a parable of enlightenment (9: 47–52); the miracle in the Fourth Gospel is
the overture to a demonstration of blindness in the Jews. Chrysostom believes
that it was performed 'from love' and to 'stop the mouths of the foolish'
(*Homily* 60.1); for Calvin it is the beginning of a satire on the Pharisees, which
continues in chapter 10. The circumstantial details are a mark of verisimilitude for Westcott (1903: 143), and are lacking in the miracle of Asclepius which
Barrett cites as a parallel (1955: 293). Bultmann perceives that blindness here,
like darkness in the prologue, is a symbol of unrighteousness (1957: 250): why
else would Christ say 'I am the light of the world'?

The quest for antecedents to this saying, first attested at 8:12, has led to Persia and to the Baptist's putative followers, the Mandaeans (Bultmann 1957: 260n). Yet Zoroastrian texts are hard to date, and those of the Mandaeans, in their present form, belong to a later epoch. Mani, who was said to have pictured the realm of deity as an extended light, commenced his preaching AD 241. The source of his theology may be 1 John 1:5, as it certainly was for Christians who were taken to task by Origen for deducing that the Godhead is a body (*First Principles* 1.1). The *Hermetica*, by contrast, seem to share with 1 Tim 6:16 the notion of an incorporeal light, but the hymn to God as light and life in tract 13 may be indebted to Jewish or Christian sources, as Dodd observes (1953a: 47). We must not forget that light in this Gospel is a metaphor, and that it characterizes not some notional essence of the Deity, but the revelation of deity in Christ. Origen already taught that Christ is called the light of men at John 1:4 because he illuminates the spirit of the believer, and in the Dead Sea Scrolls a child of light is a child of God in the sense that God has imparted knowledge to him, and assured him of a fuller revelation in the new age. This chapter then, as Bultmann saw, bears out his own contention that if anything is revealed to us in this Gospel, it is the presence of revelation in the world.

Some scholars, following Wellhausen, have argued that the quarrel with the Pharisees was patched on to an earlier narrative resembling Mark's (Martyn 1979: 32n); most readers, however (as Ashton grants, 1991: 179), have seen no cause to question the integrity of this chapter, which supplies the text for Elgar's oratorio *The Light of Life* and the title for E. Arnold's versified life of Christ (1910). Holman Hunt's painting *The Light of the World* (Keble College, Oxford) marries two Johannine works by taking Rev 3:20 for its inscription. In modern commentary the interlocutors are often invested with no other function than to elicit the revelatory discourse. The ancients took more notice of the man born blind, and if Augustine turns him into a paradigm of human impotence, Chrysostom examines his acts and motives with an interest that has not been matched (except perhaps by dramatists like Sayers) in modern times.

The Healing of the Man Born Blind

9:1. El Greco paints both confidence and compassion into the face of the Redeemer in his *Christ Healing the Blind Boy* (Prado, Madrid). From the intervention of the disciples Chrysostom guesses that Jesus stared at him intently (*Homily* 56.1).

9:2. The question is prompted, in Chrysostom's view, by the words **go and sin no more** to the paralytic at 5:14 (*Homily* 56.1); Augustine, however, holds that the man represents the whole human race, which has been made blind by the sin of Adam (*Homily* 44.1). To illustrate the Jewish belief that sin is the cause of illness, Barrett quotes *Shabbath* 55a with its proof-text at Ezek 18:20; *Genesis Rabbah* 63.6 speaks of sin committed in the womb. Calvin, however, accuses the disciples of subscribing to the Pythagorean notion of transmigration, attributed to the Pharisees by Josephus at *Antiquities* 18.2 (1959: 238). Wesley points out that in his answer Christ is not determining whether the man or his parents sinned, but whether sin was the cause of his ailment (*MCNT* at IX.2).

9:3–5. Augustine explains that both the man and his parents must have sinned, for that is the human lot, but that sin was not the cause of his condition (*Homily* 44.3). If, with the NRSV and R. H. Lightfoot, we read not **I must work** but **we** in v. 4, it appears that Christ includes the disciples in his work (1956: 201). Barrett defends the same reading, with a reference to the mission of the disciples at 20:21, and cites *Pirke Aboth* 2.15 to show that a day can mean one's span of life (1955: 295). Chrysostom, however, explains the **day** as the present epoch, whereas **night** is the outer darkness of those who will perish in the Last Judgement (*Homily* 56.2). The words **light of the world** (v. 5) recur at *Gospel of Thomas* 77 as well as 8:12; to be **in the world** was merely to be alive in current idiom, but the prologue justifies Barrett in attaching a deeper sense to Jesus' use of this locution (1955: 296).

9:6. Jesus uses spittle at Mark 7:33 and 8:23. Here, according to Irenaeus, Christ re-enacts the creation of man from clay (*Against Heresies* 5.15.5); to Chrysostom the spittle signifies that it is Christ and not the pool that effects the cure (*Homily* 56.2). Pope Gregory construes it as the 'savour of contemplation' (Aquinas 1997: 330). Calvin opines that Christ was testing the faith of his patient by a preposterous action (1959: 241); J. Lightfoot suggests that Christ was flouting a ban on the anointing of eyes with liquid on the Sabbath (1859: 342).

9:7. The healing resembles the work of another northern prophet at 2 Kings 5:3–14. Augustine writes that the man was first anointed and immersed and then baptized like a catechumen proceeding to baptism (*Homily* 45.2). Grigsby (1985), citing 7:37 with Ezek 47:1–2 and Zech 14:8, contends that this purification foreshadows the one effected by the Crucifixion. The name **Siloam** means 'waterfall' as Strauss objects (1892: 451), but J. Lightfoot had already proposed that Shelah ('**sent**') was the name of a lower pool (1859: 343); Hoskyns observes that the Septuagint of Isa 8:6 fused Siloam with Shiloh, the promised Redeemer of Gen 49:10 (1947: 355). According to Murphy-O'Connor, the creation of the pool from a spring is commemorated by an inscription from the time of Solomon; it was reconstructed in Hadrian's time and seen by Christian pilgrims. A church was also erected, but destroyed by Muslim invaders in 614 (1998: 112–15). Tacitly contrasting this immersion with the troubling of the waters at Bethesda, G. Hill extols the 'skeined light' of the 'unmoved, miraculous pool of Siloam' (1996: 69).

9:8. In Acts 3:13 and Mark 10:46 the beggars are at the gates of the Temple. Chrysostom extols the condescension of Christ, who (unlike most physicians of antiquity) relieved the poor as readily as the great (*Homily* 57.1).

9:9–10. Augustine suggests that the man's look had been altered by the opening of his eyes (*Homily* 44.8); R. H. Lightfoot asks whether anyone is the same person after baptism as before (1956: 203). Chrysostom sees his frankness as a mark of gratitude (*Homily* 57.2). For the phrase **received his sight** in v. 11 cf. Mark 8:25, 10:51–2; Matt 20:34; Luke 18:42–3. At Isa 29:18 the gift of sight betokens the coming of the Lord.

9:11–12. Why this 'colourless' reference to **the man called Jesus**? (Lindars 1972: 345). The patient is still, according to both Augustine and Bede, in the state of a catechumen who cannot preach what he has heard (Aquinas 1997: 332). Hoskyns charts the progress of his understanding: first he acknowledges Christ as the absent Jesus, then as a prophet at 9:17, and lastly as Son of Man at 9:35–7 (1947: 355–6).

The Pharisees Accuse Christ

9:13–16. The dispute about the Sabbath is reminiscent of 5:9. Barrett notes that the rabbis were divided as to whether the anointing of sick eyes should be permitted on this day (1955: 298). Augustine insists that Christ kept the Sabbath spiritually by remaining free of sin (*Homily* 44.9). The ensuing dialogue has the seeds of comedy, and Sayers, though she calls the man Jacob ben Issachar, has made a Cockney of him (1943: 190–2). Chrysostom admires the man's fortitude under interrogation (*Homily* 57.2), while Sacy suggests that Nicodemus was one of the **others** who defended Christ (1840: 386).

9:17–22a. Chrysostom describes the faith of the healed man as inchoate and insecure (*Homily* 57.2); Augustine, citing Luke 4:24, observes that hitherto he has not divined the true character of his physician (*Homily* 44.9). The Pharisees – synonymous with 'Jews' throughout this anecdote, as Barrett observes (1955: 299) – now turn upon the man's parents, but their answer proves to Chrysostom that truth is 'strengthened by the snares that are laid against it' (*Homily* 58.1). Nevertheless, he imputes their fear in v. 22 to ingratitude, and Calvin agrees (1959: 247). Maccini adduces Deut 21:18–21 and

22:13–21 to prove that it would not have been unusual to interrogate both parents (1996: 237); in Elgar's oratorio their answer in v. 20 is assigned to the mother alone, and her words are left hanging in the air.

9:22b. This measure is something more severe than the temporary excommunication which is occasionally enjoined in rabbinic texts. Furthermore, as Barrett says, the proscribed words amount to a 'Christian profession of faith', with parallels at Mark 8:29, Rom 10:9, 1 John 5:1, etc. (1955: 299). Consequently some scholars have associated the edict with the 'Blessing of the Minim', a curse on Jewish converts to Christianity which was once thought to have been recited in Palestinian synagogues as early as the year AD 85 (cf. Justin, *Trypho* 38). Martyn holds that the purpose and situation of the author are revealed by this anachronism (1979: 58); unfortunately, as Van der Horst's review of the evidence indicates (1994), we have still to determine how the decree was worded in the first century, and against whom it was aimed. Even if the extant form is primitive, our Gospel may be older if, as Horbury thinks, the 'Benediction' merely took solemn notice of an antecedent schism (1982: 61).

9:23–7. Josh 7:19 shows that the words **give glory to God** mean 'tell the truth'; but the Name, as Augustine says, is taken in vain here (*Homily* 44.11). Chrysostom, who believes that Christ is being accused of sorcery, asks why those who defame him cannot convict him as they were challenged to do at 8:46. On the other hand, he defends the circumlocution of the blind man on the grounds that facts are a stronger defence than verbal testimony (*Homily* 58.2).

The Boast of the Pharisees

9:28–30. According to Barrett, this claim to be sons of Moses is upheld by *Yoma* 4, where they are contrasted with the Sadducees, but not elsewhere in rabbinic literature (1955: 300). Lindars compares Matt 23:2 (1972: 348), and analogues to the arrogant continuation in v. 29 can be found at 7:27, 8:41 and *Papyrus Egerton* 2 (Barrett 1955: 301). Chrysostom retorts that they knew of Moses only by hearing, whereas Christ's works were performed before their eyes (*Homily* 58.3).

9:31. Henry notes approvingly that the man 'sticks to the certain matter of fact' (1991: 1979, col. 2). Chrysostom infers that the words above, **whether he be a sinner I know not** (AV), were spoken rhetorically (*Homily* 58.3). Hoskyns, citing 1 John 5:15, construes **we know** to mean 'we Christians' know (1947: 356–7). Calvin (rejecting the view of some contemporaries) endorses the maxim that **God does not hear sinners** (1959: 251); Augustine accused the puritanical Donatists of wresting it to their own cause (*Against Parmenianus* 2.8). Barrett calls it a commonplace on the evidence of Philostratus, *Apollonius* 1.12 (1955: 301), yet Scripture denies it, according to Marsh, at Ps 66:18 and Jas 5:16 (1968: 386). The adjective *theosebes* ('pious'), though regularly used by Greeks and Hellenized Jews to designate the 'godfearers' who embraced the outward forms of Judaism, is otherwise absent from the New Testament.

9:32–3. Hoskyns notes that Tobit contains the only record of such a miracle in Jewish scripture (1947: 358). Hume claims equal credit for a similar feat attributed to the Emperor Vespasian at Tacitus, *Histories* 4.81 (1962: 122–3). In Shakespeare's burlesque of the miracle, a man who is supposed to have been cured of congenital blindness is duped into showing that he is already acquainted with the names of colours (*Henry VI Part Two*, Act 2, scene 1).

9:34. Calvinists may admit that all are **born in sins**, though not that the Pharisees knew it (Hutcheson 1972: 198); Anglicans reply that this hyperbole means only, 'You were a sinner all your life' (J. Taylor 1850: 264). The accusers have deduced the man's sin from his blindness, like the disciples in v. 2.

Christ Judges the Pharisees

9:35a. 'They cast him from the Temple, but the Lord of the Temple found him' (Chrysostom, *Homily* 59.1). John Newton adopts this verse as his own confession: 'I once was lost, but now am found, / Was blind but now I see' (1979: 5) – though Hoskyns opines that **found** need not imply that the man was lost (1947: 359).

9:35b. Cf. Mark 9:23–4. Hoskyns rightly argues that the primitive reading was **Son of Man**, for which the phrase **Son of God** would have been an explicable substitution (1947: 359). The AV adopts the latter reading – perhaps, as Barrett comments, because the Son of Man is nowhere else an object of belief (1955: 302).

9:36–8. Sayers makes the man recognize Christ's voice, and adds to the poignancy of the episode by imagining that he was cast out by his parents (1943: 193–4). Marsh suspects an intentional ambiguity in the title *kurios*, which may mean either 'Sir' or 'Lord' (1968: 389); Calvin, however, grants that the **worship** in v. 38 was paid to Christ in his human character (1959: 254). Bede none the less prescribes the same posture to worshippers of God (Aquinas 1997: 340–1).

9:39–41. Jesus amplifies the Baptist's words at 3:17–21. Chrysostom typically interprets judgement as condemnation, and compares Rom 9:30–1

(*Homily* 59.1). Hoskyns, observing that Loisy applies the saying to the Gentiles and Weiss to the poor, prefers to applying it to neophytes of all races (1947: 360). Lindars, perhaps with Mark 8:38 in mind as well as John 5:27, explains that 'the response to Jesus now determines his verdict as Son of Man in the future' (1972: 351). The blindness of the Pharisees is reaffirmed at 15:22 (cf. Matt 15:14), and Theophylact asserts that they are condemned by their refusal to acknowledge the works performed before their eyes (Aquinas 1997: 342).

Interlude: The Good Shepherd

Christ, as Calvin notes, now coins two parables to shame the Pharisees: he whom they reject is the door through which true shepherds enter, and he is himself the universal shepherd of the elect (1959: 258). Elsley reports the opinion of Isaac Newton that the parable was occasioned by the sheepfolds near the Temple (1844: 455); nevertheless, such popular motifs in the primitive Church were always rooted in the Scriptures, and cognates can be found in prophetic similes for God's tutelage of Israel (Isa 40:11 and 56:8; Ezek 34:13–19, 23; 37:21–4; Ps 23:1–3; 95:7), in the language used of kings (1 Kings 22:17; cf. Mark 6:34), and in the song of the suffering servant, who is likened both to a shepherd and to a lamb (Isa 53:7 and 12; cf. 1 Peter 2:25). Beutler enumerates six traits of the shepherd in this chapter which appear to have been borrowed from the prophets or the Psalms (1991: 25). Since the Old Testament is a 'book of shepherds' – as Maurice writes, naming Abraham, Isaac and David – and since Philo improved on Scripture by making the Word of God a shepherd in his treatise *On Agriculture* 61–4 – it might seem supererogatory to look for a precursor of the Johannine shepherd outside Hebrew literature. In Zoroastrian myth the first man is a shepherd, unlike Adam, and and some Greek gods, unlike Yahweh, bore the title 'keeper of flocks'; in the Johannine parable, however, we have no reason to suppose that the fold is Eden or that Christ purports to be God. Our Gospel antedates the Mandaean sources from which Bultmann tried to glean a Gnostic prototype for the Shepherd (1957: 279–80); and it is almost certainly older than the Hermetic text *Poimandres*, the title of which was (questionably) derived by Bultmann's mentor Reitzenstein (1904) from Greek words meaning 'shepherd of men'. J. D. Turner's research (1991) has not uncovered any Gnostic myth of an earlier date in which the Redeemer is personified as a shepherd, and Bultmann's claim that only such a myth would have suggested the antithesis between good and evil minders of the flock is surely refuted by Ezek 34:17 and 34:20. No doubt the same passage lies behind the parables in Matthew and Luke, where the shepherd is God the Father; the *Shepherd* of Hermas (c.130) is the first text after our Gospel to accord this role to Christ.

Since v. 19 would be well placed at the end of the altercation with the Pharisees, some scholars reconstruct an original version in which the parable commences at a later point. There is, however, no textual authority for such enterprises, and when the shepherd returns at vv. 25–7, there is no hiatus into which the parable might be inserted. References to the healing of the blind man and its aftermath have been discerned in the parable from the earliest times; on the other hand, the claims of Christ after v. 24 propel him toward his death with a momentum that would be needlessly retarded by the introduction of a long discourse (Busse 1991: 9). Rather than surmise that the author failed to edit a narrative which had not been 'written at a single sitting' (Painter 1991: 54), one might argue that, as the Pharisees by their blindness provide a commentary on the miracle in chapter 9, so the exchange between Christ and the Jews in chapter 10 reveals the application of his parable. The flock hears the voice of the shepherd, while the Jews reject that of Christ; the shepherd lays down his life at the Father's bidding, Christ performs the works that the Father enjoins upon him; the shepherd is contrasted with thieves and hirelings, Jesus passes sentence on the false judges of the earth. The adversaries are now no longer Pharisees, but simply 'Jews' – no longer blind but deaf.

Christ the Shepherd

10:1. Augustine reads this verse as Christ's response to the Pharisees' question at 9:40 **are we blind**? (*Homily* 45.2); Elgar, with the same insight, bases the final aria of *The Light of Life* on Zech 11:17. Chrysostom says that to us the **door** is Scripture, which bars the way to heretics and the Antichrist (*Homily* 59.2). Barrett enumerates the doors to heaven in Jewish Scripture (1955: 314), and if Goodenough could prove that the door can represent a womb in Jewish imagery, the parable could be interpreted as a lesson to Nicodemus (1953: 111). In the Barmen Declaration of 1934, the 'confessing Church' appealed to this verse against the pretensions of the Third Reich (Matheson 1981: 46).

10:2. A casket of the fourth century depicts Christ as both gatekeeper and shepherd (Grabar 1968: fig. 335). Chrysostom explains that Christ is the shepherd while he protects us, and the door when he introduces us to the Father (*Homily* 59.2). Ignatius, *Philadelphians* 9, asserts that Christ is the door that admits the patriarchs, the prophets, the apostles and the Church; according to Eusebius, *Church History* 2.23, the Jews had already asked James to show them the door of Christ. Ephraem Syrus imagines a door that expands or shrinks with the merit of the one demanding entry (1990: 85). Hoskyns compares the open door at Rev 3:8 (1947: 433). In an epigram by Crashaw the door is the wound made in the flank of Christ at 19:34 (1927: 90).

10:3. The gatekeeper, though his counterpart admits the two disciples at 18:16, seems to many an intruder in this parable (e.g. J. A. T. Robinson 1962: 69). Chrysostom identifies him as Moses (*Homily* 59.2), Theophylact as the Holy Spirit (Aquinas 1997: 345), Painter as the Baptist (1991: 58), while Calvin 'does not object' to those who take him for the Father (1959: 259). Augustine compares the calling of the sheep with the writing of names in heaven at Luke 19:14, and derives an argument for the predestination of the elect (*Homily* 45.12).

10:4–5. These verses, in Chrysostom's view, reprimand the obstinacy of the rulers at 7:48 (*Homily* 59.2). Spenser laments that Christians under papal rule 'nill listen to the shepherd's voice', but stray into the wolf's maw (1970: 454). Chrysostom takes the strangers to be the insurgents Theudas and Judas, who attempted to establish the kingdom of heaven by armed force (*Homily* 59.2). Noting that other scriptures, such as Ezek 34:4, describe the recovery of lost sheep, Augustine reminds us that the visible Church is not coterminous with the elect (*Homily* 45.10–11).

10:6. The word translated 'proverb' is *paroimia*, and recurs at 16:25 and 29, but only once elsewhere in the New Testament. Busse (1991: 10–11) remarks that scholars have proposed such terms as 'allegory, similitude, parable or simply image', while he himself opts for Berger's 'image field' (1984: 39). Farrar agrees with Sanday that the Fourth Gospel contains no parable, and the others no allegory (1901: 400–1n).

Christ the Door

10:7. Both the change of metaphor and the adverb *palin* (**again**) lend colour to Schnackenburg's opinion that the speaker is no longer addressing the Pharisees, but the Johannine community (1980: 288). He adds that the image may be of Gnostic provenance (1980: 290), but Brodie cites Psalm 118:20. Lindars contends that, here as elsewhere, the words **Very truly** (*Amen, Amen*) introduce an authentic saying of Jesus (1972: 355).

10:8. Chrysostom again takes Judas and Theudas to be the **thieves and robbers** (*Homily* 59.3); he and Augustine (*Homily* 45.8) testify that others had mistaken them for the prophets. The context suggests to Brodie that the Pharisees are intended (1993: 364), and Bengel also believes them to be the target of this parable (1850: 424). J. A. T. Robinson contrasts a Zealot insurgent, the shepherd Athronges, who, according to Josephus, *Antiquities* 2.60–5, put himself at the head of a mob of bandits, showing 'no care for his own life' (1984: 465). Bunyan's interlopers, Formalism and Hypocrisy, are two (no doubt) because of the two who hung beside Christ on Calvary (1868: 103).

10:9. To **come in** is to meditate, to **go out** is to labour, explains Augustine, citing Ps 103:24 (*Homily* 45.15); Pope Gregory equates going in with faith and going out with sight (Aquinas 1997: 349). Meeks cites Jewish eulogies of Moses as the shepherd who beats off Satan and the wolves of heresy (1967: 197). Herbert weaves his own parable:

> My soul's a shepherd too; a flock it feeds
> Of thoughts, and words, and deeds.
> The pasture is thy word.
>
> (1974: 97)

10:10. Three marks distinguish Christ from the impostor, according to Chrysostom: the testimony of Scripture, the obedience of the sheep, and the gift of life (*Homily* 59.1–3). Theophylact takes the thief to be the devil (Aquinas 1997: 349), but in the eyes of Radulphus any priest who enters upon his office without humility commits the trespass censured in v. 1 (p. 1873 Migne). In *The Magician's Nephew* Lewis translates the fold into an orchard and the thief into the witch (1996: 149), but in an early Christian icon it is the serpent who scales the wall of Paradise (Troje 1916).

Christ Lays Down his Life

10:11. The shepherd on a frieze from the church at Dura, like his counterpart in the synagogue, is frequently supposed to have inherited traits from the pagan iconography of the Near East (Rostovtzeff 1934). A picture of Adam is juxtaposed (Grabar 1968: 20), perhaps because the first man was a shepherd in Zoroastrian mythology. Augustine writes that Christ is the door to other shepherds, but enters through himself (*Homily* 47.1–3). The *Teaching of Silvanus*, however, urges the believer to be his own door (J. A. Robinson 1988: 190, 195). Edersheim, who considers the parable 'a New Testament version of Psalm 23', detects an allusion to it in a question put to Rabbi Eliezer: 'is it right for the shepherd to save a lamb from a lion'? (1897: 191–4, citing *Yoma* 66b, where the allusion must be to David in 1 Sam 17:34–5).

10:12–13. Painter observes that Peter is cast as a penitent hireling in chapter 21 (1991: 63). Pope Gregory writes that a minister is a hireling if he tends the flock for gain (Aquinas 1997: 351). Augustine defends the flight of the clergy under persecution, but only when the laity are secure (Letter 180 at Aquinas 1997: 352). If, on a Gnostic reading, the sheep stand for the soul, then the wolf, according to J. D. Turner, represents the carnal appetites (1991: 48). At Ezek 34:25–9 the wolf is the heathen, and at Matt 7:15 false prophets; Luther turns the second gloss against the Anabaptists of his own day (1983: 36).

10:14–15. Chrysostom cites Rom 11:19 on God's foreknowledge of his people and Luke 10:23 on the Father's knowledge of the Son (*Homily* 60.1). Cowper interweaves v. 26 and Luke 12:32 in his hymn 'Blest Shepherd of thy chosen few' (1905: 450).

10:16. Cf. Ezek 34:23. Christ's death unites Jew and Gentile, as at Eph 2:11–16. Theophylact quotes this verse to prove, against the Manichees, that there is one Church and one Scripture (Aquinas 1997: 355). The other sheep are generally understood to be the Gentiles (see e.g. *MCNT* at X.16), but the first Jewish Christians seem to have contemplated the reunion of the 12 tribes (Matt 10:6 and 19:28, Jas 1:1), and Painter believes that the missing sheep are either 'other Jewish Christians' or members of the Johannine community who have been enticed away by rival teachers (1991: 66). The AV translation **one fold** is based on Jerome's 'erroneous' rendering (Metzger 1975: 231); Milton perhaps follows Jerome when he speaks of an 'ancient fold' containing those who shun the idolatry of Rome (1966: 198). Farrar invokes the true reading, **one flock**, to prove that the unity of God's people cannot be circumscribed by visible uniformity (1901: 401n). *MCNT* at X.16 records a dream of Wesley's, in which he was told that heaven contains no Churchmen, Baptists or even Methodists, but only Christians.

10:17–18. Though 'life' is the common rendering of the Greek *psukhe* here, it means 'soul' elsewhere, and Augustine infers that the death of Christ consisted in the temporary disjunction of the Word from his human soul (*Homily* 47). John of the Cross imagines Christ as an amorous swain who hangs himself on a tree to prove his love (1979: 43). Brodie sees a 'fading' from **I am** in v. 7 and v. 10 to **I lay down my life**, and compares the descent of the Logos in the Prologue (1993: 367). Chrysostom observes that no human being has the power to **lay down his life**, except by the sin of suicide (*Homily* 60.2). Luther contrasts the Pope, who commands but does not serve, with Peter, who exhorts the clergy to feed their flocks and make themselves examples at 1 Pet 5:1–4 (1983: 34, 40). The anthem *Surrexit pastor bonus*, set to music by Victoria and Lhéritier, supplies the missing reference to the Shepherd's resurrection.

The Pharisees not Christ's Sheep

10:19–21. As at 9:40, form-critics argue that such schisms betoken ruptures in the author's own community, or else between that community and the world. Alcuin sees the stubbornness of the Jews as an illustration of 1:5: **the light shines in darkness** (Aquinas 1997: 356). Their accusation is reminiscent of 8:48, the defence of 9:31–2. Chrysostom commends the patience of Christ for our imitation (*Homily* 60.3).

10:22. The Feast of the Dedication, or Encaenia, fell on the fifteenth day of Chislev, and is regarded as the forerunner of Hannukah by Rankin (1930). Since it was also called the Festival of Lights (Josephus, *Antiquities* 12.325), Barrett and others associate this verse with the miracle in chapter 9 (1955: 315). Theophylact notes that **winter** was succeeded by the spring in which Christ suffered; to Pope Gregory the season matches the coldness of the Jewish heart (Aquinas 1997: 358).

10:23. Josephus, *Antiquities* 15.396–401, places this porch to the east of the Temple. Theophylact exhorts us to make our own hearts a porch of Solomon against the wicked tempests of the world (Aquinas 1997: 358). R. H. Lightfoot, however, comments that the destruction of the Temple has already been predicted in chapter 2, and notes a parallel with Mark 11:27 (1956: 212).

10:24. Dodd thinks that the question arises because 'in Ezekiel the Shepherd is David' (1953a: 361); Augustine believes that the Jews are seeking a ground of accusation (*Homily* 48.3). The Greek contains the word *psukhe* (soul or life); the rendering 'Why do you take away our lives?' is implied by Chrysostom's reading (*Homily* 61.1), rejected by Erasmus (1535: 251), upheld by Bengel (1850: 427), and revived by Hoskyns with a citation of v. 17 (1947: 449). R. H. Lightfoot puts aside his own suggestion, 'why do you stimulate our souls?' (1956: 213). Barrett, collating ancient and modern Greek, concludes that the meaning is 'why do you keep us in suspense?' (1955: 316).

10:25–8. Barrett remarks that no explicit claim to be the Messiah has been advanced since 4:26 (1955: 316). Whitefield commends v. 26 as a fine text for a torpid congregation (1958: 187). Augustine regards the expression **my sheep** as a proof that those who are saved are already chosen (*Homily* 48.4). Calvin explains that the chosen sheep are predestined, and the reprobate lost through 'voluntary malice' (1959: 272). To Ryle this passage teaches the perseverance of the saints (1869: 238), though, as Theophylact notices, Judas was at this point one of the flock (Aquinas 1997: 360).

Christ One with the Father

10:29. The Vulgate and its Latin predecessor read **what the Father gave me is greater than all**: Augustine understands this to mean the Sonship (*Homily* 48). A reading which means 'in respect of what he has given to me, the Father is greater than all', is upheld by Birdsall (1960); all variants, in the opinion of Hoskyns, entail that 'God is the ultimate source of security' for his people (1947: 452).

10:30. Most orthodox readers follow the assertion of Athanasius that this verse implies union of nature (*Against the Arians* 2.5); Calvin, however, was prepared to accept that it implied no more than a harmony of wills (1959: 273). Against this position, Hilary states that *essential* unity is the ground of unanimity (*On the Trinity* 8.5); while Cyril of Alexandria remarks that the Jews were never contradicted when they accused Christ of asserting his equality with the Father (2.254–5 Pusey). Eckhart reasons that Fatherhood and Sonship are two poles of the same activity (1958: 183), while Maurice contends that the oneness of Christ with his Father is the ground of all human concord (1857: 295–6). Most scholars since Bultmann, however, agree that this verse implies that the two are one in manifestation rather than in substance (Marsh 1968: 407 etc.). Comparison of 1:14 with 14:9 suggests that the Evangelist was aware of the strand in Jewish thought which posits a similar unity between the invisible God and his manifest glory, or Shekinah (Odeberg 1929: 332). The distinction between the Father and Christ is illustrated, according to Tertullian, by the use of the neuter rather than the masculine word for one (*Against Praxeas* 22); Oecolampadius agrees that the neuter implies 'one in nature, power and majesty', but not in person (Ryle 1869: 241).

10:31–2. Cf. 5:18, 8:59. Augustine remarks that the Jews understood what the Arians fail to see when they deny that Christ is God (*Homily* 48.8); Bengel casts the same dart at the Sabellians, who believe that he was nothing but a man (1850: 428). Origen suggests that this atrocity is prefigured at Sir 27:28 (*Commentary*, Fr. 74). A passage in 'Levi's *Aquarian Gospel* fuses this discourse with 6:25–9 and Luke 3:38 to yield the argument that all men, as sons of Adam, are sons of God, and so immortal (1964: 135).

10:33. This, the only occurrence of the word **blasphemy** in the Gospel, is followed at v. 36 by a cognate verb. Imputations of blasphemy are recorded by Justin Martyr, *Trypho* 38, and the charge is laid against Jesus by the high priest at Mark 14:62. Rabbis taught that the God who proclaims himself the first and last at Isaiah 44:6 cannot have either a father or a son (Barrett 1955: 319), though, as Daube remarks, this exegesis may have been devised to refute the teaching of the Church (1956: 325–9). Protestant literalism may have reached an extreme with Hutcheson's deduction from the present tense that stones were being thrown as Jesus spoke (1972: 213).

Sons of God

10:34. For once a scripture is accurately quoted; yet the exegesis is questionable, and Lindars' defence – that Christ is not attempting to prove his Sonship, but averting the charge of blasphemy (1972: 373–4) – is already forestalled by Jungkuntz (1964). Though Barrett maintains that the usual application of Ps 82:6 in the time of Christ was to Israel (1955: 319–20), Freed finds that the Targums understand the gods as angels (1965: 61–4), and Emerton (1966) agrees that this may have been the prevailing opinion. Hilary understands the word 'gods' to mean 'holy men' (*On the Trinity* 7.24).

10:35–6. Rom 10:8 gives warrant for applying the expression **word of God** to Christ himself. As Emerton (1966) shows, the sectaries of Qumran combined Ps 82 with a warning of judgement in Ps 7:8–9, and in Hanson's view the Evangelist has made Ps 82 foreshadow the 'judgment of the pre-existent Word' on his fellow-Jews (1965, 1967). The notion of sanctification recurs at John 17:17 and 19 (cf. 1 Pet 3:15); Bengel explains it as an assertion of Sonship (1850: 428), while Lindars argues that it looks forward to the sacrifice of Christ (1972: 375). From the assurance that **scripture cannot be annulled** (or rather 'loosed' – a rabbinic locution), Ryle draws a proof of its plenary inspiration (1869: 251).

10:37–8. Hilary infers from the equality of power that Christ is Son by nature, not by adoption only (*On the Trinity* 7.26). Augustine contrasts their mutual coinherence with the presence of God in Christ's disciples by participation (*Homily* 48.10). Barrett suggests that only the resurrection of the dead would have been sufficient proof of Christ's identity (1955: 341), but Lindars believes that the work is the laying down of his own life predicted at v. 17 (1972: 375).

10:39–42. In Chrysostom's view the purpose of this journey is to remind the people of John's witness to Christ (*Homily* 61.3). Theophylact says that Christ deserts the Jews for the springs of water which prefigure the baptism of the Gentile Church (Aquinas 1997: 365–6). Calvin thinks the crowd's argument from miracles 'defective', though not fallacious (1959: 278).

Epilogue: Parable and Allegory

Allegory, the discovery of 'another sense' behind the obvious meaning of the Scriptures, is an ancient practice inspired by the example of Paul and authorized at Gal 4:24 by the participle *allêgorumena*. Even in antiquity, however, a few, like Theodore, rejected it altogether on the modern ground that it made the whim of the commentator more powerful than the intentions of the author. Others, like Epiphanius – himself a practised conjurer with the text – deplored any figurative reading of a narrative in Scripture which denied its historicity; in the same spirit, medieval interpreters distinguished between typology, which looks for adumbrations of the Gospel in Israelite history, and allegory, which converts the events and characters of that history into moral or psychological abstractions. For most of the twentieth century, the leading commentators followed Jülicher (1910) in denying that Christ himself would have stooped to either of these devices: instead, we are told, a true parable has a single point, and all the rest is garnish. Allegory – defined now as the attempt to wrest a theological truth from every element of the story (Dodd 1961, etc.) – is regarded as a sign of decadence, even when it appears in the earliest Gospel at Mark 4:14–20. On this view the *paroimia* in John 10:1–18, which demands a circumstantial exegesis, is not a parable, and Lindars denies that the Fourth Evangelist ever employed this trope (1971).

The current vogue for allegory – the term, if not the application – in literary criticism has tempered the opposition of biblical scholars to the practice. Some, like Drury (1979), hold that the antithesis between parable and allegory is untenable; others, like Brodie (1993), conduct their own experiments in this vein. It is recognized that among Christ's forebears Ezekiel wrote fables that require an allegorical exposition, while the editor of the book of Daniel used the same tool, not merely to elucidate Daniel's visions, but to explain away the unfulfilled predictions in older books of prophecy. Allegory is a form of literalism, in that it tries to redeem every letter of the sacred text; although it may be fashionable to proclaim that Christianity is 'a historical religion', neither critics nor practitioners of allegory would now maintain that every historical statement in the Scriptures is veridical. The ancients saw more history in Scripture than the moderns, but their point – which every preacher still accepts – is that the Bible would be as dead to us as a volume of annotations to Josephus if it were nothing but an infallible report of past events.

The Raising of Lazarus: John 11

Prologue: Who was Lazarus?

The raising of Lazarus is Jesus' surety for his promise of a general resurrection at John 6:54, and of course it is a prefiguration of his own. It is also not only the last but the greatest sign of his earthly ministry, for according to an ancient text, the raising of the dead is the only feat that cannot be counterfeited by the Antichrist (*Apocalypse of Elijah* 3.6–11). As the healings at Bethesda and Siloam hint at an analogy between bodily incapacity and sin, it is hard to quarrel with Chrysostom, who regards this sign as a parable of forgiveness, in which Lazarus, because no personal sin is imputed to him, serves as a type of everyman in the fallen state. Origen (*Commentary*, Fr. 80) sees Martha, in both John and Luke, as a symbol of officious Judaism, while her patient sister illustrates the secret preparation of the Gentiles. The usual response to the former charge was allegory: Augustine (*Homily* 49.2) takes for granted the historicity of all three resurrections performed by Jesus, since otherwise they would have no didactic value. Jairus' daughter, who dies within the city, represents the internal victory over temptation; the widow's son in his bier at the gates of Nain stands for the sinful act proceeding from the impulse; the burial of Lazarus at a distance from his native town is a symbol of the habit (*consuetudo*) whereby evil assumes possession of the soul. In the homelier moralism of the Puritans, Christ becomes the true physician, who discerns the cause of all sorrow and temptation. Modern scholars have turned their thoughts to the function of the story in the narrative. Dodd (1963: 367) maintains that it is the point at which the 'gift of life' is represented 'expressly as a victory over death'. Barrett (1955: 337) points out that it has both a structural function, as it precipitates the crisis, and a doctrinal one, as it demonstrates that Jesus has the power to bestow new life.

By the nineteenth century, it was necessary for the conservative Protestant to argue that no other sign boasts such credible testimony (Ryle 1869: 262). Sceptics may rejoin that there is no living character by the name of Lazarus in any other Gospel, though Mary and Martha appear in Luke as sisters. Fortna (1970: 85) has endorsed Renan's hypothesis that the tale originated in a misreading of Luke's parable of Lazarus the beggar; the two were indeed confused in ancient times (Origen, *Commentary*, Fr. 77). In addition to the objections raised by Dunkerley (1958–9), however, there are philological considerations which suggest that the Johannine Lazarus is the original. Christ's parables do not name invented characters, but he might name Eleazar, Abraham's servant in the Old Testament, and it is therefore possible that this figure was the original subject of the rich man's prayer that 'Lazarus' might be sent to warn his kinsfolk (Derrett 1960–1: 371). Whatever its source, this anecdote is embarrassing for those who hold that the Gospel is the record of an eyewitness; thus Lane Fox (1991: 303) is eager to disown it, with the supplementary argument that it interrupts the sequence of events. Brown (1966: 427–30) too asks why the progress to Jerusalem should be retarded by a journey across the Jordan at 10:40, so that Christ can return to Bethany, then take flight again to Ephraim. Lindars has ascertained that the Evangelist himself inserted the story into a second edition, fusing his own account of the anointing at Bethany with a stray tradition about an otherwise unknown Lazarus, and tinting the result with adumbrations of the Passion (1972: 386). Yet does not the author himself forestall his critics, by making the visit to Bethany an errand of love and the flight to Ephraim a sequel to the council of the Jews?

Art, of course, is not answerable to the strictures of historians. Banished by persecution to the catacombs, Roman Christians fanned their hopes by painting scenes of Lazarus' resurrection. An archive in Constantinople, plundered in 1204 by the Venetians, preserves the title of a book ascribed to him, which – in the first of many purposeful confusions of the Johannine and the Lucan Lazarus – claims to recount his sojourn in the heavens (*DCB* 3.635). Three books of the same work were alleged to have been secreted by the apostles; now that even the fourth is lost, we cannot determine whether this was the source of the tradition that the resurrected Lazarus lived another 30 years (Epiphanius, *Panarion* 66). The story that he fled from the Jews to Rome, and then from Nero to Marseilles, where he became the first of that city's bishops, cannot be traced before the eleventh century. The first poems of note devoted to him are two canticles by the 'Melodist' Romanus, who is generally dated to the sixth century (1963: 102–15). In the first each strophe ends with the salutation 'Thou art the resurrection and the Life'. The climax is the midpoint, where Christ challenges his old antagonist Death to release the body. The second poem lists the ransomed patriarchs to show that Lazarus is but one of a multitude who are raised by faith in Christ.

In the Orthodox Church, the Saturday before Palm Sunday includes the commemoration of this miracle, which is presented as a harrowing of hell and as the catalyst to Christ's triumphant entry into Jerusalem (Ware 1978: 466–75). The story is also the subject of an apocalyptic work composed in Latin at the end of the fifteenth century and translated with embellishments into French; the cartography of the underworld owes more to Augustine's sermons than to either John or Luke (Mâle 1986: 2.430–1). Lazarus also brings back a vision of hell in the Towneley miracle play, in which the principal object of the miracle appears to be the discomfiture of his countrymen (Happé 1975: 405). So too it was for Langland, though *Piers Plowman* was composed perhaps 100 years after Edward I's expulsion of Jews.

The action lends itself to dramatic or literary rather than pictorial narration, since at the instant of his resurrection Lazarus is invisible. A number of Byzantine icons show him as a shrouded, and often haloed, figure, standing at the entrance to his tomb (Weitzmann 1982: 58, 112, 115, 254, 336); but in the prolific art of medieval France he is merely an incidental figure in the major narratives (Mâle 1986: 1.177). He continues to be eclipsed by his Redeemer in the art of the Renaissance; even the *Raising of Lazarus* by Sebastiano del Piombio, which adorns the National Gallery in London, is thought to be indebted to a motif that Michelangelo had designed for the greater event (Murray 1980: 116). Rubens' dramatic etching (Berlin Museum) is perhaps the most famous representation of the miracle in more recent times.

The Journey to Bethany

11:1–3. Bethany lay close to the modern village of el-Azariyeh, which takes its name from Lazarus (J. A. T. Robinson 1985: 219n etc.). Origen treats Bethany as a station in the spiritual progress of the reader, with a questionable etymology of the name as 'house of obedience' (*Commentary*, Fr. 77). Because the anointing is not described until 12:3, the allusion to it here is often discounted as an editorial interpolation (Schnackenburg 1980: 322). The sisters are the first characters to call Jesus 'Lord' before they have seen his power (cf. 8:11, 9:38), and the recurrence of this title in the mouth of Martha at Luke 10:40 strikes Farrar as a 'literary miracle' (1901: 454n).

11:4–5. Cf. John 9:3 and Matt 9:24 par.; against a false perfectionism, Ryle comments that even friends of Christ fall ill (1869: 270). For Kierkegaard the true 'sickness unto death' is the failure to be an individual before Christ (1954: 146–54). Although Christ's love prompts some to identify Lazarus as the 'disciple whom Jesus loved' (13:23), Edwin Arnold speculates that 'El' Azar' is the young man whom Jesus loved for his sincerity at Mark 10:21 (1910: 188). Dickinson rejoins that 'Love can do all but raise the dead' (1970: 702).

11:6–8. The harshness of the word **therefore** betokens Christ's determination to make the event redound to his Father's glory, even at the cost of delaying his journey (R. H. Lightfoot 1956: 219). Hippolytus explains that he did not heal at a distance lest the source of the miracle should be mistaken (1897: 217). On Judaea and the **Jews** see chapter 5.

The Work of Christ

11:9–10. Cf. 12:35, *Gospel of Thomas* 24. Dodd detects the beginnings of a Christological parable (1963: 373–9). Hanson (1991: 150) cites Jer 13:16 in the Septuagint to show that Jesus has assumed the role of a prophet. Since Christ was light at 9:5, he becomes the **day**, and the **hours** his 12 apostles in Augustine's gloss (*Homily* 49.8); Erasmus, however, understands the **day** as that of 8:56, and the **hours** as a rhetorical abridgement of the time that remains to Christ before his passion.

11:11–15. Neither here nor at 1 Thess 4:13 is **sleeping** merely a euphemism for death, as in Hebrew Scriptures. It is fanciful to imagine that the unconverted Paul was present to hear these words, as the poet Romanus imagines (1963: 104); but Romanus knows what Lindars forgets (1972: 391), that all the

Classical authors who employ 'sleep' as a synonym for death were writing verse. Augustine neatly observes that the man is dead to his sisters, sleeping to the Lord (*Homily* 49.11). Strauss gave the *coup de grâce* to pious rationalists, who preserved the historicity of the episode at the cost of saying that Lazarus was not dead in the literal sense (1892: 484–8).

11:16. Dodd construes this saying as an exhortation to martyrdom (1953a: 367); North adds that Jesus is honouring his own precept (15:13) that a disciple must lay down his life for his friends (2001: 51). Thomas is silent at Mark 3:18. R. Taylor, to whom the Gospel was an allegory of the zodiac, takes Thomas for Thammuz, god of the deciduous year, and Didymus for Didymaeus, a title of Apollo (1831: 184–9). To Alcuin the name implies double-mindedness (Aquinas 1997: 608). Yet, as R. S. Hawker demonstrates, the literal meaning 'twin' can yield some matter for a sermon: 'There were two brethren in the field; the one/Shall have no memory underneath the sun' (1904: 126).

11:17–19. Four days was the interval after which Jewish law regarded a death as irreversible (J. Lightfoot 1859: 367). Chrysostom likens the days to successive stages of corruption: born in sin, we flout the Law in our hearts, then defy the written Law, and finally trample even upon the Gospel (*Homily* 49.12).

Christ and Martha

11:20–1. Henry notes that Mary's inactivity has been attributed to grief or to her ignorance of Christ's coming (1991: 1990, col. 2). If her stillness is purposely reminiscent of Luke 11:39, Origen may be correct to see an allegory of the quiet soul's receptiveness to God (*Commentary*, Fr. 80). Most students agree with Chrysostom (*Homily* 49.13) and Barrett in understanding Martha's observation that her **brother would not have died** as an expression of faith; yet, as Schnackenburg notes, some criticism seems to be implied, as in Luke 11:41 (1980: 388). Donne retorts that those to whom Christ is present do not die (1958: 191–4).

11:22–6. North sees this as a variant, and v. 41 as a verification, of Matt 7:7ff (2001: 71–101). Martha's faith is reminiscent of Job 19:25, while the answer of Christ supplies the introit to Roman Catholic and Anglican rites of burial. Bengel (1850: 432) and Dodd (1953a: 364–6) both note that v. 25b is a gloss on 'resurrection', and v. 26 on 'life'. Bultmann applies both predicates to the hour of critical decision, and maintains that both were intended to subvert the conventional doctrine of resurrection (1957: 306, 312).

11:27. R. H. Lightfoot chides the imperceptive Martha for her failure to grasp the promise of new life (1956: 222). Feminists may reply that she avoids the hesitation of the blind man (9:38), and implicitly confesses all that Jesus says of himself at v. 25.

Christ and Mary

11:28–32. In keeping with Luke 11:40, Mary prostrates herself but offers no testimony to Jesus. Her silence may be (a) ignored, as when the Towneley miracle play puts words of promise into her mouth (Happé 1975: 406–7); (b) explained dramatically, with Farrar (1901: 455–6), as a symptom of extreme emotion; or (c) interpreted mystically, with R. H. Lightfoot (1956: 225), as the sign of an understanding that is too deep for expression.

11:33. Cf. 11:35, 38. 'Sighed – and forgot [his] power to save' offers Langhorne (*EE*, 17). The Greek verb *ebrimêsato* connotes anger – a testimony to the Lord's austerity, says Bengel (1850: 433), whereas Lindars suspects an exorcism, and Chrysostom contends that sin is the object of Christ's anger (*Homily* 49.18). Torrey posits an Aramaic source in which the sense of the verb is 'quivered' (1923: 341). Ryle, who takes the Greek to mean 'he troubled himself', appeals to Rupertus: 'had he not troubled himself, no-one else could have troubled him' (1869: 309).

11:34. This question seems to compromise the omniscience of the speaker. Augustine (*Homily* 49.20) and Chrysostom (*Homily* 49.20) plead the analogy of Genesis 3:9, where God cannot really have lost sight of Adam.

At the Grave

11:35. The shortest verse in the Bible (though the Evangelist could not know this), a substitute for the agony in Gethsemane (Chrysostom, *Homily* 63.2) and a proof that he possessed a human soul (Tertullian, *Flesh of Christ* 13). Newman adds that the spectacle of his sympathy consoles us, that as God he was peculiarly aware of the enormity of death, and that in his prescience he knew what pains the miracle would bring upon himself (1982: 159–65). Hanson seeks a typological explanation, citing Ps 42:4 (1991: 156). Cf. 2 Kings 9:11 on weeping as a sign of prophetic insight in Elisha.

11:36–7. In the Jews' questions Farrar detects a sneer (1901: 458), R. H. Lightfoot a murmur of sincere bewilderment (1956: 224).

11:38. Origen compares the release of Joseph from the well, which is itself a prefigurement of the Resurrection (*Commentary*, Fr. 84). He is also one of the few to find significance in the fact that Christ groans once 'in

Sebastian del Piombo, *The Raising of Lazarus*. National Gallery, London.

spirit' when far away (v. 33) and once 'within himself' as he nears the tomb. Cf. 12:27.

11:39–40. In the Orthodox liturgy, it is the stench that demonstrates the superiority of Jesus to the miracle-working prophets of the Old Testament

(Ware 1978: 470). The words **said I not** (AV) have been referred to 11:4, 25 and a previous dialogue with Martha and Mary (Ryle 1869: 321). According to Sacy, the stone is a feeble image of our encumbering sin (1840: 450), and Natalis Alexander adds that Christ has it moved by other hands to show that sinners must collaborate in their own deliverance (1840: 468).

11:41. Origen (*Commentary* 28.6) is the first to note that Christ gives thanks before he has made a prayer and before there is any visible sign that the miracle has been accomplished. He attributes Jesus' certainty to his preternatural wisdom; Hanson (1991: 155–6) notes the Jewish exposition (Targum) of Isa 53:7, which declares that the prayers of the just are granted even before they are uttered; Origen (*Commentary* 28.6) had already appealed to Isa 58:9.

11:42–3. Wiles cites Christ's apology in partial justification of patristic teaching on the impassibility of Jesus (1960: 145–7). German scholars, from Bauer to Schnackenburg, have taken it as evidence that the Jesus of the Fourth Gospel never prays with the humility of a man. In the Orthodox liturgy (Ware 1978: 470) the loud call in v. 43 is a parable of Christ's summons to the sinner (cf. Chrysostom, *Homily* 49.22), while for Grundmann it is foreshadowed at 10:3 and 5:25–9 (1984: 316). Origen, the great literalist, deduces from the prayer of thanks that the soul has already come back to the body (*Commentary* 28.6).

11:44. A *Secret Gospel of Mark*, attested in Alexandria c.200, contains a picturesque variant of this episode (Koester 1990: 296). Contrasting the vocabulary with that of chapter 20, Kersten and Gruber plausibly conclude that the Evangelist does not wish even the grave-clothes of the friend to resemble those of his Redeemer (1992: 228–36). Origen sees the gradual unbinding as an allegory of our slow release from sin by obedience to the words of Christ (*Commentary* 28.8). Radulphus explains that after Christ has summoned us, the Church must strip us of sin as the disciples now relieved Lazarus of his clothes (p. 1868 Migne). The spectators are shown in various postures of wonder in Rembrandt's painting of 1632, but in its successor of 1642 a quiet faith prevails, while the corpse remains invisible (Vissen 't Hooft 1957: 134, 136). In Blake's illustration the statuesque demeanour of Christ prefigures his upright posture on the Cross (Aberdeen Gallery).

The Prophecy of Caiaphas

11:45–6. Jews still denotes natives of Judaea, as at v. 8, if not strictly of Jerusalem (v. 19). Since the Gospel harps on the incredulity of the Jews, Fortna assigns these verses to an earlier redaction, in which miracles were always the cause of faith (1988: 231). Origen asks whether those who bore the tidings were incredulous observers or believers hoping to bring about conversion (*Commentary* 28.10).

11:47–8. In a mystery play, *The Council of the Jews*, the priests are afforced, in a parody of the ecclesiastical processes against heresy, by two anonymous doctors (Happé 1975: 411–31). The musical *Jesus Christ Superstar*, in which Caiaphas sings of 'blood and destruction because of one man', confirms the plausibility of the Johannine account in the twentieth century. To Farrar, on the other hand, this 'Sanhedrin' (as he renders the Greek *sunedrion*) is an instrument of revenge (1901: 459).

11:49–50. Caiaphas speaks with the characteristic rudeness of a Sadducee; he is certainly echoing John 3:8, and perhaps once again addressing Nicodemus. For all that, he is relegated by Dante to the inferno of the hypocrites (*Inferno* 23.115–17). For his maxim that one may die for the people Barrett finds a precedent at *Genesis Rabbah* 94.9 (1955: 337). Both Judaism and early Christianity believed that a martyr may be an *antipsuchon* or soul's ransom for the living, but neither allows the community to sacrifice a victim of its choice. Origen compares the appropriation of this saying by the Pharisees to heretical perversions of the Scriptures (*Commentary*, Fr. 85); Tolstoy declares all capital punishment the work of Caiaphas (1936: 440); Robertson takes the same view of the doctrine that a wrathful God punished Jesus in our place (1905: 106).

11:51. On priests as occasional prophets Ryle quotes 2 Sam 15:27 (1869: 340), and Lindars, Josephus, *Antiquities* 13.299 (1972: 407). Barrett concludes that an author who speaks of the priesthood as an annual office cannot have been a Jew (1955: 339). Chrysostom's assertion that the office, once held for life, had been commuted to a year because of the internecine rivalries of the candidates, has been traced to a misreading of Josephus, *Antiquities* 18.2.1.2. Origen construes the text to mean simply that he was high priest in 'the year of our Saviour's death' (*Commentary* 30.12). Grundmann suggests that the Romans demanded an annual confirmation of the priest's tenure (1984: 304).

11:52. Barrett cites 17:21 on the unity of the Church, and contrasts Jer 23:2 on the gathering of the nations (1955: 339). An allusion to the Eighteenth Benediction of the synagogue, which prophesies the gathering of the dispersed, has been suspected (Grundmann 1984: 309). It is difficult to determine whether the task of the Messiah has been extended here to include not only Jews of the Diaspora but the elect among the Gentiles (Henry 1991: 1996, col. 1).

11:53. Langland, *Piers Plowman* 15.594–5, conflates the plot with Mark 3:22: 'Ac thei seiden and sworen, with sorcerie he wroughte / and studieden to struyen him, and struyden hemselve.'

11:54. Christ's journey may be explained as the flight of an outlaw (Lane Fox 1991: 300) or as a return to his Samaritan headquarters (Cullmann 1976).

Origen finds a lesson in the name, which he takes to signify fruitfulness (*Commentary*, Fr. 86).

Epilogue: The Decay of Miracles

Since the early nineteenth century – when a 'resurrection man' was one who kidnapped bodies for medical experiments – numerous artists have resuscitated Lazarus, with the same blend of incredulity and contempt that Frankenstein felt for his creation. In 1823 the painter Haydon admired the sublimity of his own *Raising of Lazarus* (1950: 471–7); yet Blake had already imagined that the body, when raised by Los the creator, broke into quarters representing four divisive phases of Church history (*Milton*, plate 24). In Browning's 'Epistle of Karshish', a sceptical physician recounts the narcotic seizure of Lazarus and his bewilderment on recovering his senses (1902: 512–16). In a poem by C. S. Lewis, St Stephen admits that the man who was thus compelled to die twice was a martyr (1994: 139), while the Lazarus of Edwin Arlington Robinson, having learned that there is 'something worse than death', can only hope that Jesus knows the purpose of his temporary return (1997: 144–53). At least he finds an audience, but Eliot's Prufrock, fusing the Johannine with the Lucan Lazarus, suggests that if he came back with his tidings, a listless voice would tell him 'no, that is not what I meant at all' (1974: 16). While Tennyson asks whether 'something sealed the lips of the Evangelist' (*In Memoriam* 31 in 1953: 238), Lagerkvist's Barabbas troubles Lazarus in vain for news of the undiscovered kingdom (1952: 50–1). In Epstein's sculpture the dead man seems reluctant to emerge.

Even a disorientated Lazarus may furnish the poet with a simile for a returning prisoner (Causley 1975: 112) or a lover's awakening from the stupor of passion (Wolfe 1925: 68–9). Sylvia Plath's 'Lady Lazarus' is a symbol of indomitable womanhood and the resilience of the Jews (1965: 16–19). Even poets, however, can be openly incredulous. Ann Sexton, in 'Jesus Summons Forth', puts Lazarus in heaven, green and dead 'as a pear', while Jesus strives to reanimate his body (1991: 196). Carol Ann Duffy's 'Mrs Lazarus' spurns the resurgent spouse who was already dead to her before his burial (1999: 49–50), while Dannie Abse's 'No Lazarus' confines the resurrection to Madame Tussaud's (1998: 54). Thom Gunn lets the corpse stir, only to close his eyes for ever (1993: 7–8). In Nikos Kazantzakis' novel *The Last Temptation*, the revenant survives just long enough to arouse disquiet in the living. When, however, Barabbas tries to murder him, he melts away as, for many in the twentieth century, faith in the miraculous has melted at the touch of criticism (1961: 423).

Prologue: The Chronology of the Passion

Chapter 12 marks the inception of a narrative that is common to all four Gospels: Christ is anointed for burial, excites applause and enmity by riding into Jerusalem, foresees the crime of Judas, and shares a meal with his disciples. Yet the details of the anointing in this Gospel are peculiar, the entry into Jerusalem vestigial, and the defection of Judas almost ostentatious by comparison with the Synoptics. Above all, we miss the words of institution at the Last Supper, and whereas the Synoptics agree that the supper was eaten to celebrate the Passover, this Gospel states at 18:28 that the priests had yet to consume the paschal lamb, and thus implies that the death of Christ coincided with the sacrifice of this animal on the Day of Preparation. The coincidence appears to have been intended by the Evangelist, who makes the Baptist hail Christ as the Lamb of God at 1:29; and Asiatic Christians, who synchronized the remembrance of the Passion with the Day of Preparation in the Jewish feast, declared that the apostle John had ordained this mode of reckoning (Eusebius, *Church History* 5.24.16). Since, however, they seem to have invoked tradition rather than the Gospel, the discrepancy between the texts was ignored until the early modern era. One solution then in vogue alleged that since the Passover fell on a Friday by the Mosaic rule, Christ kept it on this day, although the priests now made a custom of deferring the observation to the Sabbath lest there be two consecutive days of idleness (Hutcheson 1972: 271). J. Lightfoot, who denies this, holds that 18:28 refers to the feast of mirth (Chigagah) which succeeded the eating of the paschal lamb (1859: 421). By the early nineteenth century, however, Edward Gresswell could declare it to be the general view that 18:28 referred to the general celebration, but that Christ celebrated his own feast on the previous day, alone or with 'a portion of the Jews' (1830: 80ff). The Qumran scrolls gave rise to another theory: that the disciples had adopted the Essene calendar, and celebrated their Passover a day before the priests (Daniélou 1957: 26–7).

The anointing of Christ's feet is paralleled only at Luke 7:37–41, where the setting is not Bethany, the host is Simon the Leper, and the woman is not named. At Mark 14:6–9 and Matt 26:6–13, the setting is Bethany, but Christ's head receives the unction. Augustine holds that Luke speaks of another occasion, while this is the anointing commemorated. He adds that it has been displaced by the other two narrators, and that both the feet and the head will have been anointed (*Harmony of the Gospels* 2.78–9). A sonnet by Hemans fuses the Marcan and Johannine accounts to extol 'One lowly offering of exceeding love' (1912: 527). In Caldara's oratorio, *The Magdalen at the Feet of Jesus*, the same woman is the Magdalen, Martha's sister and the penitent of Luke 7, and her soul is a battleground between love and lust. The Latin anthem *Lauda mater ecclesia*, set by Lassus, declares that, like her brother, she returned from the jaws of hell.

The Anointing at Bethany

12:1–2. Sunday falls **six days** (by inclusive counting) before the Friday, while the Sabbath (at which one might arrive by counting back from Friday or inclusively from Thursday) is an unlikely day for a journey (Lindars 1972: 415). Alcuin construes the six days as the days of creation, the supper as faith, Martha as service, Lazarus as regeneration, and Bethany as obedience (Aquinas 1997: 399). Martha is busy, as at Luke 10:40; Chrysostom explains that she owned the house, while Mary, as a disciple, was excused from service (*Homily* 65.2).

12:3. Comparing the savour of martyrdom at 2 Cor 2:16, Augustine derives the obscure noun *pistike* (**pure nard**) from the Greek *pistis*, 'faith'(*Homily* 50.9, 51.6). Lindars infers from the wiping that the woman's act prefigures the washing of feet at 13.5 (1972. 417). Maurice, half in sympathy with Judas, holds that only a woman could commit this extravagance without sin or affectation (1857: 327). The woman's answer is given by Charlotte Mew: 'You can change the things for which we care, / But even You, unless you kill us, not the way' (1981: 27).

12:4–6. For the variant 'of Kerioth' here for **Iscariot** and at 6:71 see Barrett (1955: 344). This treachery also follows the anointing at Matt 26:14 and Mark 14:10: 'For thirty pence he did my death devise, / Who at three hundred did the ointment prize' (Herbert 1974: 48). Farrar pronounces avarice the 'besetting sin' of Judas and his 'race' (1901: 571); medieval legends trace his sin to the rapacity of his wife (Kermode 1979: 95) or to the loss of his purse, which forced him into the clutches of Pilate, a Jewish usurer (Sisam and Sisam 1970: 54–6). In Sturge Moore's 'Judas', John, who has 'the poorest head for figures', misjudges Judas when he separates the copper coin from the silver (1932: 244–5). According to the Muslim *Gospel of Barnabas*, on the other hand, Christ's failure to reprimand the theft convinces Judas that he is not a prophet (1907: 182). In Andreyev's *Judas Iscariot*, he is told of the crime but, knowing the appointed role of Judas, loudly forgives him (1947: 46).

12:7–8. Cf. Matt 26:11–12, Mark 14:8. Since the ointment has not been **kept**, Torrey proposes to retranslate into Aramaic: 'should she keep it for the day of my burial?' (1923: 341). Burgon takes the received text to mean 'She was keeping it to embalm my corpse, but has now anointed me in anticipation' (1998: 84). One reading, not approved by modern commentators, makes this verse an injunction to reserve *part* of the ointment for the burial; in Beaumont's dialogue, based on 11:21–34, Mary complains that this portion has been spent instead on Lazarus (1967: 2.250). On the **poor** see Deut 15:11; as Ryle observes, the passage presupposes a duty to feed them (1869: 357).

12:9–10. Just so, says Victor of Vita, those who deny Christ's Godhead vex the Church (*Vandal Persecution* 2.51). Chrysostom writes that Lazarus, as a man of rank, could not be expelled so easily as the blind man (*Homily* 66.1). To Marsh the introduction of Lazarus hints that the anointing was a token of Mary's faith in the Resurrection (1968: 457).

Entry into Jerusalem

12:11–12. Deserting must be understood metaphorically of conversion, as Lindars notes (1972: 420). Christ goes up to Jerusalem on the day on which the lamb was confined in preparation for sacrifice (Aquinas 1997: 400).

12:13. The **palms** are unique to this Gospel; Hosykns compares 1 Macc 13:51 and Symmachus' version of Song of Songs 7:8 (1947: 421). Barrett, citing Lev 23:40 and *Sukkah* 3, describes the *lulub* waved at the Feast of Tabernacles as a combination of myrtle, palm and willow (1955: 348). For Tertullian palms announce the triumph of martyrs over the Antichrist (*Scorpiace* 12.10), and Augustine takes the branches for songs of praise (*Homily* 51.2). Coakley collects five instances of such junketing from the Hellenistic era (1995: 471), citing Josephus, *Antiquities* 17.285, to show that this acclamation of a **king** would have been more typical of the Jews than the expectation of a kingdom at Mark 11:10 (1995: 475). Theodulph of Orleans combines the two salutations: 'Thou art the king of Israel / Thou David's royal son' (*A&M* 98). Westcott argues that the significance of the entry is enhanced if Psalm 118 (which contains the word **Hosanna**, 'save me', at vv. 25–6) was composed 'for the Feast of Tabernacles after the Return' from Babylon (1903: 137). The *Lenten Triodion* warns that those who take up this shout must take up the cross (Ware 1978: 490). In the musical *Jesus Christ Superstar*, it becomes a chorus, crude and repetitive if not parodic. Herbert thinks this ovation as unseasonable as the visit to the tomb:

> I got me flowers to straw thy way;
> I got me boughs from many a tree:
> But thou wast up by break of day,
> And brought'st thy sweets along with thee.
> (1974: 62)

12:14–15. The story is shorter than in Mark and Matthew; the citation of Zech 9:9 is not only abridged but modified by the substitution of **do not be afraid** for 'rejoice greatly'. Barrett can suggest only that the memory of the Evangelist has betrayed him (1955: 348). Distinguishing ass and colt, as at Matt 21:2, Augustine equates the former with the unbelieving Jew, the latter with the receptive Gentile (*Homily* 51.5).

12:16. For the glorification, cf. 1:14, 7:39, 12:28. Augustine discerns an allusion to the Resurrection, as at Mark 9:9 (*Homily* 51.6). Barrett cannot reconcile the ignorance of the disciples with their accolades (1955: 349). Temple infers from the final clause that the author has in mind the more significant acts related by the Synoptics (1961: 187).

12:17–19. Marsh suggests that those who expected a military deliverer were now at odds with those who had divined from the raising of Lazarus that Christ's power was to be exercised over death (1968: 461). Bengel observes that those who hear are taught by those who have seen (1850: 436–7). Chrysostom thinks that the Pharisees who say the world has gone after him (v. 19) are unconfessed disciples (*Homily* 66.2); yet the world is more often Christ's adversary, as at 9:39 and 16:33, and R. H. Lightfoot comments that the crowd will soon **go after him** as its prey (1956: 251).

The Grain of Wheat

12:20–2. Lindars, noting that Greek-speaking Jews are called 'Hellenists' at Acts 6:1, opines that these Greeks are godfearers like Cornelius at Acts 10:1 (1972: 427). Bede compares the Ethiopian eunuch in Acts 8 (Aquinas 1997: 403–4); in Barrett's view the author may have meant only that these neophytes 'were not Jews' (1955: 351). Philip seeks Andrew as he sought Nathanael at 1:45. His native town Bethsaida (cf. 1:44, 6:5) is not in Galilee, but Brodie tries to draw a lesson from the yoking of a 'Semitic' name with that of a territory which is [once] associated with the Gentiles at Matt 4:15 (1993: 413). R. H. Lightfoot appeals, more aptly, to Isa 9:1–7, where Yahweh revisits Galilee after turning away his face at 8:17 (1956: 251).

12:23. Cf. 11:16, and 3:14 for the Son of Man upon the Cross. Borsch suggests that the exaltation corresponds to the 'handing over' at Mark 14:41 (1967: 309); he also shows from Isa 33:10 and Ps 94:2 that vindication often accompanies exaltation (1967: 286–7).

12:24. 'Forth he came at Easter, like the risen grain' (*NEH* 115); but Dodd sees in this 'parable' an earnest of the general resurrection at 1 Cor 15:30 (1963: 366–8). Grain once dead does not revive, but Irenaeus writes that it becomes the body of Christ in the Eucharist, feeding life in us (*Against Heresies* 5.22). Just as Bede declares that Christ 'died alone but rose again with many' (Aquinas 1997: 404), so Hutcheson represents the Church as the 'harvest' of his passion (1972: 251). For Boehme it is Adam's flesh that dies in Christ, who added the external seed of flesh to the interior seed of the weakened soul, inherited through Mary (1945: 240, 249).

12:25–6. Matt 10:39, Mark 8:35, Luke 9:24 are adduced by Dodd as independent variants of v. 25 (1963: 338–43). Augustine warns us not to take our hatred of the soul to the point of suicide (*Homily* 51.10), and Theophylact deduces that we must hate it in the present world but not in the world to come (Aquinas 1997: 405). Brown compares v. 26 with Matt 10:38 on the assumption of the Cross (1966: 475). Chrysostom explains that he says **the Father**, not 'I', **will honour him** because the audience did not know him as God (*Homily* 67.1).

The Glory of the Cross

12:27. At Matt 26:38–9 and Mark 14:34–5 Christ prays that the cup may pass from his lips. Lindars compares Ps 42:5–6 and the Thanksgiving Hymn from Qumran, *1QH* 8.32 (1972: 430–1). Chrysostom explains that the Word was voluntarily subject to the infirmities, though not to the sins, of the flesh that he assumed for our salvation (*Homily* 67.1). Lloyd-Jones contends that the only fear that is worthy of the Son of God is fear of separation from the Father (1996: 109). Bultmann protests, however, that the petition dramatizes the inevitable perplexity of every human soul when the call of faith countermands the inertia of the flesh (1957: 327–9). Christ is troubled at 13:21 and 11:33, while **save me** would appear to be a Greek echo of **Hosanna** in v. 15; but the pain, the prayer and the final resolve combine to make this scene an analogue to – or, as Ryle would urge (1869: 396), a foretaste of – the agony in Gethsemane as related by the Synoptics.

12:28. Augustine suggests that the Father glorified Christ for the first time in the creation or in the Virgin Birth (*Homily* 52.4); 17:5 seems to favour the first solution. Lindars recalls the second petition of the Lord's Prayer (1972: 431). Noting that God's glory was associated both with the earliest sign at 2:11 and with the last at 11:4, Marsh concludes that his voice in v. 30 interprets both the foregoing miracles and those to come (1968: 467).

12:29–30. Cf. the voice at Christ's baptism (Mark 1:11, Matt 3:17). Pope Gregory writes that audible signs without vision are imparted through an angel (Aquinas 1997: 408). Lindars agrees that, in contrast to 5:37, this verse does not imply any 'direct speech from God' (1972: 432–3). Barrett, however, assumes that the voice is divine, and not the mere echo or *bath qol* of which we hear in rabbinic literature (1955: 354).

12:31. The only exorcism in the Gospel, though the whip at 2:15 and the finger at 8:6 belong to the apparatus of exorcism elsewhere (Luke 11:20; Betz 1992: 62). Barrett sees an allusion to the casting out of the blind man in chapter 9 (1955: 355). Augustine understands **world** (as at 3:18) to mean the wicked (*Homily* 52.6), but Sacy contends that the judgement is one of mercy (1840: 392–3), while Natalis Alexander explains that, having rendered justice to God on the Cross, Christ is preached in all lands, and thus the devil is riven out of human hearts (1840: 392–3). The devil is styled the **ruler of the world** at 2 Cor 4:4 and in a Midrash on Ex 24:7 (Hoskyns 1947: 426). As Ryle observes, the Reformers were particularly diligent, and particularly divided, in their comments on the word **judgement**: to Barnes it meant the crisis of the world; to Zwingli, discrimination between believers and unbelievers in the present; to

Calvin and Beza the Reformation; to Grotius the deliverance of the world; to Bengel the decision as to who should possess it hereafter; and to Pearce the condemnation of the Jews (Ryle 1873: 399).

12:32–3. Cf. Hos 11:2 for the drawing, John 3:14 for the lifting up, and 21:19 for a similar aside on Peter's death. Chrysostom explains that he needs to **draw** us because we are fettered by a tyrant (*Homily* 57.3). Kierkegaard contrasts drawing with enticing, and argues that Christ solicits us from above after repelling us through his earthly humiliation (1967: 153–6). Athanasius writes that the arms of the Cross enabled Christ to embrace the world (*On the Incarnation* 25). In Langland's simile God puts forth his finger in Christ to draw us into his palm, the Holy Spirit (*Piers Plowman* 17.140–53 at 1987: 212). Knight compares Shakespeare's predilection for having his tragic heroes die 'upstage' (1968: 154). V. Turner observes that the 'universalism' of **all people** has no parallel in the Synoptics (1959: 246–7) – nor, we may add, at 6:44. Many, with Erasmus, understand **all** to mean 'of all races and degrees' (1535: 254). Jacobus adds 'all enterprise, all art and science, all wealth and power in the world' (*MCNT* at XII.32).

Faith and Doubt

12:34. In the phrase **abides for ever** Ryle sees the 'universal teaching' of the Old Testament at Isa 9:7, Ps 110:4, Ezek 37:25 and Dan 7:14 (1869: 409). The subsequent question responds to 3:14 and 8:28; it echoes 9:36, and in Hoskyns' view contrasts the Son of Man at Dan 7:13–14 with the unknown figure whom Jesus now proclaims (1947: 427). Chrysostom suspects that they asked in malice (*Homily* 68.1), Augustine that they revealed their own intentions (*Homily* 51.6). As Ashton notes, however, Christ's executioners were not Jews (1991: 493).

12:35–6. Oecolampadius understood this echo of 8:12, 9:5 and Isa 42:7 as a response to the question in the previous verse, who is this Son of man? (Ryle 1869: 411). Dodd reckons this among the Johannine parables. Augustine argues that to be in **darkness** is to deny the death of Christ (*Homily* 52.13). For **children of light** cf. Luke 16:8, Eph 5:8, *Gospel of Thomas* 50; Origen deduces at *First Principles* 1.8.4 that human beings may become angels.

12:37–40. For Baur this disappointing end to the ministry gives notice of a rupture between the Jews and the Evangelist's community, and hence betrays the late date of the Gospel (1878: 156). In the quotation of Isa 53:8 at v. 38, Christ displaces Israel as God's servant. Lindars posits two stages of exegesis, since this verse quotes the Septuagint, but 12:40 translates the Hebrew of Isa

6:9 (1972: 437), Matt 13:14, Mark 4:11, etc. The Hebrew construction (followed also at Mark 4:11, but not at Matt 13:14) implies predestination (R. H. Lightfoot 1956: 253), and Kysar observes that while the will does not suffice for faith, it is the cause of unbelief (1986: 202; cf. Augustine, *Homily* 53.3). Hutcheson takes understanding in v. 40 to be knowledge efficacious for salvation (1972: 263).

12:41. Cf. 8:56 and Isa 6:1. Chrysostom explains that Isaiah beheld the Son in the Father because 'the dignity is one' (*Homily* 68.2). Barrett compares a Targum on Isaiah 6:5, which argues that the prophet beheld 'the glory of the *Shekinah*' (1955: 360).

The Judgement of the World

12:42–3. Hutcheson finds a warrant for Christian excommunication here (1972: 265), and, as Newman reminds us, those who praised the Pharisees were 'religious and conscientious' (1982: 407). The Pharisees, in Calvin's view, were made cowards by the ambition that taints all rulers (1961: 59). Barrett notes a play on the ambiguity of *doxa*, which signifies both 'glory' and 'good repute' (1955: 360).

12:44. We have heard the Baptist's **cry** at 1:15 and that of Jesus at 7:28 and 37. Chrysostom suggests that he now rebukes his secret disciples for their timidity (*Homily* 69.1). Borgen, in search of a primitive apophthegm, discovers parallels to what follows at Matt 10:40, Mark 9:37, Luke 9:48 and 10:16, John 5:23, 8:19, 13:20, 14:7, 9 and 15:23 (1976a). Forestalling modern proposals to excise these repetitions of earlier statements in the Gospel, Bengel calls them an epilogue and summation of Christ's teaching (1850: 441).

12:45–8. Cf. 1:18, 4:7, 8:12, 9:5, 12:35. Chrysostom observes that if we draw from the stream we draw from the fountain also (*Homily* 69.1). Collating v. 47 with 5:22–7, Augustine explains that Christ did not come to **judge** until the end of his earthly ministry (*Homily* 54.5–6). Condemnation follows rejection of Christ at Matt 10:33, Mark 8:38, Luke 9:26 and 12:9. Hutcheson remarks that threats, no less than promises, advance the Gospel (1972: 267).

12:49–50. Since Christ himself is the Word, Augustine takes him to mean that he judges not as Son of Man but as Son of God (*On the Trinity* 12.26). John 5:27, however, is against him, while for Calvin the Word that judges is the Gospel (1961: 63). Hoskyns holds that rejection of Jesus in any form is rejection of God (1947: 431).

Interlude: The Character of Judas

The name 'Judas Iscariot' might have been a barbed invention, for all Jews were called after Judah, son of Jacob, and an Aramaic word for 'traitor' has been adduced as a cognate for 'Iscariot'. Nevertheless, the consensus of modern scholarship on the surname is foreshadowed in some Greek manuscripts, where 'Iscariot' is replaced by the gloss 'of Kerioth'. The Kerioth of Josh 15:9 was a zealot headquarters in the first century, and in G. Moore's *The Brook Kerith* Judas is the officious mouthpiece of an Essene Christ (1952: 116, 139, 151, 184). In medieval legend he is simply a tool of Satan, in whose mouth his writhing soul is placed by Dante (*Inferno* 24.61–9). The legend that he was born of incest merely compounds his sin (Paffenroth 2001: 70–8), though in another legend he is granted a few days' respite from his torments (Webb 1965: 62), and Matthew Arnold, correcting our Evangelist, explains this as a reward for an act of charity to a leper (1950: 156–8).

Writers later than Arnold have perceived that none of the twelve does more to assist the work of Christ. Rodgers declares that at the Last Supper 'Judas was part of Jesus' (1952: 60); Eliot's 'flowering Judas' heralds the coming of Christ at springtide (1974: 39); and in R. Buchanan's 'Ballad of Judas Iscariot', the murderer's spirit bears his own corpse to the supper of the Bridegroom (1882: 27–38). Mark Rutherford's (1925) hypothesis that Judas hoped to precipitate the arrival of the Kingdom has been widely endorsed; in Kazantzakis' novel *The Last Temptation* he is a spirited fanatic who tries to force the hand of Jesus (1961: 14ff), and in the musical *Jesus Christ Superstar* he is a militant, disgusted by the growing effeminacy of his master. In a story by Paul Claudel he accuses Christ and Mary Magdalene of concocting the scene described in chapter 12 (1960: 186–8); nevertheless, the aim of his accusation, according to Masefield, was to secure a reprimand, not a capital sentence (1925: 37). Eva Gore-Booth insinuates that Judas lives in each of us – 'What all men share must all men execrate' (1925: 97). Christ's injunction, **what thou doest do quickly** (AV) (13:27) almost justifies Bob Dylan's insinuation that 'Judas Iscariot had God on his side'; though it also lies behind Charlotte Mew's pronouncement that 'We do not, all of us, know what we do; / But Judas knew' (1981: 41).

The Foot Washing

13:1. On the date of the Supper, see preface. The world, or *kosmos*, now conceived as the adversary, is mentioned '40 times in the last discourse' (Barrett

1955: 365); as Chrysostom notes, **his own** are no longer the Jews of 1:11 (*Homily* 70.1). The words **loved to the end** may mean 'to the utmost', but are frequently construed, as by Augustine, to mean that he loved to the point of death (*Homily* 55.2). Lindars follows Bernard in maintaining that the aorist tense **loved** singles out one event, most probably the foot washing, as a fore-taste of the Passion (1972: 448).

13:2. At 12:2 and 1 Cor 11:20 the word **supper** denotes the eucharist; for Origen, this final meal of the day represents maturity (*Commentary* 32.2). Hutcheson thinks that only the Passover ends here, while Christ sits down to a 'common supper' at v. 12 (1972: 271). In Calvin's view the sin of Judas is all the greater because it is instigated by the devil (1961: 65), while Greban makes 'Sathanas' (v. 27) work on his envy of Christ and impatience under poverty (1962: 26–34). The intrepid R. Taylor speculates that **Iscariot** is a corruption of the name Issachar, that both Judas and the Issachar of Gen 49:14 personify the constellation Cancer, and that his father **Simon** is Simon Peter, whose jeal-ousy is apparent at Acts 1:16–25 (1831: 170–3).

13:3–5. The others, argues Maurice, are to be purged of the infection that has already eaten up the heart of Judas (1857: 349–50). The humility of Christ is enhanced, in Chrysostom's eyes, by the fact that he waits for the others to sit and fills the basin himself (*Homily* 70.1–2). Origen remarks that neither Abraham at Gen 18:4 nor Joseph at Gen 43:22 procured water for their own guests (*Commentary* 32.4). Augustine likens the pouring of the water to the shedding of his blood (*Homily* 55.7), and Santucci compares the writing of a will (1974: 154). Tertullian was perhaps the first to detect an allusion to baptism (*On Baptism* 12.3), and Hoskyns gathers evidence that Latin baptismal practice once included a *pedilavium*, or washing of feet, which Ambrose (*On the Mysteries* 6.32) explained as an exorcism of inherited sin (1947: 444–6). Today the ablution survives as a rite for Maundy Thursday, the day before Good Friday, though the story is recited on Wednesday of Holy Week in the Ortho-dox Church (Ware 1978: 537). To Brown the act of Christ is most intelligible as a prophecy of his coming humiliation (1971: 566–8). Barrett notes that Jewish slaves were excused from the performance of this duty, though he denies that wives and children were degraded by the custom which required them to wash the feet of the *paterfamilias* (1955: 366).

13:6. The phrasing implies to Chrysostom that someone, whom he sup-poses to be 'the traitor', was washed before Peter (*Homily* 70.2). Cf. Mark 14:43, which is sometimes rendered 'Judas, first of the twelve'. Cyril of Alexandria declares that we can no more ask why Jesus chose this ingrate than why God chose Saul or Adam (2.358, Pusey). Edersheim, by contrast, holds that the Incarnation entailed a voluntary forfeiture of 'divine knowledge in the choice of his human actions' (1897: 503).

13:7. Ambrose suggests that baptism is the thing to be learned hereafter (*On the Mysteries* 31), while Origen holds that Christ, with an allusion to Isa 52:7, was preparing his disciples to be evangelists (*Commentary* 32.6). Hugh Blair draws the general lesson that the future is concealed from us by a gracious providence (1824: 488–90).

Dialogue with Peter

13:8–9. Barrett compares the rebuke to Peter at Mark 8:33 (1955: 367), and Origen implies that he forgot his master's indifference to the washing of hands at Matt 15:2 (*Commentary* 32.9). To Lindars he 'represents faith without understanding' (1972: 350). For Cyril of Alexandria these verses contain an allegory of baptism, but only because this is itself a symbol of the humility to which we are bound by faith (2.347–8 Pusey).

   13:10. The guest in this brief simile is said to have been **bathed** (*leloumenos* might connote a ritual lustration), and hence to have no need of **washing** (a repetition of *niptein* from vv. 5 and 8–9). Barrett maintains that the verbs are synonymous metaphors for the cleansing of the disciples by Christ's death (1955: 368). Elsley cites *Yoma* 3.3 to show that **bathed** implies sanctification, but **washing** the mere ablution of feet and hands (1844: 465). Augustine warns that, while the whole of a man is bathed in his unrepeatable baptism, the feet of Peter represent the abiding sins of the flesh, for which we must do continual penance (*Homily* 56.4). Sacy includes even penance in the principal ablution, and takes the feet for the venial sins to which we succumb every day through the fragility of nature (1840: 520). Henry contends that, while the elect are irrevocably clean through justification, it behoves them to wash their feet by 'constant watchfulness' (1991: 2007, col. 1). Others follow Brown in regarding the words **except the feet** as an accretion (1971: 568).

   13:11. Origen takes **not all of you are clean** to indicate that Judas was now abandoned to the curse of Rev 22:11 (*Commentary* 32.9). Chrysostom adds that the others, though clean in mind, were not yet cleansed by the death of Christ (*Homily* 70.2). **13:12–15.** Barrett suggests that the action of Christ, hitherto a parable of his forthcoming sacrifice, has now become an example of humility, because he renounces his privilege as **Lord** (1955: 369). For the term 'example' (*hupodeigma*) in v. 15 cf. Heb 4:11, 8:5, 9:25, Jas 5:10 and 2 Pet 2:6. The humility shown here by Christ, argues Cyril of Alexandria, was expressed not merely in his condescension to the world but in his eternal generation, since that too was an act of obedient love (2.345–6 Pusey).

13:16–17. Cf. Matt 10:24–5, Luke 6:40. The words **Very truly** betoken a 'traditional saying' for Lindars, who construes the following words as an allusion to the apostolic status of the disciples, and defends the words **if ye do them** (AV, omitted in some variants of v. 17) by referring to Luke 11:28 (1972: 453).

Christ Foresees his Death

13:18. Barrett wonders whether **I know whom I have chosen** means (a) 'I know that Judas is not one of the chosen', or (b), 'I chose him and I know why', as at 6:71 (1955: 370). Henry is certain only that they are 'few among the many' (1991: 2008, col. 2). Origen guesses that Judas is excluded, as a servant of the devil rather than Christ (*Commentary* 32.8). The quotation is from Ps 41:9, and, as Brodie says, is especially vivid when juxtaposed with the washing of the feet (1993: 45). Hanson compares the Qumran document *1QH* 22–5, where a quotation of the same passage is succeeded by an invective against the 'son of destruction', a formula reminiscent of 17:12 (1991: 175). Augustine compares 1 Cor 11:27 on those who eat the Eucharist to their own damnation (*Homily* 59.1).

13:19–20. Cf. 8:24 for the words **I am** without a predicate; Lindars cites Isa 43:8–13, where the power of Yahweh is manifested even to the blind by the truth of his prophecies (1972: 455). Juxtaposing v. 20 with Matt 10:40, Luke 9:37, Mark 10:37 and Luke 10:48, Dodd discovers the residue of a common oral tradition (1963: 343–7).

13:21. According to Augustine, Christ was **troubled** by sorrow for Judas or (as at 11:33) by the imminence of his own passion (*Homily* 61.1 and 5). Origen holds that, though the trouble arose in the human spirit of Christ, because it was united with the Logos and thus capable of divine foresight, the soul was the actual seat of the perturbation, as 12:27 indicates (*Commentary* 32.18). To Puritans the commotion is no metaphysical riddle, but a comfort to the saints (Hutcheson 1972: 283). Leonardo chose this dramatic moment for his fresco of *The Last Supper*, giving a sinister turn to the head of Judas and ejecting John the Evangelist from Christ's bosom, where he reposes in the more static compositions of Perugino, Ghirlandaio and the medieval artists (Clark 1988: 144–53).

13:22–3. Cf. Matt 26:22, Mark 14:19 and Luke 22:23 for the perplexity of the disciples. Chrysostom thinks that each of them trusted Christ's assertion more than his own unsullied conscience (*Homily* 72.1). The **beloved disciple** now appears for the first time since 1:35. Stibbe (1992: 78–80) identifies him on several grounds as Lazarus (cf. 11:5); John, Mark, Paul and doubting Thomas have also been proposed (Kragerud 1959: 42–6). Catchpole (1998) makes a case for Nathanael, Gunther (1981) for the Jude of 14:22 on the assumption that he is also the brother of Jesus at Mark 6:3. Most commonly he is taken to be John, son of Zebedee, who is not named in this Gospel, yet is a prominent character in the other three. Since the altercation at Mark 10:41 is not recorded in this Gospel, it is hardly 'inconceivable', as Stibbe contends, that John bar Zebedee would have been accorded the place of honour so soon afterwards (1992: 79). With Maurice we may reply that the partiality of Christ is no proof of merit in the disciple (1857: 360).

13:24–5. This text caused John the apostle to be known as 'the recliner' (Burgon 1998: 52). Jeremias argues that a Jew would not have reclined at any meal except the Passover (1957: 20); Barrett submits that, if this is implied, the author has been led into contradiction by his negligent use of material from the Synoptics (1955: 372). Origen sees an analogy between the beloved disciple in the bosom of Christ and Christ himself in the bosom of the Father at 1:18 (*Commentary* 32.20). Cornelius Agrippa has him sleeping, as though the knowledge of divine mysteries presupposed an obnubilation of the senses (1993: 488). Augustine, citing the Latin, proposes that if the **breast** is superior to the **bosom** in v. 23, it signifies the increment of grace which prepared the disciple to hear the answer to Peter's question (*Homily* 60.4). Steiner, contrasting the 'sacred love' of this dinner with the 'profane love' of Plato's *Symposium*, asks none the less if an 'aura of homoeroticism' does not hang over the Johannine account (1996: 404). Hölderlin too, in 'Patmos', depicts a Greek banquet in which Jesus and this disciple share the 'mystery of the Vine' (1961: 196–7). In *The Secret Dinner*, a medieval dialogue, Christ imparts to John the mysteries of creation, the sacraments and the Second Coming (Nelli 1968: 31–60).

13:26. Ruth 2:14 proves to Ryle that the passing of the sop was so common a gesture as to escape notice (1873: 39). Barrett cites the Passover Haggadah to show that the dipping of bread was also a custom of the festival (1955: 373). According to a mystery play, this gift illustrates Paul's warning that the sinner eats the body of the Lord to his own damnation: Judas has 'sold [his] master and eaten him also' (Happé 1975: 450–1).

Judas Departs

13:27–8. Satan is also introduced at Luke 22:3. While Christ does not use the name Satan in this Gospel, he hints at diabolic possession at 6:70 and 8:44.

Origen notes that in v. 2 the devil has not yet *entered* Judas (*Commentary* 32.14); Chrysostom explains that he was vulnerable because Christ's action had severed him from the twelve (*Homily* 72.1). Augustine says that Christ foretells the sin but does not enjoin it (*Homily* 62.4); Elsley, quoting Plautus for an instance of this 'proverbial' expression, adds that Grotius takes it to signify acquiescence (1844: 466). Sayers makes Judas reply in an undertone with the salutation 'King of Israel' (1943: 247).

13:29–30a. Barrett notes that the meal is once again assigned to the day before the feast (1955: 374). In the word *euthus* ('**immediately**') Kermode sees a finality that is absent from the 40 Marcan uses of this connective (1979: 92). Origen suspects that Judas had not consumed the bread, lest the gift of Christ should drive out Satan (*Commentary* 32.16). In Robert de Boron's *Book of the Grail*, his empty chair is the ancestor of the Arthurian Siege Perilous (Matthews 1997: 184).

13:30b. Cf. 9:4. 'Judas arose and departed; night went out to the night,' writes Robert Nichols (Squire 1921: 345; cf. Origen, *Commentary* 32.24). Poussin portrays his exit into the shadows on the left-hand side of his *Eucharist* of 1647 (National Gallery, Edinburgh). Lindars notes that the Passover meal was consumed at night in accordance with an interpretation of Ex 12:8 (1972: 460). Marsh compares Luke 22:53, where Christ surrenders to his captors with the words 'this is your hour' (1968: 495).

The New Commandment

13:31–2. The glorification is prompted by Christ's knowledge of the sequel to Judas' exit; he makes his own the Father's pledge at 12:28. Hilary proves from the text that Son and Father are one in majesty (*On the Trinity* 11.42); Origen contrasts the veiled glory of Moses at Ex 34:29ff, but warns that Christ is glorified only when the Father is glorified (*Commentary* 32.26). From the illogicality in the use of tenses, Hoskyns infers that the glorification is 'past, present and future' (1947: 450).

13:33. The word 'children' (*teknia*), used only here in this Gospel – and only after Judas has departed, as Ryle points out (1873: 51) – occurs seven times in the First Epistle of John. Augustine takes the words **you cannot come** to mean that they were not fit for death (*Homily* 64.4), while Chrysostom believes that they were spoken to rouse their love (*Homily* 72.3). Hutcheson takes the reference to the Jews to imply 'you are not to seek me carnally, as they did' (1972: 287); Henry observes, however, that the disciples are not told, like the Jews at 7:34, that they will not find (1991: 2010, col. 3).

13:34–5. The **new commandment**, which recurs at 15:9, has its roots in Leviticus 19:18. Barrett, who compares the teaching of Rabbi Hillel, denies that any restriction of love to the household of faith is intended, as at Gal 6:10 (1955: 377). For Sacy the new factor is in the words **as I have loved you** (1840: 530). Wesley, however, opines that it is 'new in the school of Christ' because he 'had never before taught it to them expressly' (*MCNT* at XIII.4).

13:36–8. The 'Jews' ask a similar question at 7:35. Lindars notes that Peter has appropriated the words used of the good shepherd at 10:11 (1972: 465). Chrysostom writes that Christ allowed Peter to fall for his own instruction (*Homily* 73.1). The foolish boast has a parallel at Mark 14:29, and Christ's reply at Luke 22:34, where again the prediction occurs in the course of the Supper. Augustine thinks it presumptuous of Peter to aspire to do for Christ what Christ has not yet done for him (*Homily* 66.1). Perhaps he misunderstands because, as R. H. Lightfoot observes, the 'usual terms' for Passion and Resurrection are avoided in this discourse (1956: 266).

Epilogue: The Weight of Glory

Luther opposes Law to Gospel, insisting that the purpose of the latter is to tear us from the natural man's 'theology of glory', which makes heaven the prize of merit, and to bring us before the Cross, where every human pretence of righteousness is extinguished, and a new, though forensic, innocence is imputed to us through the work of Christ (*Heidelberg Disputation*, 1953: 276–307). Karl Barth agrees that the true road in Christology is the one that celebrates not the ascent of man to God but God's descent to man (1956: 157–210). Albert Schweitzer holds that Christ was the first to take this path, when he renounced the expectation of an imminent catastrophe and perceived that it was his own death, as the Son of Man, that would usher in the kingdom (1954: 387–90). If there is any Gospel that proclaims this evangelical paradox without evasion, it is the Fourth, in which, as Christopher Smart declares: 'the Glory of God is always in the East, but cannot be seen for the cloud of the crucifixion' (1954: 69).

For all that, we must not forget that suffering (*pathos*) in Greek is simply the antonym of action. In the Fourth Gospel Christ's death is his exaltation and sacrifice, but lugubrious rehearsals of his pains on the Cross are the fruit of monastic piety. This Gospel lends no countenance to Jürgen Moltmann's theory that the Cross enabled God to feel 'com-passion' with the woes of bereavement, servitude and poverty (1990: 179–83). If the title 'Lamb' at 1:29 implies that Jesus died as a sacrifice, it is not his pain but his voluntary subjection to the power of his accusers that completes the plan of God. The pattern of abasement followed by vindication is often anticipated in the Old Testament (Dan 7:13, Isa 53:1–12, Ps 8:5–6). The suffering Messiah, on the other hand, was perhaps unknown before the time of Jesus. It is possible, as Meeks contends (1967: 212, etc.), that a distinction had been drawn between the prophetic Messiah and his royal successor; but only in later texts is the Messiah ben Joseph of northern Israel a warlike man of sorrows, whose death makes way for the peaceable enthronement of the southern Messiah ben David (G. W. Buchanan 1978: 27, etc.). Even if the roles of king and prophet were already fused in some accounts of Moses, we are not told that he suffered for his own glory or the redemption of his people (Meeks 1967: 204). In the Fourth Gospel, glory is disguised but not deferred as in Jewish prophecy: the northern prophet is sovereign in two kingdoms when he rides his ass to the southern capital. It is all the more remarkable that there is no Transfiguration in this Gospel, and no visible revelation of divinity in the resurrection body; on earth the sole theophany is the scandal of the Cross.

Prologue: The Spirit in Christian Doctrine

It is in this chapter, where Christ foretells his departure and prepares to pray on behalf of his disciples, that a new name and a new mission are conferred upon the Spirit. In Paul we learn that the Spirit can be grieved, has a mind, and intercedes with groanings (Eph 4:30; Rom 8:27), but only in the Fourth Gospel does the title 'Paraclete' indicate unequivocally that the Spirit is a person. Taking the place of Christ within believers after his bodily departure, he enables the community to proclaim its dangerous gospel and prepare a habitation for Son and Father on their return. From this clear differentiation of character and activity, the Church at length concluded that the Spirit is not merely the disembodied Christ but another person or hypostasis of the

Godhead. Eastern and Western orthodoxy disagree as to whether 14:26 makes the Son responsible for the origin of the Spirit or only for his earthly mission.

Protestant controversialists, especially the Puritans, insist that the spirit of truth inhabits only the private conscience of believers, and cannot guarantee the infallibility of an institution (Chillingworth 1841: 23ff). Since there can hardly be a common doctrine where there is so little common knowledge, such authors as Milton turned back to the Scriptures and discovered that, while such a verse as 14:26 may imply that the Spirit is a person, there is little to confirm that he is God (1973: 285). Even the personality of the Spirit was denied by Servetus and Socinus during the Reformation, and today perhaps the majority of exegetes agree with Lampe that the Paraclete acquired his personal traits in the Gospel only because he functions as a surrogate for Christ (1977: 7–11, 92). Bultmann's view that the Spirit completes the mission of the Word (1955: 69) is reinforced by Barrett's point that *parakalein* was a term for Christian preaching (1955: 385); Dodd, taking 4:24 as a universal gloss, concludes that 'Spirit' signifies the divine life which is imparted to the faithful at the climax of Christ's ministry (1953a: 226–7). This last discourse of Christ he likens to a Hermetic dialogue (1953a: 420–3), though he adds that in chapter 16 the 'eschatological discourse' of Mark has been coupled with the 'esoteric teaching' of the Saviour in other Gospels (1953a: 390–3). No Hermetic work, in fact, can be shown to antedate the present Gospel; on the other hand, the valedictory speeches culled by Brown from the Old Testament and other Jewish works do not allow for interjections (1970: 596–601). Such punctuated monologues as the *Dialogue of the Saviour* and the *Sophia Jesu Christi*, discovered in 1945 at Nag Hammadi and commonly labelled 'Gnostic', may be imitations of the Johannine passages, rather than witnesses to a more ancient stereotype.

Christ's Farewell

14:1. The **fear** may have been occasioned, as Augustine suggests, by Christ's response to Peter at 13:38 (*Homily* 67.2). Barrett notes a parallel at 2 Esdras 10:55 (1955: 380). Verse 9 supports Erasmus in his conjecture that the next words mean 'If you believe in God, you believe in me' (1535: 256).

14:2. Bishop Bull takes these **mansions** to be the chambers assigned to righteous souls after death in *1 Clement* 50, 2 Esdras 4:35–6 and the Targum on Isa 26:20 (Huntingford 1829: 376–80). Lindars compares the 'dwellings of the holy' at *1 Enoch* 39.4, and suggests that heaven was imagined on the model of God's earthly house, the Temple (1972: 470). Irenaeus learned from certain elders that they signify different levels of beatitude (*Against Heresies*

5.36.2), and to John of the Cross seven mansions house the seven degrees of love (1991: 183). To R. Taylor the esotericist, the word **mansions** (AV) proves that the 12 disciples stand for signs of the zodiac (1831: 229). Lord Dowding (1943) gives the title *Many Mansions* to a book on the varieties of posthumous survival; this is also the title of Harvey Cox's (1988) meditation on his 'encounter with other faiths' and of Dan Cohn-Sherbok's recent collection of articles designed to promote the mutual toleration of religions (1992). David Bell attaches it to his survey of 'development and diversity in mediaeval theology' (1996); likewise the Empress Helena was said to have been versed 'in every mansion of the scriptures' (Edwards 2003: 67). The 'realised eschatology' implied here is also adumbrated at 14:23, where the Son and the Father come to make their abode, or *monê*, in the faithful; 'mansion in the sky' is none the less a synonym for Cloudcuckooland in 'Delta Dawn', a popular song of 1972.

14:3–5. Chrysostom observes that the disciples can follow where the Jews at 8:22 cannot (*Homily* 73.2). In support of his doctrine of predestination, Augustine contends that it is not the mansions but the inhabitants who are still to be **prepared** (*Homily* 68.2). He adds that, had Christ remained visible, faith would have been superfluous; H. Drummond, however, argues, that an object is often more conspicuous when it is at a distance (1953: 140). Hutcheson commends to us a twofold way, by suffering and by duty (1972: 295). The whole of the ensuing discourse is briefly enucleated in John Newton's saying, 'Christ has taken our nature up into Heaven to represent us; and has left us on earth, with his nature, to represent him' (1979: 155).

14:6. Were he only the goal, writes Meynell, we should never find the way (1923: 65). Athanasius reasons that, as **truth** is inalienable from the Godhead, he who is Truth must be eternal (*Against the Arians* 1.20). Herbert mingles prayer and exegesis:

> Come, my Way, my Truth, my Life:
> Such a Way, as gives us breath:
> Such a Truth, as ends all strife:
> And such a Life, as killeth death.
> (1974: 164)

Augustine explains that we go *by* the **way** *toward* **truth** *in* **life** (*On the Word of God* 54). Hilary divines that the **way** is the antidote to error, **truth** to falsehood, **life** to death (*On the Trinity* 7.33). Theophylact identifies the **way** with practice, **truth** with contemplation, **life** with the faithful coadunation of the two (Aquinas 1997: 453). To Natalis Alexander, Christ's example is the **way**, his teaching **truth**, and his grace our **life** (1840: 70).

Knowing the Father

14:7–8. Chrysostom finds that Christ now improves on 6:44 by revealing the equality of Father and Son (*Homily* 73.2). Origen, applying the verse to the Son as second person of the Trinity, takes 'see' to mean 'understand' (*First Principles* 2.4.3). It seems to Augustine that Philip has failed to apprehend what some of his colleagues know already at 14.4 (*Homily* 70.2).

14:9. Luther sees this answer as a rebuke to the 'theology of glory', which forgets that humble faith is our only vision in this life (1961: 291). Locke was an infamous champion of the 'Socinian' view that Christ reveals the Father as he is revealed in all good men who are called his sons (1790: 171–2). Ryle suggests that Christ used Philip's name 'to prick his conscience' (1873: 73), while to Brodie it seems that the 'discourse moves . . . inward', as when Lazarus is addressed by name at 11:43, Mary at 20:16, and Peter at 21:15–17 (1993: 462).

14:10. Cf. 17:21 and Gal 2:20 on Christ in the believer. Chrysostom takes this to mean that Father and Son are united in operation, so that neither can be regarded as a sole agent (*Homily* 74.2); Augustine rebukes both the Arians, who deny that the two are equal, and the Sabellians, who deny that they are two (*Homily* 71.2). Athanasius characteristically maintains that if the Son were not eternal and almighty, we could not see the Father in him (*Against the Arians* 1.21). Yet, even as a Unitarian, Coleridge wrote 'Who thee beheld thy imag'd Father saw' (1974: 65), while Swedenborg contends that the Father dwells in the Son as the soul dwells in the body, so that only the Incarnation makes them two (1933: 132–3).

14:11–14. Christ adopts the plural, proving the Hutcheson that the others were as ignorant as Philip (1972: 299). Lindars regards v. 12 (whose authenticity is guaranteed by the formula **very truly**) as an embellishment of 5:19–20 (1972: 475–67). Augustine, citing Rom 4:5, declares that the promise of **greater works** is made good in the conversion of the Gentiles (*Homily* 71.3); Elsley refers it to the gift of tongues, imparted for that purpose at Pentecost (1844: 468). Ryle allows no miracles after the apostolic age (1873: 79), and the undertaking to grant prayers **in his name** (echoed in 1 John 5:14) is a proof to Barrett that the invocation is 'by no means magical' (1955: 384).

The Paraclete

14:15–16. The first sentence resembles 1 John 3:22–4 and 5:3. Augustine holds that the next verse follows logically, as love implies the possession of the Spirit

(*Homily* 74.2). From 1 John 2:1 he infers that Paraclete means 'advocate' (*Homily* 74.4); Brown prefers the rendering 'intercessor' at 1 John 2:1, and holds that in the Gospel the term must mean more than 'advocate' even as an epithet for Christ (1970: 1140). Alcuin glosses Paraclete as 'Comforter', i.e. giver of strength (Aquinas 1997: 462). Mandaean texts cited by Bultmann speak of a 'helper'; Lindars, while he remarks that Job 16:2 in the Septuagint suggests 'consoler', prefers the translation 'counsellor' because it can also function as a synonym for 'advocate' in America (1972: 479). Erasmus, however, defends 'consoler' on the grounds that consolation is the object of the foregoing speech. Johnston observes that *p'raqlit* has the meaning 'intermediary' in an Aramaic Targum, though it is there applied to angels (1970: 80–118).

14:17. Texts from Qumran (e.g. *1QS* 3.17–19) set a spirit of truth against a spirit of falsehood, and the Spirit is here the antitype of the devil at 8:44, as Lindars notes (1972: 480). Bede remarks that if he is the Spirit of truth, he is also the Spirit of Christ, although at the same time he is given from the Father (Aquinas 1997: 463). Henry More the Platonist maintains, against Enthusiasts or pretenders to inspiration, that because the Spirit receives truth from the *logos*, or divine reason, he never chooses any other seat than the rational faculty when he works upon the soul (1662: 39).

14:18–19. The Greek says 'I shall not leave you orphans'. Barrett quotes Plato, *Phaedo* 116a, on the orphandom of Socrates' disciples (1955: 387). Unlike Socrates, Christ returns, and Augustine applies v. 19 to the whole interval before the Second Coming, since this is **a little while** to God, and Christ remains visible to the eye of faith (*Homily* 75.2–3).

14:20–1. Alcuin holds that the key to knowledge of God is fulfilled by 'love and observance of the commandments' (Aquinas 1997: 467). Augustine throughout his commentary insists that if love and knowledge are bestowed by the Spirit, they do not originate in our free will (e.g. *Homily* 74.1, citing Rom 5:5). The words **I will reveal myself** are spoken, in Theophylact's view, to ensure that his risen body will not be mistaken for a phantom (Aquinas 1997: 467–8). Augustine remarks that Christ's love is the cause of faith in the present world and of vision in the next (Letter 112.10).

14:22–5. Jude, the 'brother of James', replaces the Thaddaeus of Luke 6:16 and Acts 1:13. Barrett suggests that he speaks for puzzled Christians who awaited an immediate glorification of Christ in full view of the world (1955: 389). Christ's answer echoes 10:18, 12:48–9, 1 John 4:8, etc. Noting that in v. 24 he speaks only of one **word**, Augustine explains that the words of Christ (as at 6:68) are his own, but he is the one Word of the Father (*Homily* 76.5).

14:26. Pope Gregory holds that the Spirit is both the advocate who intercedes for sinners and the comforter who sustains them in their penance

(Aquinas 1997: 470–1). Augustine distinguishes the Son who speaks from the Spirit who teaches (*Homily* 77.2). Barrett notes that the Spirit calls to memory the words and deeds of Christ, and not, as a similar phrase at *Corpus Hermeticum* 13.2 implies, the cosmic mysteries (1955: 390).

Christ Prepares his Departure

14:27. The word *shalom* includes health and prosperity (Lindars 1972: 484), and might almost be rendered 'salvation'. Augustine understands this to mean inward peace, as there is none in the outer world (*On the Word of God* 9); Chrysostom adds that such external peace may ruin virtue (*Homily* 75.3), and observes that these words were meant to allay the fears of the disciples. In conjunction with Ps 133:1, this verse has served as an exhortation to ecclesiastical harmony (Optatus, *Against the Donatists* 1.1).

14:28. See the epilogue to chapter 17 on the relation between the Father and the Son. Ryle understands the word **because** to imply 'rejoice that I go to recover my primordial glory' (1873: 102). Tertullian quotes the text to prove against those who denied the Trinity that Father and Son are not identical. After the Nicene Council of 325, the orthodox were more concerned to reject the implied subordination of Son to Father, though Athanasius grants that the words imply some inscrutable precedence in the Godhead (*Against the Arians* 1.58). Once the complete equality of the persons was asserted, the favoured expedient was to assign the difficult sayings of Christ to one of his two natures: 'As man he went, as God he stayed,' says Augustine on this passage (*Homily* 78.1). The theory survives in Liddon's Bampton Lectures, where he pleads that it would be meaningless for a mere man to avow his inferiority to the Father (1906: 202–4).

14:29–30. Chrysostom sees that the object of the previous verse was not so much to measure the Second Person against the First as to imply that the Father is capable of a greater work than has yet been manifested through the Son (*Homily* 75.4). The prince of this world is familiar from 12:31, 16:11, 2 Cor 4:4, Eph 6:12, etc.

14:31. Strauss rejects the hypothesis that Christ, on the point of rising, was detained by love, and argues that the reference to betrayal in the previous chapter prompted an illogical reminiscence of the words **arise, let us go hence** (AV) which Mark 14:42 ascribes to Jesus in Gethsemane (1892: 380). For Cyril of Alexandria this verse proclaims the transition from love of self to love of God, and hence from slavery to sonship (2.531–5 Pusey). Against Torrey's retranslation into Aramaic and Bultmann's transposition of chapters 17 and

14, Barrett suggests that chapter 14 and chapters 15–17 offer 'alternative versions of the last discourse' (1955: 379; cf. 392).

Epilogue: The Disciples

Christ is interrogated in this chapter by three disciples, who would scarcely be remembered but for their role in the present Gospel. All three lent their names to other texts, though only the letter ascribed to Jude became canonical. In the apocryphal *Acts of Philip* the hero turns ascetic and has one of the Johannine Maries as his sister Mariamne. The *Gospel of Philip*, often characterized as a Valentinian work, is typically Gnostic in its appeal to knowledge as a criterion of salvation, and not less so in its assumption that such knowledge is imbibed through the physical ceremonies of baptism and chrism or anointing (J. A. Robinson 1988: 139–60). No sacraments appear in the *Gospel of [Judas Didymus] Thomas*, which, like that of Philip, survives in a Coptic rendering discovered at an Egyptian site in 1945 (J. A. Robinson 1988: 124–38). A loose collection of sayings, some of which are thought to be primitive, it has more in common with the Synoptic Gospels than with the Fourth, although its precepts for the repression of the body and its appetites suggest that the Johannine Christ has been adopted as a pattern. As parallels Dunderberg (1998) adduces the frequency of aphorisms commencing with 'I am', a claim to equality with the Father, disparagement of the Law, a threat to the Temple, denunciation of ignorance under the imagery of darkness, and an allusion to Christ's epiphany in the flesh. Thomas' propensity to doubt becomes a virtue in saying 13, where he alone perceives his ignorance; since, however, resurrection is simply the dissipation of this ignorance, he has no occasion to test the wounds of Christ.

If, as is often surmised, the *Gospel of Thomas* emerged from Syria, it was the forerunner of the apocryphal *Acts of Thomas*, in which he becomes the evangelist of India (*NTA* 2.451). Hence Chrysostom exclaims that he who was too afraid to accompany Christ to Bethany at 11:16 outran his colleagues after the Resurrection (*Homily* 62.2). To an esotericist of the Renaissance, he is one of 12 good genii, excelling in faith as John excels in piety and the Magdalen in contemplation; or again he is the seventh sign of the zodiac, the seventh stone on the breastplate of the high priest, the occupant of the seventh throne in the judgement of the world (Agrippa 1993: 528, 574). Puritans, less credulous of legend and unable to admire a doubter, failed to catch the sardonic tone of Thomas at 11:16, but lamented the failure of his resolution at 14:5 (Henry 1991: 2012, Col. 2). Though Westcott thinks him stolid (1903: 167), other

Anglicans find him 'quiet and reflective', commending the 'apologetic value' of his slowness in belief (Hastings 1913: 728). This is the bud that flowers in Charlesworth's theory (1995) that the one who 'validates' Christ's resurrection is the disciple whom he loved. More modest is the hypothesis of Schenke (1986), that the *Gospel of Thomas* drew upon a Syrian tradition which inspired the Fourth Evangelist's portrait of the beloved disciple; the direction of influence is, however, reversed by Raymond Brown (1962).

Prologue: The Place of this Speech in the Gospel

Dialogue now gives way to monologue, and house to garden. Chrysostom suggests that this transition was intended to calm the minds of the disciples (*Homily* 76.1). The vine comes in so abruptly that one poet suspects a miracle:

> Appear no more, proud Olivet,
> In tawny olives; from this time
> Be thou with purple vines beset.
> (Hall 1906: 214)

A frail bridge between this chapter and its neighbours is constructed by an early Christian oracle, which declares that all the creatures of the Word are wreathed like clustering grapes about the Holy Spirit (*Theosophy* 4 in Beatrice 2001: 11). Yet, if the company left the house immediately, it is possible that the sight of a local vineyard prompted the following discourse (Maurice 1857: 384). Westcott suggests that everything after chapter 14 was spoken when the party had reached the Temple, where they beheld the Golden Vine (1903: 237). Critics hesitate to describe this sermon as a parable, if only because the Fourth Gospel employs a different term, *paroimia*, which shares with *parabole* the labour of rendering the Hebrew word *mashal* in the Septuagint. Brown retains the Hebrew term (1970: 668–79), while Lindars speaks of allegory (1972: 487); Brodie, however, substitutes the word 'parable' with cursory discussion (1993: 477). While Christ appears as a character in some Synoptic parables, he is never the principal subject, and the clue to his identity is the word 'Son' rather than an extended metaphor. The shepherd and the vine in the present Gospel are, by contrast, types of Christ himself – one gathering in the flock at the cost of his life, and one bestowing life upon the Church when his visible presence is withdrawn.

The vine beside the Temple led some pagans to imagine that the Jews worshipped Dionysus (Tacitus, *Histories* 5.5, etc.). Churchmen denied this, but in a Christian afterthought to the Greek *Apocalypse of Baruch*, the tree of knowledge in Eden is a vine; a sapling planted by Noah from the same root yields sweet fruit in place of bitter, and appears to be a cipher for the Cross (Sparks 1985: 911–12). It was 'Christ the true vine' who took the vow of abstinence from wine at Matt 26:29, says the Orthodox liturgy (Ware 1978: 546), while a eucharistic hymn by Heber salutes him first as bread, then as vine of heaven (Wesley 1876: 267). Bultmann regards the vine as a scion of the 'tree of life', which German scholars had found to be ubiquitous in the cults and myths of the ancient Mediterranean (1957: 407–8). In reply, Raymond Brown adduces a eucharistic liturgy which renders thanks for the vine of David at *Didache* 9.2 (1971: 671). Even setting aside the Synoptic parables of the labourers and of the wicked tenants, the vineyard was already a symbol of Israel in Isa 5 and Ezek 17:1–10. In Ezek 15 the prophet weeps for the vine which symbolizes the apostate people of Jerusalem (cf. Vawter 1964), and Jeremiah employed the same image to characterize the remnant (6:9). Dodd has drawn attention to the eulogy of Israel as the vine transplanted from Egypt in Ps 80:8–9 (1953a: 411); it is clear, then, that the vine stands for the kingdom, as the shepherd represents the ideal king.

The Vine

15:1. Against those who denied the three hypostases in the Trinity, Dionysius of Alexandria retorted that the dresser of the vine and the vine itself must be distinct (Athanasius, *On the Opinion of Dionysius*). For Hilary the vine signifies the passivity of Christ's human form, while the gardening is the active work of God (*On the Trinity* 9.55). Augustine suggests that the metaphor contrasts Christ with the withered vine of Jer 2:21 in the Septuagint (*Homily* 80.2), and for Hoskyns the supersession of Judaism is the husbandry of the Father (1947: 475). The Orthodox rite for Tuesday of Holy Week prays to God, the 'husbandman of all good trees and fruit', to fructify the barren mind (Ware 1978: 530). *My Father is the Gardener* is the title of a novel by Colin Urquhart (1984), and the thirsting soul of the novice is portrayed by Teresa of Avila as a garden watered secretly by God (1957: 101). In the second Eden of Marvell's 'Garden', the vine coexists with apples that are ripe to fall and therefore not forbidden (1952: 52).

15:2. Chrysostom glosses the pruning as the tribulation that follows the death of Christ, enriching the harvest of good works (*Homily* 76.1); Augustine explains that fruits of piety supervene on God's planting of his own ordinances in place of the seeds of wickedness (*On the Word of God* 59). To Elsley the pruning signifies the removal of false opinions, such as the expectation of a temporal kingdom (1844: 471). Brown notes that the pruning of the fruitless branches occurs in early spring, the time of this discourse (1970: 675); to Cyril of Alexandria their barrenness signifies faith without the vital sap of love (2.247–9 Pusey).

15:3–4. Cf. 13:10; *Gospel of Thomas* 40 threatens destruction on every vine that grows outside the Father. Many scholars note the play on *hairein* (take away) and *kathairein* (**cleanse**). Augustine cites 1 John 1:8 to prove that all need cleansing, and adds that Christ is now at once vine and gardener, as though to illustrate the perfect unity between himself and the Father as at John 10:30 (*Homily* 80.2). Chrysostom adds that the purpose of the whole simile is to comfort the disciples, to remind them of their own part in Christ's mission, and at the same time to admonish them that their power proceeds from him (*Homily* 76.2–4). R. H. Lightfoot contrasts the passages in which Jesus is said to be 'with' the disciples: e.g. 1:39, 4:40, 11:34, 15:33, 16:4 (1956: 291). Augustine turns this verse against those who teach that human freedom is sufficient for good works (*Homily* 81.2).

15:5–6. To **abide**, says Alcuin, is to believe, obey and persevere (Aquinas 1997: 479–80). Hoskyns suggests that the fruits are produced symbolically in the miraculous draught of fish at 21:6 (1947: 476). Boehme exhorts us not to count our merits, but to 'draw the sap' and leave the fruits to Christ (1945: 284). Alcuin, with an eye to Matt 13:39–40, maintains that the reapers in v. 6 are angels, and the fire everlasting torment (Aquinas 1997: 480). As Brown observes, modern scholars are reluctant to attribute such a menacing eschatology to the Fourth Evangelist (1970: 679). Maurice instead sees a reference to inward desiccation, which may become 'fixed and lasting' in the obstinate (1857: 387–8). A parallel may be sought at *Gospel of Thomas* 43, where we hear that any vine that is planted 'without the Father' is 'doomed to wither' (cf. also Matt 15:13).

15:7–8. Both the parable of the sower at Mark 4:16–19 par. and the grafting of the olive in Rom 11:16–20 may be cited as analogues to the whole simile. Jer 11:6 prefigures the burning, while the promise of answered prayer is reminiscent of Matt 7:7 and Luke 6:41. Theophylact writes that the fruits of the apostles in v. 8 are the Gentiles (Aquinas 1997: 481).

The Price of Love

15:9–10. Augustine holds that the promised glorification of believers (reminiscent of 5:20, 10:15, 14:23–4) does not make us equal to Christ, but rather annihilates our good works (*Homily* 82.1–2). Nevertheless, he adds that the phrase **my love** may signify Christ's love for us or ours for him (*Homily* 82.3). Alcuin suggests that Christ fulfilled the commandment of his Father by obedience unto death, as at Phil 2:8 (Aquinas 1997: 483). We too, says Radulphus, cannot love without obedience, any more than we can obey without love (p. 1891 Migne). Calvin, however, opines that such commandments, being impossible, are given to expose our helplessness (1961: 97).

15:11–12. These words, according to Chrysostom, are spoken to allay the grief which the death of Christ will bring to his disciples (*Homily* 77.1). Christ's **joy**, according to Bultmann, becomes ours through the ripening of faith (1955: 83). The commandment to love one another is no longer new, as at 13:34, and may be compared to Lev 19:18, Mark 12:31, Rom 13:8–10. Jerome, in his *Commentary on Galatians* 6:10, reports that the apostle John repeated the words 'My little children, love one another' on his deathbed. The pagan exclamation, 'see how these Christians love one another' is reported by Tertullian, *Apology* 30. To the objection that we cannot feel love by choice, Maurice answers that we must learn it by submission (1857: 390).

15:13–14. This ordinance, foreshadowed at 10:11 and usurped by Peter at 13:37, is enjoined on all 'brethren' at 1 John 3:16. In Wilfred Owen's parody of the Crucifixion, the precept 'love your enemies' (Matthew 5:44) overrules the limited charity of these passages: 'But they who love the greater love / Lay down their lives; they do not hate' (1985: 111). In fact, Pope Gregory had already extended the application of v. 13 by citing Luke 23:34, where Christ forgives his killers (Aquinas 1997: 484). The next verse enlarges the circle of Christ's friends, which hitherto has included Lazarus, Mary and Martha at 11:5 (cf.

11:11) and the anonymous disciple at 13:23. All these perhaps inherit the 'friendship with God' vouchsafed to Israel's patriarchs at Ex 33:11, Jas 2:23 and Philo, *Migration of Abraham* 45 (Barrett 1955: 398). Bridges sets this verse against the dictum of Aristotle that it would be absurd for a man to call God his friend (1953: 697), while Traherne implies that friendship with the Redeemer makes us worthy of the titles: 'I am his image, and his friend; / His son, bride, glory, temple, end' (1980: 42).

15:15. Cf. *Gospel of Thomas* 13: 'I am not your master.' Augustine, equating servitude with fear, maintains that there is one kind that is cast out by perfect love (1 John 4:18), while a second, godly kind remains for ever (*Homily* 85.2). **All things** (AV) are restricted by Chrysostom to 'all those that it was right for them to hear' (*Homily* 77.1); these, according to Gregory, include 'the joys of spiritual love' and 'the pleasures of the heavenly country' (Aquinas 1997: 486). Westcott comments that, while revelation is here said to have been fulfilled in word and vision, 16:12 implies that it will not be complete until the Resurrection (1903: 221). M. Smith compares *Greek Magical Papyri* 1.54, in which a superhuman visitant in the form of a bird enables the magician to perform miracles and enjoy a reputation as a god, while his protector remains invisible to the uninitiated (1985: 98–100).

15:16–17. Cf. Rom 8:30 on predestination and Matt 7:11 on God's benevolence, though only this Evangelist enjoins petitions in the name of Christ. Barrett shows that comparisons with Gnostic and esoteric literature fail, because the adepts always take the credit for their own salvation (1955: 398). R. H. Lightfoot remarks that the word which denotes the appointment of the disciples is the one that refers to Christ's laying down his life at 15:13 (1956: 292); Lindars adds that the verb **go** enjoins a mission, from which Judas has been presciently excluded at 13:18 and 6:70, as it was known that he would not cleave to the vine (1972: 492). Augustine explains the sequence of thought in v. 17 with the comment that love is the **fruit** of v. 16 (*Homily* 87.1)

The Hatred of the World

15:18–19. Christ, according to Chrysostom, foresees the persecution of his followers, and reminds them that his love, the ground of theirs, is manifested in submission to the world's hatred (*Homily* 77.2). From the perfect (rather than aorist) tense of the verb, **hated**, Brown infers that 'the hatred endures' to shape the thought of the community (1970: 686). These verses have given rise to the common dictum that Christians are 'in the world but not of the world', though, as Lindars protests, they are not told to withdraw from all mundane activities (1972: 495).

15:20–1. Cf. 13:16. Citing Acts 9:4, where Christ makes his own the perse-cution of the Church, Brown remarks that friendship and painful obedience are not so incompatible as v. 15 implies (1970: 683, 686). Chrysostom infers from v. 21 that the Father suffers with Church (*Homily* 77.2). Augustine, quoting Wis 15:3 but also remembering Matt 5:10, takes this verse to mean that the righteous suffer for the name of Christ (*Homily* 88.2), but the parallel at 1 John 2:12 perhaps alludes to injuries done to the Johannine sect by other Christians.

15:22–4. Temple imputes to the Jews a voluntary darkening, though not a wilful defiance, of the conscience (1961: 263); Pope Gregory implies that their sin is wanton, and therefore unforgivable (Aquinas 1997: 494). To the words **seen** and **hated** in v. 24 Crashaw rejoins 'They saw Thee not, that saw and hated Thee' (1927: 96). Noting that Christ says **sin**, not 'sins', Augustine allows their ignorance to absolve them of the great sin of unbelief, but nothing more (*Homily* 89.1). Natalis Alexander points the moral that if the Jews were culpa-ble, Christians who dishonour Christ are unforgivable (1840: 605).

15:25. The sentence may be imperative – 'Let the word be fulfilled' – but most agree with the AV that the construction is elliptical: 'This cometh to pass, that the word might be fulfilled' (cf. Barrett 1955: 402). Since neither Ps 39:15 nor Ps 69:5 coincides perfectly with the present saying, Brown adds *Psalms of Solomon* 7.1 (1970: 689). The Psalms are also part of the Law ('your law') at 10:34. Jocz compares a saying of Rabbi Johanan ben Torta from the Babylonian Talmud, *Yoma* 9b (1962: 43).

15:26. Chrysostom reads this and the following verse as a reply to the unspoken question 'Why have you sent us to preach in a hostile world?' (*Homily* 77.2). Theophylact adduces the words **I will send** as a proof of equality between the first two persons of the Trinity (Aquinas 1997: 495). Augustine adds that the Spirit is said to **proceed** and not to be born, because it would be absurd for him to be the Son of the Son (*Homily* 99.6).

15:27. Brown suggests that all disciples have been with Christ **from the beginning** in so far as they are said at v. 16 to have been chosen (1970: 683). As Hoskyns says, they give no additional testimony, but bear witness in the Spirit (1947: 481); cf. 1 John 4:13–14. *MCNT* at XV.27 quotes Lange: first one must be sure of one's salvation, then one awaits the power from on high, and then one undertakes the duty of witness.

Future Sufferings of the Disciples

16:1. Marsh compares Mark 14:29, where Peter swears that he will not take offence when others stumble (1968: 539). Barrett cites 6:61, the only other occurrence in this Gospel of *skandalizein*, together with *Didache* 16.5 and other texts which illustrate the meaning 'fall away' (1955: 403).

16:2–3. Barrett cites Mishnaic and Midrashic texts commending those who shed the blood of heinous sinners, and praises the Evangelist for perceiving the 'sincerity of . . . the Jewish opposition' (1955: 404). Chrysostom reads v. 3 as a consolation (*Homily* 78.1).

16:4–5. Augustine takes the **time** to be the 'night' foretold at 9:4 (*Homily* 93.4). To reconcile this verse with the Synoptic accounts, where all predictions occur before the Last Supper, he argues that the subject of Christ's words here is the future testimony of the Spirit (*Homily* 94.1). Since the words **none of you asks** appear to contradict 13:36, he refers them to the time of the Ascension (*Homily* 94.3). Temple suggests that 'self-concern', which 'prompted' the question at 13:36, now 'stifles it' (1961: 267).

16:6–7. Marsh notes, as an instance of 'Johannine irony', that Caiaphas at 11:50 and 18:14 is the only other character who pretends to know what is 'expedient' for others (1968: 539). Augustine explains that the 'form of a servant' (Phil 2:7) had to be removed to make way for the coming of the Spirit (*On the Trinity* 1.19).

The Spirit as Judge

16:8. The verb *elenkhein* may mean to 'expose', 'reprove', 'convict', 'refute' or 'argue'. Hutcheson maintains that the dispensation which convinces the elect convicts the reprobate, whether they have turned against their saviour, as in v. 10, or against their Lord, as in v. 11. J. Clarke relates all three to the Cross: the world will learn that it crucified the Saviour, will see the Ascension vindicate his righteousness, and will know that Satan has now been judged as the murderer of Christ (1740: 149). Natalis Alexander asserts that the Jews distinguished criminal trials from suits concerning equity and judgements about the Law; accordingly, Christ is acquitted of criminality in v. 9, and absolved of all wrongdoing in v. 10, while Satan is proved incompetent to try him in v. 11 (1840: 615). Barrett (1955: 405) cites Philo, *The Worse Serves the Better* 146 on the elenctic character of the Word. Augustine suggests that Christ **reproves** the Jews in his flesh and the world through the Holy Spirit (*Homily* 95.1); Locke maintains that all three rebukes of the Spirit are administered in no other form than preaching (1790: 93–4).

16:9. Barrett sets out three possible translations: (a) he will convict the world of error regarding sin; (b) he will convict the world of its own sin, because that sin is now revealed in disbelief; (c) he will convict the world of its own sin, which consists in disbelief (1955: 406). Chrysostom, accepting (c), declares that infidelity is compounded by rejection of the Spirit, as at Matt 12:31 par. (*Homily* 78). Lindars, however, denounces (c) as impossible and endorses (b), inferring from the presence of the word **righteousness** in adjacent texts that **sin** is not one transgression but a state (1972: 502). This verse and the next two are digested by Westcott into the proposition that a person once convinced of his sin must either submit to judgement or accept the imputed righteousness of Christ (1903: 228).

16:10. Augustine, citing Hab 2:7, writes that the absence of Christ, as the pre-condition of faith, is the test of righteousness (*Homily* 95.2). Lindars adduces parallels to the term **righteousness** (not used elsewhere in the Gospel) in the Qumran Scrolls at *1QH* 4.30–7, 7.16–19 and 28–31 and *1QS* 11:10–15; he concludes that the Evangelist is not drawing on Paul directly, but on their 'common Jewish background' (1972: 502). Sacy maintains that the failure of the Jews to prevent the Ascension was a proof of their incapacity to estimate the merits of Christ (1840: 614); for others (e.g. Natalis Alexander (1840: 615)) this miracle is the Father's ratification of his innocence. For Henry it confirms two kinds of righteousness: the hitherto unrecognized goodness of Christ, and the immunity bestowed upon the faithful by his death (1991: 2023, col. 2).

16:11. Augustine construes this to mean that the world is wrong to complain of the devil, who is now permitted to vex us only for our own edification (*On the Word of God* 60). Cf. 2 Cor 4:4 on the 'god of this world' with Eph 6:12 on 'principalities, powers and rulers of darkness'. For Blake the Law is Satan, the 'God of this world' who condemns the innocent (1969: 771).

16:12–13a. Lindars suspects an 'apologetic motive', as the Evangelist is aware of his own additions to the original deposit (1972: 504). To support the reading **guide** in v. 13 against **teach** in the Latin Vulgate, Lindars refers to Ps 25:5 and 143:10 and Wis 9:11 (1972: 505). Brodie remarks that similar terms are used of the Spirit at 4:25 (1993: 499). Augustine denies that the text refers, as heretics pretend, to secret doctrines which were to be imparted only to a self-elected circle of the wise (*Homily* 97.1); Anglicans have invariably denied the Roman argument that this truth is protected by the infallibility of the Pope (Hobbes 1973: 304). As Wesley expresses it, truth means only 'evangelical truth' (*MCNT* at XVI.13).

16:13b–14. Likewise Christ never speaks without the Father: 7:17, 12:49, 14:10. Tertullian styles the Spirit the 'vicar of Christ' at *Prescription of Heretics* 28.6; Ashton is content to follow Windisch in describing him as the *doppelgänger* or *alter ego* of Christ, but adds that neither glory nor any other visible property is attributed to him in the present Gospel (1991: 1967). Augustine says that the Spirit glorifies Christ by pouring love into our hearts, and thus enabling us to understand the equality of the Persons in the Godhead (*Homily*

100.1). Newman remarks that though the Spirit 'did more than Christ for the Apostles', he could not fail to manifest the one who sent him (1982: 213).

16:15. Cf. 8:38, 12:49 and 14:10 on the Son. Why say this? In order, answers Chrysostom, to show that his own authority is not compromised when his followers submit to the Holy Spirit (*Homily* 78.2). Hilary deduces that, if Christ possesses all that belongs to the Father, the Spirit receives his mission and his properties from both (*On the Trinity* 8.20). The Greeks reply by distinguishing the essence of the Spirit from his commission on earth (Mastratonis 1982: 290–300). Most modern critics would agree with Brown that Christ is speaking of the plenary revelation of the Father in his earthly ministry (1970: 709).

Words of Consolation

16:16. Cf. 7:33, 14:19. Barrett notes the apocalyptic sense of **you shall see** at 1:50, 11:40 and Mark 13:26 and 14:62 (1955: 410). Bede maintains that Christ alludes to his crucifixion and burial when he says **ye shall not see me**; Alcuin applies the words **and ye shall see me** to the interval between the Resurrection and the Ascension (Aquinas 1997: 511–12). The RSV has **you shall not behold me**, then **you shall see me**. Maurice suggests that **behold** connotes intellectual vision, and **see** the recovery of that vision through the bodily senses (1857: 404–5). Ryle quotes, but denies, the view of Alford, that Christ is seen in part at the Resurrection, then more fully at Pentecost and in perfect fullness at the Second Coming (1873: 172–3).

16:17–18. Comparison with 7:36 suggests that the followers of Christ are still as ignorant as the Pharisees. Augustine suggests that the words **I go to the Father** at 14:28 were clear, while the words **a little while** will remain obscure (like Mark 9:10) until the Resurrection (*Homily* 101.1); hence the words **you shall see me** are a promise to the Church (*Homily* 101.6). Ashton argues that the 'indefinite hope' of a Second Coming has been 'realised and transformed' in the Evangelist's community by the advent of the Spirit (1991: 463).

16:20–2. Cf. Gal 4:19, Rom 8:22. 'Welcome my grief, my joy,' sings Crashaw (1927: 95). Alcuin takes the woman to personify the Church, while Bede maintains that, just as in natural birth we emerge from the womb into the light of day, so in death we pass from the darkness of the present world into eternal light (Aquinas 1997: 513–14). Chrysostom remarks that he speaks of a man's birth, not a child's, as though to allude to his own resurrection (*Homily* 79); Augustine declares that the child is a male because no worldly good is more desired (*Homily* 101.5). Verse 21 contains a reminiscence of Isa 26:17–18 (Septuagint) and 66:7–10 (Brown 1970: 731): the former alludes to the Resurrection, the latter contains the promise 'you shall see' and is succeeded in v. 22 by an echo of Isa 64:14 (Septuagint). According to Scholem, the 'birth-pangs of the Messiah' became a common theme in Jewish eschatology (1971: 8, 10). Lindars finds the most 'impressive parallel' in one of the Dead Sea Scrolls (*1QH* 3.8ff), whose obscure description of a labouring woman may allude to the Messianic child of Isa 9:6 (1972: 509). Feuillet (1966) associates the afflicted woman of Rev 12:2–5 with the woman of this parable and the mother of Jesus at 19:25. Hoskyns scoffs at Loisy's conjecture that the woman's pangs prefigure the laborious conversion of the synagogue (1947: 488).

16:23–4. Contrast 15:16. Dodd suggests that a reminiscence of Matt 7:9 has reached the Evangelist from the 'private teaching' of Jesus (1953a: 392). Lindars holds, as usual, that the words **truly, truly** betoken a 'traditional saying' (1972: 510). He concurs with Augustine in understanding **ask** to mean both 'seek' or 'pray' and 'inquire' (*Homily* 101.4); Barrett, however, argues that the latter represents the typical usage of *erôtân* in this chapter (1955: 412).

16:25. Cf. Mark 4:34 and Matt 13:13 and 34 on speaking in parables to the multitude, John 11:4 on *parrêsia* (**speaking plainly**), and the challenge of the Jews at 10:24. At Num 12:8 God reveals his similitude, having ceased to speak in darkness. On *paroimia* as a translation of *mashal* see Simonis (1967: 75–9); R. H. Lightfoot remarks that the words of Christ, like his miracles, are signs that require decipherment (1956: 289). Henry maintains that the frankness (*parrêsia*) of Christ was displayed at Pentecost in Acts 2:4 (1991: 2025, col. 3), but Chrysostom refers to the 40 days between Resurrection and Ascension (*Homily* 79.1). Pope Gregory opines that the Father is **shown** in the glory of the Resurrection (Aquinas 1997: 518).

16:26–8. Cf. 1 John 5:14–15. Alcuin applies v. 26 to the world to come, but maintains that in the present world we are still to petition the Father **in his name**, as at 15:16 (Aquinas 1997: 517). Augustine, quoting 1 John 4:10, maintains that God does not wait for us to love him, for the love that he loves in us is his own creation (*Homily* 102.5). Hilary distinguishes between his coming forth 'by nature' and his presence in the world 'by dispensation' (*On the Trinity* 6.31). Barrett styles v. 28 a 'complete summary, in John's manner, of the Christian faith' (1955: 414).

The Disciples Profess their Faith

16:29. Augustine, noting that Christ at 16:25 undertook to dispense with proverbs at some future hour, concludes that the disciples were so ignorant that they failed to perceive their own lack of understanding (*Homily* 103.1).

Brodie (1993: 503) remarks that the dialogue echoes Peter at 'his best' (6:69) and at his 'most brash and overconfident' (13:36–8).

16:30. Perhaps 2:24–5 confirmed Augustine in his reading **you do not need to ask anyone questions** (*Homily* 103.2), but Brown cites Josephus, *Antiquities* 6.11.8, to show that the ability to anticipate a question is a trait of the Messiah (1970: 725–6), while Bream (1969) suggests that some depreciation of pagan oracles is implied. It is not clear whether anything should be made of the discrepancy between *ek tou patros* in v. 28 and *apo tou patros* here: both locutions demand the English rendering **from the Father**.

16:31–2. Cf. 1:50. Bede offers two elucidations of the train of thought: (a) 'You are late in believing, for **the hour is come**', etc.; (b) 'You believe correctly, but **the hour is come**', etc. (Aquinas 1997: 520–1). In the **scattering** (cf. 8:16, 29) most scholars see an allusion to the quotation of Zech 13:7 at Mark 14:27 and Matt 26:31. As the flight of the disciples from Gethsemane is not recounted in the present Gospel, Barrett suggests that the prophecy is fulfilled at 21:2 by their return to Galilee (1955: 415). Hoskyns quotes the *Gospel of Peter* on the dispersion of the twelve (1947: 493), while Dodd finds other instances of 'humiliation' at 6:68–70 and Mark 8:29–33 (1953a: 416n).

16:33. Cf. Rev 5:5, 6:2, 17:4 and 1 Cor 15:27. These words recapitulate the whole of the foregoing discourse, according to Augustine (*Homily* 104.1). R. H. Lightfoot remarks that, notwithstanding God's love for the world at 3:16, it remains a battlefield (1956: 294). Chrysostom discovers a promise of victory in the closing words, as Christ could not have overcome the world if the world had overcome his saints (*Homily* 80). Hoskyns compares the words 'there was no man with me' at Isa 63:3, and thinks it possible that the author wished to explain the cry of desolation at Mark 15:34 (1947: 491–2). Noting that many have wished to detach this verse from its predecessor, Brown is content to argue that **this** must refer to the promises of vv. 26–7 (1970: 727).

Interlude: The Prayer

It is widely agreed that Christ assumes the prerogative of the high priest when he makes the following prayer – the 'Holy of Holies', even to a Methodist (*MCNT* at XVII.1) – though Theodore called it rather 'a sermon in the form of prayer', to countermand the inference that Christ is a lesser being than the Father (Wiles 1960: 144). The sacerdotal tincture may surprise us in a Gospel that ignores the institution of the sacraments, but it would not seem so remarkable if we were as sure as the ancients that the Evangelist, before he came to Christ, had been a 'sacrificing priest who wore the mitre' (Eusebius, *Church*

History 5.24). In the text he makes a more modest claim, on his own behalf or that of his informant, of acquaintance with the high priest (18:15); nevertheless, alone of our four Evangelists, he concedes to Caiaphas the power of prophecy and a motive for his conspiracy that is not entirely selfish (11:47–53). The Asiatics held that it was 'John' who had prescribed their date for Easter; the letters of Ignatius to the Asian churches, steeped as they are in Johannine vocabulary, also use strong words to uphold the dignity of bishops and the necessity of communion through the eucharist with the flesh and blood of Christ.

The eulogy of Christ as the great high priest (*Magnesians* 9.1) is only one of the motifs that Ignatius shares with the Epistle to the Hebrews, and, although it is often noted that Christ never makes petitions to his Father in this Gospel, the Puritan John Owen maintains that at 17:24 he enters on the task of intercession which is accorded to him at Heb 8:1 and 1 John 2:2 (1850: 285). Sacrifice and priesthood are pervasive themes of another Johannine writing, the Apocalypse, but the priesthood of all believers which it proclaims at 5:10 is not endorsed in our Gospel. Again we may seek analogies with the hallowing of the Father's name in the Lord's Prayer, but in this case the petitionary clauses are intercessory, not supplicatory, and the speaker implies that he is the one through whom the prayers for sustenance and deliverance will be answered. God is Christ's Father before he can be 'Our Father', and, as Wesley perceives, the subject of the prayer expands to comprehend the apostles, then the whole nation of believers, then the world (*MCNT* at XVII.1).

Return to the Father

17:1. Chrysostom interprets the elevation of the eyes as a sign of fervour (*Homily* 80.1). The reference to the **hour** suggests to Bultmann that the prayer was placed initially between 13:1 (which follows 13:30 in his revision) and the annunciation of Jesus' death at 13:31 (1957: 371ff). The hour is understood by Hilary as that of the Crucifixion, which inspired the centurion's glorification of Christ as Son of God at Matt 27:54 (*On the Trinity* 3.10–11). Augustine, however, argues that, while the seed is sown in the **hour** of humiliation, the **glory** is to be reaped in the Resurrection (*Homily* 104.3); **glorify me** means 'raise me from the dead, that I may make you known to the world beyond Judaea' (*Homily* 105.1).

17:2. Barrett notes that **all flesh** (AV) is a Semitism unique to this passage of the Gospel (1955: 418). Chrysostom says that **all flesh** is to be contrasted with the Jews, and that Christ is the redeemer of all humanity 'so far as it lay with him' (*Homily* 80.2). Hilary maintains that this return of glory for glory is a proof of the Son's equality with the Father (*On the Trinity* 3.12).

17:3. Barrett quotes rabbinic comments on Prov 3:6 and Am 5:4 to show that knowledge of God in Judaism means primarily the observance of the Law; as evidence of allusion to a 'Hellenic' commonplace, he offers only *Corpus Hermeticum* 1.3. On the God of the Jews as the one true God he collates 1 John 5:20 with Philo, *Special Laws* 1.332, etc. (1955: 419–20). When this verse was urged against the equality of the persons in the Trinity, Basil the Great replied that Christ chose not to reveal his deity before the Resurrection (Letter 8). The contrast is thus, as Athanasius argues, between the living God and the idols of the nations (*Against the Arians* 3.38). Bishop Berkeley accordingly took this verse in 1731 as an exhortation to spread a 'holy practical knowledge' of God in the English colonies (1837: 394–401).

17:4–5. Chrysostom avers that Christ had been glorified in heaven by the angels before his ministry **on earth** (*Homily* 80.2). Those who denied the eternal divinity of Christ endorsed a variant in Tatian's *Diatessaron*, which implied a more recent communication of glory (Laurentin 1972: 77). The orthodox position states that only his human element can advance in glory, and only in relation to our knowledge (Hilary, *On the Trinity* 3.15). Augustine adds that the human Christ can boast of his pre-existent glory only because the exaltation of his manhood was eternally predestined; conversely, he construes the words **I glorified** as a use of the past tense to illustrate the certainty of the future (*Homily* 105.5). In John Owen's view, the glory of God the Father had not been hidden from the Jews, but was now augmented by the 'love, grace, goodness and compassion of the Son' (1850: 56).

Intercession for the Disciples

17:6a. Augustine understands the revealed **name** to be 'Father', since the name 'God' was already known to the Jews (*Homily* 106.1–4). Lloyd-Jones cites the name Jehovah-Shalom, 'the Lord is peace' from Judg 6:24 (1996: 221). Barrett cites Isa 52:6 and Ex 3:15 to show that the name 'embod[ies] the (revealed) character of God' (1955: 421).

17:6b–8. The word must be communicated in words, writes Marsh, citing 7:16 (1968: 564). Augustine takes the **keeping of the word** to mean obedience to Christ's precepts, and the **belief** of the disciples to be a steadfast disposition which could not yet be ascribed to them at 16:31–2 (*Homily* 106.6). Since the Greek employs verbs rather than nouns, R. H. Lightfoot infers that faith and knowledge are not so much states as processes (1956: 301); Calvin explains that the two are not contrasted here because nothing is known of God but by faith, and true faith has the certainty of knowledge (1961: 140).

17:9–10. 'I pray not for the Jews,' declares Christ's mother in the Byzantine *Apocalypse of the Theotokos* 26 (M. R. James 1893: 125–6). Augustine understands **world** to mean those who are governed by worldly appetites (*Homily* 107.1); Temple interprets it as 'the whole system of nature, including human nature' (1961: 302). Calvin declares that Christians are enjoined to pray for the world, but their prayers are efficacious only for the elect (1961: 140). Chrysostom observes that we do not cease to belong to the Father when we are **given** to the Son (*Homily* 81.1); Augustine characteristically derives from v. 10 a proof of their equality (*Homily* 107.2).

17:11a. References to God's holiness are legion in the Old Testament; Brown cites *Didache* 10.2 as another example of early Christian usage (1970: 759). Hoskyns adduces 1 John 5:19 to show that holiness is the property that separates the Father from the ignorance and wickedness that the devil has introduced into the world (1947: 500). Chrysostom takes the statement **I am no longer in this world** to mean 'I am shall no longer be here in flesh, though present in spirit' (*Homily* 81.1).

17:11b. Appealing to the Syriac Sinaitic text, a new papyrus and the general character of the Gospel, which 'never elsewhere questions the unity of the disciples', Lindars follows Barrett in recommending the omission of **that they may be one**, etc. (1972: 525). Augustine takes this petition to show that Christ and his Father are one in nature, as human beings are (*Homily* 107.5). Ficino Platonizes: 'John's theology teaches that they who contemplate the divine reason are finally united to it as it is united to God' (1559: 198e).

17:12a. Augustine surmises that the Father preserved the disciples invisibly, even while Christ kept them **in his name** (*Homily* 106.6). Temple compares Phil 2:9, and adds that, while the name may be Adonai, it is God's 'revealed character, not the spoken sound' that is intended (1961: 304). The Valentinian *Gospel of Truth* declares that the name of the Father is the Son (J. A. Robinson 1988: 49). Henry puts three senses on the expression: (a) for the sake of thy name, (b) in the knowledge of thee, (c) in thy power (1991: 2031, col. 2).

17:12b. To Maurice the predestination of Judas is an 'unfathomable abyss' (1857: 419); to Calvin it explains itself, and is mentioned here to forestall any challenge to the divine foreknowledge (1961: 143). R. H. Lightfoot suggests that the **scripture** may be Ps 41:9, cited at 13:18, or Ps 109:8, cited at Acts 1:20 (1956: 301). The phrase 'son of perdition' is characterized as a Semitism by Erasmus (1535: 262); yet Danker (1960–1) quotes Menander to show that this may be a Greek locution. Murphy (1958) finds in documents from Qumran that the Hebrew equivalent may signify Sheol, corruption or the punishment of the wicked. Barrett observes, in the light of 2 Thess 2:3 that Judas is here cast in the role of the Antichrist (1955: 424). Hoskyns warns that the fall of Judas is mentioned because it is 'typical', and to show that our crimes are not forgiven because they are foreknown (1947: 501).

Church against World

17:13. Cf. 15:11. Christ, according to Bultmann, proclaims the 'hour of discrimination', in which his followers cannot escape the choice between eschatological and natural existence (1957: 386). Here and throughout the chapter Mandaean parallels abound in his commentary. Lloyd-Jones exhorts us to cultivate a decorous joy without 'boisterous' hilarity (1996: 280).

17:14. As the disciples have not yet suffered persecution, Augustine suggests that the past tense is employed to denote the ineluctable future (*Homily* 108). Censuring the adoption of the present tense in the NEB, Lindars suggests that Christ is echoing 15:25 (1972: 527). Chrysostom declares that it is the hatred of the world that makes the disciples worthy of divine favour (*Homily* 82.1). A final clause, **as I do not belong to the world**, is accepted by Barrett (1955: 425), but Brown thinks it more probably an addition 'in imitation of 16' (1970: 761).

17:15. The prayer resembles Matt 6:15, though the longer version of the Lord's Prayer goes on to reserve for God the Father the **glory** vouchsafed to the disciples in this chapter (*Didache* 8.2). Brown defends the translation **evil One**, rather than 'evil', by appeal to 1 John 2:13–14, 3:12 and 5:18–19 (1970: 761). The evil foreseen, says Bede, is that of schism (Aquinas 1997: 535); Chrysostom takes the word to mean apostasy (*Homily* 82.1).

17:16–17. Augustine explains that Christ himself was never **of the world**, and his disciples are so no longer (*Homily* 108.1). He adds that God will **sanctify** them through the truth who, according to 14:6, is Christ (*Homily* 108.2). Chrysostom however, sees a reference to the gift of the Holy Spirit (*Homily* 82.1), while Erasmus takes the word to signify only that the preaching of the apostles will be holy, like that of their master (1535: 262). The notion that they 'are consecrated to death' is rejected by Barrett both here and at v. 19 (1955: 426). Wesley, however, discriminates between the 'separation of the disciples' here and the sacrifice of Christ in the following verses (*MCNT* at XVII.17, 19).

17:18–19. The perfect **sent** has better attestation than the present 'send'; perhaps, as Brown conjectures, there is a reference to the mission in Samaria at 4:38 (1970: 762). Harvey comments that Jewish law demanded the revocation of the first agent before the sending of the next (1976: 106). The words

I sanctify myself are understood by Chrysostom, quoting Rom 12:1–2, to mean that Jesus offers himself as a sacrifice (*Homily* 82.1). Observing that the Greek verb *hagiazein* is attested only in Scripture and in texts that betray the influence of Scripture, Hoskyns reads this verse as an interpretation of Mark 14:22–5 (1947: 502–3). Lindars submits that the Evangelist 'is building on the tradition of eucharistic words, which he paraphrases for the present context' (1972: 529). Brown compares 10:11, 11:51 and 15:13, all verses in which one dies on behalf of others (1970: 766).

Prayer for Unity

17:20–1a. Christian tradition assumes that, after the departure of Judas, only eleven were left to be the immediate beneficiaries of this prayer (Marsh 1968: 570). Chrysostom opines that it is a ground of comfort to them that they are the means of saving others (*Homily* 82). Eckhart's contention that the saints become **one** by becoming identical with the Son of God (1977: 27–9) is generally reckoned heterodox; orthodoxy teaches that Father and Son are one in nature, while we are one by will and adoption only (Augustine, *Homily* 110.1). Hoskyns, however, feels bound to add, with Loisy, that the Church is 'one concrete organic union of charity' (1947: 504).

17:21b–2. Either Christ prays **that the world may believe** (Augustine, *Homily* 110.2), or his prayer implies **that the world will believe** because of the unanimity of the Church (Chrysostom, *Homily* 82.1). To Augustine **glory** in v. 22 means immortality (*Homily* 110.3), to Chrysostom 'miracles, doctrine and unity' (*Homily* 82.2). Cyril of Alexandria distinguishes our 'somatic' participation in Christ through the Eucharist from the supervenient glorification through the Holy Spirit (3.2–3 Pusey).

17:23. Cf. Zech 2:12–13 on the sending of the angel so that the wicked nations may know that God has sent him (Brown 1970: 771). Barrett favours the reading of Codex Bezae, **that I love them** (1955: 429); Brown upholds the commoner reading **that you love them**, and the common identification of **them** as Christ's disciples rather than the world (1970: 771). Sabellians, writes Chrysostom, are put to shame by the mention of the two persons, Arians by the assertion of their unity (*Homily* 82.2). Augustine adds that the Father's love of the Son is the cause of his loving those whom the Son elects (*Homily* 110.4).

17:24a. Christ prays, according to Hoskyns, that the theology of the Cross may be transformed into a theology of glory (1947: 504–5). Barrett contends that 'the ordinary language of prayer breaks down' when Christ expresses a will that he knows to be identical with the Father's (1955: 429). Temple finds it 'intimately personal' that he should address the Father without an epithet (1961: 313).

17:24b. Isaac Watts argues from 1 Cor 15:28 that Christ discloses his glory to the elect before the Resurrection, and infers the separability of the soul (Huntingford 1829: 337–9). The Greek word for **creation** is *katabole*, 'founda- tion', occurring also at Matt 13:35, Luke 11:50, Eph 1:4 and Heb 4:3. It is not found in the Old Testament, and Brown's citation of the *Assumption of Moses* (an apocryphal text, not free from Christian tampering) is hardly sufficient evi- dence of a Jewish pedigree (1970: 772). On the pre-existence of Christ cf. 1:1–4, Col 1:15.

17:25–6. Westcott remarks that the prayer, like the discourse that precedes it, ends on a note of confidence (1903: 284). The Son's 'unique apprehension of the Father', argues Temple, is the ground of all that we can know of him (1961: 315). Bultmann takes v. 26 to signify that the creature is restored to its proper standing with the Creator through revelation (1957: 400); to Natalis Alexander this disclosure of **his name** consists in publishing his compassion for the sinner (1840: 657).

Epilogue: One Glory or Two?

Käsemann (1968) is certainly right to urge that Christ presents knowledge as the key to salvation in the present chapter; like that of the early heretics whom we call Gnostics, this knowledge, or *gnosis*, includes the divine disclosure of events before the creation and an awareness of the inscrutable Father through the elusive witness of the Son. Neither Käsemann nor the Gnostics would deny that this knowledge is rooted in the 'historic events' narrated in the Gospel (Lindars 1972: 516–17); the deeper question is whether one is saved by the 'objective' work of Christ or by 'subjective' apprehension of him as Saviour. This disjunction implies another: is Christ God in so far as he makes God known to us, as Moses was God to Pharaoh at Ex 7:1, or was he God already before we knew of him, and even, to use the language of this chapter, before the foundation of the world?

The frequency of the title 'Son' in this Gospel is no evidence of natural affin- ity, for sonship in both Testaments means above all the right of inheritance, and we at least obtain this not by nature, but by adoption. As Ashton demon- strates, it is the privilege and duty of a son in Hebrew thought to act as his father's plenipotentiary, and conversely, the appellation 'son' might be given to such an emissary, whatever his relation to the sender (1991: 303–28). The pro- logue to the Gospel, when it states that the Word was God, implies at least that

Christ as Logos has this representative function, and that nothing can be known or desired of God but what is manifest in him 'from the beginning'. At 17:5 the auditory metaphor is supplanted by a visual one: the word *doxa*, elsewhere rendered as 'reputation' or 'appearance', often stands in biblical Greek for the Hebrew Shekinah, or 'glory'. In writing of the Diaspora, this word implies a benign accommodation of God's infinity to the limits of his world. Here it denotes an attribute that the Son shared with the Father before the world began, but aboriginal parity of honour does not amount to an identity of essence. Athanasius pleads that if Christ is the image of the Father, we ought to worship him according to the rule that allots the same reverence to the statue of the king as to the king himself (*Against the Arians* 3.5); Eusebius, however, had already made the proviso that the statue and the king are not the same (*Gospel Demonstration* 5.4.10).

Opponents of 'subordinationism' draw a strong inference from such verses as 10:30 and 17:5, and then demand a congruent interpretation of verses such as 17:3, in which the Father is styled the one true God. A Eusebius, on the other hand, will invoke the natural sense of 17:3 against the strong inference from 17:5. Those who agree with Bultmann that the true saviour in this Gospel is the word of revelation will prefer not to speak of coessentiality, but of a perfect adequation between the content of the message and its bearer. Rahner defines the Word as the self-expression of the Father (1975: 126–7), while Von Balthasar, remembering the theology of the Shekinah, concludes that the glory of Christ is the *kenôsis*, or self-emptying, of the Trinity in the world (1989: 211–28). Both are dogmaticians, and the exegete will hesitate to embrace the modern vocabulary of the first or the Pauline idiom of the second; he can rejoice at least that the Incarnation of Christ, as witnessed in the Gospels, is now the accepted key to a Trinitarian theology.

Prologue: Historical Considerations

It is commonly held that the record of the trial in Mark and Matthew must be fictitious because the Sanhedrin was forbidden to meet at night, and it was not a crime under Jewish law to style oneself 'the Christ, the Son of God'. In the Fourth Gospel the first interrogation is informal, the charge is a political one, and sentence has already been pronounced at 11:50. Indignant commentators have continued to deplore the 'irregularity of the process' (Henry 1991: 2038, col. 3). It is, however, the greater legality of the Johannine trial that commends this narrative even now to scholars of distinction who make no profession of Christian belief (Millar 1990). At the same time there are those who, while they acknowledge the 'intrinsic plausibility' of the account, protest that when some detail needs to be verified by historical parallels, as at 18:12, it proves to be no more credible than the others (E. P. Sanders 1993: 66–73). It remains true that whatever is most probable is most likely to be invented, and anyone who imagines that the Evangelist became an artless chronicler when he finished the prayer of Jesus should remember that in these chapters we are reading the libretto for oratorios by such masters as Cipriano de Rore in the Renaissance, J. S. Bach in the classical era, and Arvo Pärt in modern times.

In the Garden

18:1. Augustine surmises that the events related in the Synoptic tradition took place between the end of Christ's discourse and the crossing of the brook (*Homily* 112.1). Wesley suggests that the garden 'belonged to a friend' (*MCNT* at XVIII.1). Alcuin opines that Cedron means 'of cedars', and that the brook represents the draught of death, which 'blots out in a garden what was committed in a garden' [that is, in Eden] (Aquinas 1997: 546). Barrett however, noting that this 'popular etymology' has prompted emendation in some manuscripts, concludes that the name means simply that the dry brook flowed in winter (1955: 432). Hoskyns derives it from a word meaning 'black' (1947: 508). Brown notes, with some incredulity, that this journey has been likened to David's flight across the Kidron at 2 Sam 15:23 (1971: 806). I do not know whether anyone has built on the remark of Jeremias that the valley of the Kidron was made fertile by the blood of sacrifices (1969: 44).

18:2. That Judas knew his location proves to Chrysostom that Christ did not mean to hide (*Homily* 82.1). As Barrett observes, 'the betrayer' (*ho paradidous*) is 'almost a technical term' at Matt 26:25, 46, 48; Mark 14:42, 44; Luke 22:21; John 13:11, 18:2, 5 (1955: 432). Augustine characterizes Judas as the wolf of 10:12, with further allusions to Zech 13:7, Mark 14:27 and Matt 7:15 (*Homily* 112.2). Theophylact says that mountains were the places in which the disciples, including Judas, were accustomed to receive the loftiest teachings (Aquinas, 1997: 546).

18:3. '[W]ith lights and torches now they find the way / To take the Shepherd whilst the sheep do stray' (Aemilia Lanyer in D. Clarke, 2000: 243). A *speira* is a band of Roman soldiers, and this term suggests to Winter (against the tenor of the whole narrative) that Jesus was arrested for insurrection (1961: 129–30). Whereas Augustine assumes that the troops were granted by the governor (*Homily* 112.2), Chrysostom, who had seen Constantinople become the prey of Gothic mercenaries, suggests that they were bribed (*Homily* 83.1).

Hoskyns finds that the lanterns are 'normal equipment for a military unit' at Dionysius of Halicarnassus, *Antiquities* 11.40 (1947: 509).

The Arrest

18:4. Christ does not await the kiss of Judas (as at Mark 14:45): as Henry says, the second Adam did not conceal himself as the first had done (1991: 2036, col. 1). The statement that he **knew all**, says Lindars, prepares us for his effect upon the newcomers at v. 6 (1972: 540). Ashton hears an echo of the prophecy at 7:34 (1991: 487).

18:5. Jesus of Nazareth is Christ's name on the Cross, and in the mouth of the demoniac at Mark 1:24. The words **I am he**, repeated at 18:8, were addressed at 4:16 to the Samaritan and at 6:20 to the disciples. As Hutcheson writes, the word of comfort is now a word of dread (1972: 375) – although the Roman troops could not have known, as Henry does, that **I am** is the name of God in the Greek of Ex 3:14 (1991: 2036, col. 2).

18:6. Christ is more forbearing than Elijah at 2 Kings 1, but this discomfiture is still the 'normal effect of a theophany', as Lindars divines from Dan 10:9, Acts 9:4, 22:7, 26:14 and Rev 1:17 (1972: 541). Barrett compares Ps 55(56):10 Septuagint: 'my enemies have fallen backwards' (1955: 434). Augustine sees a presage of Christ's future power as judge (*Homily* 112.3). Pope Gregory remarks that the elect prostrate themselves, while the reprobate 'see not where they fall' (Aquinas 1997: 548).

18:7–8. Christ's death 'buys' the lives of his disciples, comments Marsh (1968: 586). Hutcheson remarks that the Lord does not put his sheep to the test before they can bear it (1972: 376). Erasmus scoffs at commentators who seek a charter for clerical immunities in the command to **let these go** (1535: 263). Chrysostom suggests that Christ is giving the guards an opportunity to escape the sin of murder (*Homily* 83.1). Augustine finds that even the foes of Christ are unconscious agents of his will (*Homily* 112.3).

18:9. Cf. 6:39 and 17:12; Christ's words are now treated as a prophecy, as at 18:32. Chrysostom applies this pledge to the present world as well as to the next (*Homily* 83.1). Lindars argues that the Evangelist, who does not describe the flight of the disciples, is correcting the application of Zech 13:37 at Mark 14:27 (1972: 542).

18:10. Cf. Luke 50.22 for the **right ear**, though he, like Matthew and Mark, names neither the aggressor nor the victim. Benoit states that the right ear was considered the more valuable (1969: 43), while Theophylact suggests that Peter acquired the sword for the sacrifice of the lamb (Aquinas 1997: 549). Barrett suggests that the danger would have justified the illicit carriage of weapons at this season (1955: 435), but Chrysostom reminds us of the injunction to turn the other cheek at Matt 5:39 (*Homily* 83.2). Brown notes the theory that Malchus was an Arab (1970: 812). Augustine thinks that the author's purpose in naming him was to enable readers to verify the miracle; but since the name connotes royalty, he adds that it prefigures the reign of Christ (*Homily* 112.5).

18:11. Theophylact suggests that he calls his passion a **cup** to signify his willing acceptance of it (Aquinas 1997: 550), though Mark 10:39 and 14:36 suggest a different reading. Calvin derides 'fanatics' who infer that we should not avert death with medicines, but agrees that the verse prohibits the use of unlawful force against enemies (1961: 157).

Christ before Annas and Caiaphas

18:12. Cf. Acts 21:31 for the title 'chiliarch': literally the commander of a thousand and technically the commander of a cohort. Hoskyns argues that the whole cohort must have been present, though the word **detachment** in v. 3 is often taken, on the evidence of Polybius 11.23, to betoken a third of the full 600 (1947: 509). Winter suggests that the dignity of the officer has been exaggerated in this narrative (1961: 29).

8:13–14. Henry opines that the 'lamb' was led to the slaughter through the sheep-gate, which is located on Mount Olivet at Neh 3:1. Cf. Matt 26:57 for the name 'Caiaphas', which Bultmann supposes to have been interpolated in this and the following verse (1957: 497). Bede ascribes to God the desire that 'they who were allied in blood should be allied in guilt' (Aquinas 1997: 551). Josephus, *Antiquities* 18.26–35 records that Annas held the office from AD 6 to 15, but as his successors included his four sons as well as Caiaphas, his son-in-law, Barrett finds it plausible that he should still 'retain great influence' (1955: 438). Farrar suggests that he became a deputy, the 'second priest' of 2 Kings 25:18 and Jer 52:24 (1901: 567n). Luke styles him the high priest at Acts 4:6, and Brown appeals to Josephus, *Jewish War* 2.126, where Jonathan is described as high priest 15 years after being ejected from the office (1970: 820). In the mystery play *The Buffeting*, Annas tries to curb the ire of Caiaphas and protests against the beating (Happé 1975: 472–83); in Sayers he acts as a gadfly to his son-in-law, and seizes the opportunity to conduct an 'irregular investigation' (1943: 171, 261). In later Jewish sources, his name is a byword for corruption (Evans 1995: 123–37); on a fourth-century casket both prelates wear Roman dress (Grabar 1968: fig. 333).

18:15. The **other disciple** has been identified as Nicodemus and even as Judas (Brown 1970: 822); Schnackenburg is the most distinguished adversary of the prevalent opinion that he is both the beloved disciple and the narrator (1982: 235). Chrysostom assures us that he mentions the connection with the high priest not as a boast, but rather to deprecate the inference that his entry into the house was an act of courage (*Homily* 83.2). Barrett finds it 'improbable' that such a man could be John the son of Zebedee (1955: 438). Nevertheless, the *Gospel to the Hebrews* states that when he was a fisherman he brought his catch to the high priest, and Polycrates at Eusebius, *Church History* 5.24, that John was a priest who wore the mitre. His acquaintance who is styled the **high priest** must, as Westcott shows, be Caiaphas, since he receives this title at vv. 13 and 24, whereas only Luke 3:2 applies it to Annas jointly with his son-in-law (1903: 255). Ryle quotes the fancy of Hengstenberg that 'John had earlier sought from the high priest . . . what he found in Christ' (1973: 259).

Peter's Denial

18:16. Barrett quotes 2 Kings 4:6 (Septuagint) for an earlier instance of a female doorkeeper (cf. Mark 14:68–9), and adds that the Greek allows us to identify either her or the other disciple as the one who beckoned Peter into the house (1955: 439). Bultmann, however, contends that the doorkeeper ought to have been a man, and an Ethiopic variant supports him (1957: 499).

18:17a. Some deduce from the word **also** that the 'other disciple' was already 'known as such' (Marsh 1968: 589). The reply to Brown's question, 'why was he not in danger?' (1970: 824) is, as Bengel already saw, that he was acquainted with the high priest (1850: 167–8).

18:17b. Brodie finds in Peter's words a 'direct contradiction of the divine "I am"' at 18:5 and 8 (1993: 529); Theophylact opposes some who argue that he lied to avoid a punishment which would separate him from Christ (Aquinas 1997: 554). Lindars compares the Baptist's laudable reply at 1:21 to those who were seeking a Messiah (1972: 549). Pope Gregory takes the **fire** in v. 18 to signify love of the present world, which supervenes upon the waning of our inward love for God (Aquinas 1997: 554).

The Mock Trial

18:19. 'A guilty criminal examineth his judge,' sneers Avancini (1950: 136), thinking perhaps of Mic 5:1: 'They shall smite the judge of Israel'. Chrysostom,

Theophylact and Alcuin agree that the high priest, having no charge to bring, was asking Christ to incriminate himself (Aquinas 1997: 555). Dodd suggests that they hoped to find him guilty of the sorcery and heresy alleged against him in later Jewish invective (1963: 95). Barrett compares the *Acts of Justin*, where the prefect asks what dogma is professed by the defendants (1955: 540).

18:20. Christ elects at 11:54 not to teach in *parrêsia* (i.e. in public), and only at 16:25 does he adopt plain speech (*parrêsia*) with his intimates. Augustine understands the word *parrêsia* here to mean 'in the hearing of many', rather than 'plainly' (*Homily* 113.3). In *The Buffeting* Caiaphas turns the fact against him: 'Great wordis hast thou spokyn; then thou was not dom' (Happé 1975: 472).

18:21. Westcott observes that a man was not expected to incriminate himself (1903: 257); Hoskyns points the moral that the Gospel is known only through the witness of Christ's disciples (1947: 514). Wesley, however, takes Christ to mean that Pilate will not believe him (*MCNT* at XVIII.21).

18:22–3. The blow is reported at Matt 26:65–8, Mark 14:65, Luke 22:63–4; Paul suffers similar ignominy at Acts 23:2–4, and Mark 14:48–9 ascribes the same remonstrance to Christ at his arrest. To Temple the abuse proves that 'the meeting was informal' (1961: 328). Alcuin sees a fulfilment of Lam 3:30, 'he gave his cheek to the smiters' (Aquinas 1997: 556), and Handel in the *Messiah* weaves this verse into his lament for the 'man of sorrows', based on Isa 53:4.

18:24. Chrysostom concludes that the accusers were at a loss (*Homily* 83.3). Bede wonders whether 'they sent him bound as they had brought him' or had released his bonds in the meantime (Aquinas 1997: 557). Mahoney (1965) emends the text to remove the word **bound**. The Syriac Sinaiticus, and even one Greek manuscript, make this verse follow directly after v.13, making Caiaphas the chairman of all the proceedings, as he is in the other Gospels. Hoskyns replies that, if the current version is not the original, it is difficult to see how it would have arisen (1947: 512). Westcott presumes that Caiaphas had been present at the earlier 'private' session (1903: 257).

18:25. Romanus blames this temptress more than the other questioners (*Cantica* 31.4 at 1963: 244); and so perhaps does Luigi Tansillo in the third stanza of his *Lagrime di S. Pietro*, set to music by Orlando Lassus. Since Mark 14:66–72, Matt 27:69–75 and Luke 22:58–9 all assign the second challenge to a single interlocutor, Augustine suggests that a number of persons challenged Peter at once (*Gospel Harmony* 3.6); hence in the *St John Passion* of Bach, the accusation is levelled by a chorus. Strauss, however, enumerates eight denials from the four Gospels, and disdains to reconcile them (1892: 660).

18:26–7. Notwithstanding rabbinic prohibitions on the keeping of cocks in Jerusalem, Jeremias quotes evidence of their presence from the Mishnah (1969: 47–8n). Brodie juxtaposes the three denials with three occurrences of **I am** on the lips of Christ at 18:5, 6 and 8 (1993: 531). Bede counts two denials, taking the first to stand for those who disbelieved before the Resurrection, the second for those who rejected even that; carnal lust is signified by the first provocation, diabolic intrigue by the second (Aquinas 1997: 559). Fruitless shame is expressed in Bach's vivacious aria 'Oh, take flight', but the chorale that follows indicates a salutary repentance. In the same way, Prudentius says, the sinner desists when he hears the voice of Christ, our herald of celestial dawn (*Cathemerinon* 1.53–64). Henry, however, reasons that since Peter went unpunished, though his denial would have been incredible to the bystanders, he had no occasion to sin (1991: 2042, col. 2). His case is none the less better than ours, according to Kathleen Raine:

> The cock crows out the night, and we remain
> outside eternity, the lover's dream
> the soldier's sleep, the locked gates of the tomb
> ghosts of our days, longing for night again.
>
> (1956: 23)

The Interview with Pilate

18:28. Ryle compares the 'false scrupulosity' which fasts at Lent and riots at the carnival (1873: 278–9). Chrysostom suggests that Christ had instituted a new Passover on the previous evening, or else that the name 'Passover' has been given to the whole season (*Homily* 83.3); Alcuin contends that the Passover of the priests was in fact the 'great feast' of the fifteenth day of Nisan, which followed the immolation of the lamb on the fourteenth day of Nisan (Aquinas 1997: 560). Brown calculates the time as 6.00 a.m. (1971: 844), and it could hardly have been earlier if, as Westcott observes, a criminal could not be condemned at night (1903: 258). The praetorium is generally assumed to have been the former palace of Herod on the West Hill (Brown 1970: 845).

18:29–30. Absurd, says Chrysostom, to entrust the punishment to Pilate without involving him in the trial (*Homily* 83.4). Noting the charges laid by the priests at Luke 23:5, Augustine decides that 'each Evangelist said what he thought sufficient' (*Gospel Harmony* 3.8).

18:31. Theophylact holds that Pilate is rebuking the Jews for their silence, Alcuin that he is deferring to their knowledge of the Law (Aquinas 1997: 562). Sacy construes his behest ironically: 'Judge for yourselves if your law allows the condemnation of an innocent man' (1840: 712). He maintains a level bass in Bach's oratorio, though the chorus is loud and daunting.

18:32. Cf. 12:31–2. *The Buffeting* allots these words to Annas in his alter-cation with Caiaphas (Happé, 1975: 476). Origen surmises that the law of the Jews forbade an execution during the feast (*Commentary* 20.25); Hutcheson adds in corroboration that 'Herod delayed the intended execution of Peter till after Easter, Acts xii, 4' (1972: 386). Chrysostom understands them to mean either that the Romans did not allow the Jews to inflict a capital penalty, or else that the crime was against Rome, not against Israel (*Homily* 83.4). J. Lightfoot assembles rabbinic texts which relate that the Sanhedrin had lost (through neg-ligence, as he infers) the right to inflict a capital penalty (1859: 221–4). Against Lietzmann and Juster, Sherwin-White concludes that Rome would not have conceded this right to native authorities in such an unruly province, discounts as 'lynchings' the deaths of Stephen (Acts 7:54ff) and James the Just (Josephus, *Antiquities* 20.9.1), believes that the process threatened against the adulteress at 8:1–12 was equally illegal, and insists upon the word 'secretly' in Origen's account of the executions carried out by Jewish tribunals (1963: 32–44).

18:33–5. Pilate's question appears to presuppose the accusation at Luke 23:2 (so Alcuin at Aquinas 1997: 564); in the *Acts of Pilate*, however, the Jews expressly prefer a charge of blasphemy (*NTA*, 1.455). Ryle takes the rejoinder of Christ to mean, 'Why, if you, the governor, have not heard any ill of me are you prepared to believe these men?' (1873: 286). Where Chrysostom admires Pilate for exposing 'the evil intentions of the Jews' in his answer at v. 35 (*Homily* 83.4), Westcott hears only disdain for his native subjects (1903: 260). Corelli makes him reluctant to believe that Jesus can be one of them (1935: 77).

Christ's Defence

18:36. Cf. 17:16, 18:11, Matt 22:53. Chrysostom rebukes those who imagine that, because Christ's **kingdom is not from this world**, he is hostile to the Creator (*Homily* 83.4). Theophylact explains that, though he reigns here, his authority is from above (Aquinas 1997: 565). Ryle maintains that the verse enjoins the pious and temperate use of political power in ecclesiastical affairs, but not the complete disjunction of Church and State (1869: 287).

18:37. As Brown points out, only Pilate employs the word **king** (1970: 434). In Masefield's play *Good Friday*, it is the putative claim to kingship that robs Jesus of support (1923: 454–5). The rest of Christ's reply echoes 8:32, 10:4 and 14:6. As Augustine recognizes, he speaks to the world and not directly to his interrogator (*Homily* 115.1). Ryle cites commentators who distinguish between Christ's birth as man and his coming into the world as God (1873: 291).

18:38. '*What is truth?* said jesting Pilate, and would not stay for an answer' (F. Bacon 1972: 3); to Wesley the question means 'Is truth worth hazarding your life for?' (*MCNT* at XVIII.38). Yet Chrysostom supposed that he asked in earnest (*Homily* 83.4–5). Butler admires his relativism (1985: 307); the silence of Christ persuades Voltaire that truth is unattainable (1961: 236–7). Augustine suggests that Pilate hurried out to concert the ruse that now occurred to him (*Homily* 115.5). Bengel, however, argues that Christ's answer was lost on one who recognized not truth but power as the source of kingship (1850: 268).

18:39. Bede thinks that this unattested custom was not prescribed by law, but handed down from the forefathers in memory of the captivity in Egypt (Aquinas 1997: 567). Westcott notes a rabbinic parallel for Pilate's offer to release **your king** (1903: 261), and Theophylact holds that his irony is directed at the Jews, not at his prisoner (Aquinas 1997: 568). Henry, while accusing the priests of adding this custom to the law of God, points out that Pilate appeals to the multitude because he knows that the priests will not agree (1991: 2042, col. 1).

18:40a. Cf. Mark 15:7–11. R. H. Lightfoot suspects that **shouted** bespeaks not merely passion but demonic influence (1956: 325). A variant of Matt 26:16–17 implies that the name of the other man was Jesus and Barabbas his patronymic (Hastings, 1906: 171). Alcuin construes **Barabbas** as 'son of their master the devil' (Aquinas 1997: 568): Christ is thus the true Bar-abbas ('son of the father'), as at Matthew 10:25 he is the true Beelzebub ('master of the house'). Gresswell, who opines that the execution of Barabbas had been postponed to enable Pilate to offer this choice, maintains that the imminence of the Passover (on the Johannine chronology) made it necessary to carry out the sentence without delay (1830: 91).

18:40b. At Mark 15:7 and Luke 23:19 Barabbas is an insurgent; Meeks discovers him in the robber of 10:1 (1967: 68). In Hugo's *Fin de Satan*, he owes his release to a priestly stratagem (1886: 332). Brandon insinuates that he and Christ had rebelled in concert (1968: 175–6), and the charge that Christ was a brigand can be traced to the second century (Horbury 1984). The scenario is reversed when children take a thief for Jesus in the film *Whistle down the Wind*.

Epilogue: The Character of Pilate

Nothing in Pilate's governorship suggests that he would have mollified an insult to the religion of his subjects when he had the opportunity to inflame it. Soon after he was installed as procurator by Tiberius in AD 26, he provoked a riot by allowing the Roman legionaries to house their painted standards in the Temple (Josephus, *Jewish War* 2.169). Later he wrested funds from the Temple treasury to finance the construction of aqueducts (ibid., 175–7), and even after the fall of his protector in Rome, Sejanus, he put down a Samaritan rising with such bloodiness that Tiberius recalled him at the instance of the Jews. His evil repute outlives him in Josephus and Philo; early Christian sources, however, paint him in better colours, alleging that he became a convert after his reluctant execution of the Saviour (*NTA* 1.482–4), and that when he sent the record of his proceedings to the Senate, Tiberius decreed that Christ should be worshipped as a god (Tertullian, *Apology* 5). Such impostures prompted the fabrication of the more hostile *Acts of Pilate* during the last great persecution of the Church (Eusebius, *Church History* 9.5.1, 9.7.1).

In the Towneley play, *The Scourging*, Pilate vents his malice with a candour that is elsewhere reserved for devils, but in the York play he seems sorry for his office (Happé 1975: 507–10 and 685). In Masefield's play *Good Friday*, he acknowledges no god but Rome (1923: 456), and Caldwell makes him a superstitious bureaucrat, who fears neither God nor man as he dreads the Emperor (1959: 512–16). For Hugo he is a prudent hoarder of revenues, coldly indifferent to his victim and yielding readily to the bias of his accusers (1886: 376, 382). The Pilate of Anatole France (1892) forgets this murder when he recounts the indiscretions that disgraced him. By contrast, Sayers credits him with fierce expostulations before he bows to threats and numbers (1943: 282–6). In Bulgakov's *The Master and Margarita* he avenges Christ by contriving the assassination of Judas (1967: 324–46), and on the eve of his fall in E. Arnold's *Light of the World* he bemoans his cowardice toward 'that one Man / whom, of all Jews, I hated not, nor scorned' (1910: 43; cf. 19:5 below).

Prologue: Gospel Parallels

Since this chapter coincides most frequently with Mark's account of the Passion, it has often been proposed that Mark was its source. Though Dodd put his weight against it, an affirmative reply was upheld by Lee (1957); almost at once, however, Buse (1958) asked why the Fourth Evangelist makes no use of materials that are not assigned to stratum A in Vincent Taylor's commentary on Mark. In similar fashion, Wills adduces Matera's (1982) distinction between the primitive and the redactional in Mark to prove the independence of the Fourth Evangelist (1997: 138). Parallels arise, according to Wills, because both Mark and the Fourth Evangelist have fashioned Christ according to the same religious and literary types. One is that of the scapegoat, represented in

Scripture by the persecuted man of God and in Greece by the putative bearer of pollution (1997: 40–1). Another is that of the prophet – a role sustained by the entry into Jerusalem, the oracle against her, the arrest, flagellation and trial before a magistrate, the reticence of the victim, his prediction of his death and the death itself (1997: 160). In fact, the first two concomitants of the prophet are vestigial in the Fourth Gospel, and its Christ does not maintain a consistent silence though he says too little to justify Wills' assimilation of him to another Greek type – that of the indomitable philosopher who beards the crooked Emperor in his den (1997: 137). A fourth is that of the hero (1997: 43–50); but only the resurrected Christ was worshipped, whereas a hero cult is centred on the tomb.

In two of the three fifth-century representations of the Passion described in Hastings, John and Mary are in attendance (1906: 313), and the Johannine narrative lends peculiar details to two illustrious paintings of the seventeenth century: Rembrandt's *Three Crosses* and Poussin's *Crucifixion* (Wadsworth Atheneum, Hartford). For the most part, however, it is difficult to ascertain whether a painter of the scene has used this Gospel as his text. Within the Church, although the other accounts of Jesus' life have often been accommodated to the chronology of the Fourth Gospel, the liturgy of the eucharist and the calendar of Easter have been derived from the Synoptics. Even the cause of the execution is not made clear, for while the rubric above Christ's head implies a charge of sedition, there is no evidence that the governor has heard one. Though he acquits his prisoner three times, his sagacity only proves that he acts against his conscience, so that even his apologists, like Chrysostom, complain of his pusillanimity (*Homily* 84). J. Clarke points out that his actions are illegal, since they flout the law which required ten days to elapse between trial and sentence (1740: 163). No doubt this Gospel contradicts Moltmann's claim that the oppressors of the Jews were the only murderers of Jesus (1990: 163–4); no doubt it makes of 'Jew' an invidious epithet which inspired the tirades of Luther (to name but one); yet its aim, as Ryle points out, is not to incriminate one race but to expose the 'judicial blindness' which God sends on those who are pious only in their own conceit (1873: 301).

The Buffeting

19:1. For the flogging of criminals before execution, cf. Josephus, *Jewish War* 2.25. Augustine represents the act as a sop to the Jews (*Homily* 116.1), and Masefield as a ruse to spare the prisoner (1925: 67–8). To Avancini the blows represent the plagues of sin as in Ps 32:11 (1950: 157). Christ's face retains a dolorous tranquillity in most paintings, even where, as in Giotto's *Flagellation*, he is watched by an eager crowd (Arena Chapel, Padua). In that of Fra Angelico his mother's averted countenance exhibits more emotion (Museo di San Marco, Florence). He suffers no contumely from the Jews in the previous chapter, as he does at Luke 22:64, 23:11, etc., and, as Frazer seems to apprehend, this Gospel is thus the chief obstacle to his theory that the Crucifixion coincided with the feast of Purim, at which the Jews re-enacted the hanging of their enemy Haman in the book of Esther (1914: 412–23).

19:2–3. Cf. Matt 27:27–31. Chrysostom blames the cruelty of the soldiers on the Jews (*Homily* 84.1), but they were following Roman custom, for the scene resembles the buffeting of the mock king which was a feature of the Roman Saturnalia (Frazer 1914: 414–15, quoting Dio, *Oration* 4). Lindars (1972: 564) refers to Philo's account of the taunting of a maniac (*Against Flaccus* 36–9), but this has more in common with Matt 27:29, and De la Potterie sees no mockery in the present passage (1960: 239). The thorny crown is a centrepiece of medieval piety: 'Of sharp thorne I have worne a crowne on my hed, / So rubbid, so bobbid, so rufull, so red' (Gray 1975: 26, attributed to Skelton). To Hutcheson the ram caught in the thicket as a substitute for Isaac in Gen 23:13 prefigures this coronation (1972: 393). Grünewald's addition of a bandage suggests that a latter-day Christ would face a firing-squad (Alte Pinothek, Munich).

The Sentence

19:4–5a. At Matt 27:24 Pilate absolves himself *before* handing Jesus over to the soldiers. In the crown of thorns (cf. Matt 27:28) Bede recognizes the sins which Christ took on him (Aquinas 1997: 570), just as Marvell upbraids the 'thorns with which I long, too long . . . My Saviour's head have crowned' (1952: 9).

19:5b. Ryle finds mockery here (1873: 308), Augustine a plea to 'spare the outcast' (*Homily* 116.2). Barrett, citing Caiaphas' speech at 11:51–2, concludes that Pilate has 'accidentally' recognized the heavenly Son of Man (1955: 454). Lindars suspects an unconscious reminiscence of Zech 6:12: 'Behold the man whose name is the branch' (1972: 566). Cyril of Alexandria explains that we should still be Satan's prisoners had Christ not achieved his victory *as man* (2.653 Pusey). The Latin words *Ecce Homo* furnished Seeley with a title for his life of a 'human Jesus' (1895); Nietzsche attached them to a panegyrical survey of his own works (1908, often reprinted and translated). Rossetti's sonnet on the Crucifixion – 'Shall Christ hang on the Cross and we not look?' – is a simultaneous commentary on this verse, 8:28 and 12:32 (1995: 434). In Rembrandt's *Ecce Homo* of the 1650s, the group includes Barabbas, and perhaps also a stone effigy of Adam (National Gallery, London). Dürer shows his opinion of the

Rembrandt, *Ecce Homo*. National Gallery, London.

governor by attiring him as a Turk (Panofsky 1955: 60). In an *Ecce Homo* ascribed to Leonardo, Hemans detects 'all depths of love, grief, death, humanity' (1912: 529). Yet the statuesque pose of Christ belied his human weakness in most Renaissance paintings; even his human contours disappear in Bacon's triptych of 1944 (Tate Gallery, London).

19:6a. The Latin *Cru-ci-fi-ge* occupies four stark, unaccompanied notes in the *Passio* of Arvo Pärt. For Chrysostom this exclamation shifts the blame from

Pilate to the Jews (*Homily* 84.2). Crossman contrasts the shout of **Hosanna** at 12:13 (*A&M* 102).

19:6b–7. Wroe is one of many who find Pilate's invitation to murder 'ridiculous' (1999: 252). Chrysostom commends the silence of Christ as a fulfilment of Isa 53:7–8 (*Homily* 84.2). In the crowd's reply the words **he made himself the Son of God** echo 5:18, 10:36, but are wanting at Luke 23:23.

19:8–10. Bede infers that Pilate was afraid 'lest he should slay the Son of God' (Aquinas 1997: 572). His question means, according to Abbott, 'How could you possibly be the Son of God?' (1906: 297). Behind it, according to Wroe, 'lay every unsettling, half-grasped phrase [he] had heard that day' (1999: 253). Ryle suggests that, being at odds with his conscience, he hoped for a word on which he could take a 'firm stand' (1873: 312–13). For the silence of Christ cf. Luke 22:63–5 and 23:9, Mark 15:5, Matt 27:14, 1 Pet 2:22–3. Pilate's second speech (cf. Mark 15:4, Matt 27:13) prompts Chrysostom to ask why he did not exercise his **power to release** the accused (*Homily* 84.2).

19:11. Chrysostom urges that **given** implies that Pilate is permitted, not predestined, and therefore guilty (*Homily* 84.2). Augustine argues that he sins from fear and not, like the author of the **greater sin**, from envy (*Homily* 116.5). Theophylact identifies this sinner as 'Judas or the multitude' (Aquinas 1997: 574); the name of Caiaphas is also frequently suggested. Ryle concludes that the pronoun personifies the whole Jewish people (1973: 315). Brown compares Acts 4:27–8, where Pilate is treated 'as a tool of God' (1970: 878). The verb *paradidonai* ('to give up') here retains the sense of 'betray', as at 6:64, 6:72, 12:4, 13:2ff, 18:2ff; but that is not its meaning at vv. 16 and 30 below.

19:12. As this is not Pilate's first attempt to set Christ free, Hoskyns judges him unintelligent or superstitious (1947: 524). Observing that not all scholars are prepared to admit the currency of the title 'friend of Caesar' before Vespasian (AD 69–79), Brown (1970: 879) compares 'friends of the king' at 1 Macc 2:18 and Josephus, *Antiquities* 12.7.3. Philo records that Pilate was swayed by a similar innuendo on another occasion (*Embassy to Gaius* 301–2), while Maier (1968) suggests that the fall of Sejanus in AD 31 – or even the anticipation of such an event – would have robbed him of a protector.

The Road to Golgotha

19:13. **Gabbatha** is not a true equivalent for the Greek name **Lithostratos** if, as Hastings says, it denotes a 'convex' structure and not a 'level, tesselated surface' (1906: 631). The pavement may have been a portable one such as Emperors carried (Suetonius, *Julius* 46), or the rostrum in the market-place

(Josephus, *Jewish War* 2.9.3), or perhaps a portico in the palace of Herod where the governor resided (Hastings 1913: 350). De la Potterie (1960) denies that the judge's bench of Matt 27:19 is the seat described here, and the Greek text could mean either that Pilate sat or that he caused Christ to be seated. There are parallels for the former sense at 12:14 and 8:2, while the latter can draw support from Justin Martyr, *1 Apology* 35 (Barrett 1955: 453) and *Gospel of Peter* 7 (*NTA* 1.184).

19:14a. The Crucifixion is said at Mark 15:25 to have taken place at the third hour, not the **sixth**; Augustine explains that Christ was crucified first by the tongues of Jews and then by the soldiers (*Homily* 117.1). Mahoney (1965) contends that Mark is speaking only of the time when the lots were cast. Elsley cites Archbishop Usher's opinion, reinforced by Nonnus and a Paschal sermon attributed to Peter of Alexandria, that the original text read **third hour**, as in Mark (1844: 483–4). Ryle traces to Grotius the common solution, that the sixth hour means the quarter which terminated at the sixth hour, but commenced with the blowing of trumpets at the third (1873: 321). Barrett suggests that the author wished to synchronize the death of Christ with the slaughter of lambs and hence with the Day of Preparation (1955: 454); yet Alcuin (who accepts the Synoptic chronology) takes **preparation** to mean the day before the Sabbath, as at Ex 16:22 (Aquinas 1997: 575).

19:14b–15a. Chrysostom thinks that Pilate has now despaired of moving the Jews (*Homily* 84.10–12), Theophylact that he exhibits Christ's humility as a satire on their malice (Aquinas 1997: 576). Lindars sees no mockery here, but 'almost a confession of faith' (1972: 571).

19:15b. With one accord, writes Chrysostom, they denied the kingdom of God (*Homily* 84.2); Matthew Henry remarks that the Jews who would have no king but Caesar have had none since. Meeks detects a parody of a festal hymn which proclaims that only God is king of Israel (1967: 77). On Brown's chronology, this renunciation of the covenant takes place at the hour when the priests began to slaughter the paschal lambs (1970: 895).

19:16–17a. 'Lo, the faint Lamb, with weary limb / Bears that huge tree which must bear Him,' writes Crashaw (1927: 270). Poussin, Bruegel, Giorgione, Dürer and Tiepolo are among those who have painted the stumbling Christ. Lipsius was perhaps the first to protest that they impose the whole Cross on Jesus, who in fact will have carried nothing but the beam (J. Clarke 1740: 164). There is no trace here of the story that the Cross was borne by Simon of Cyrene (Matt 27:32 par.); Augustine's solution is that Jesus and Simon bore it in turn (*Gospel Harmony* 3.10). The Evangelist may have wish to countermand the 'docetic' story that Simon took the place of Jesus on the Cross (Irenaeus, *Against Heresies* 1.24.4), or he may, as Dodd suggests, have known the saying that 'every man must bear his own cross' at Luke 14:27 (1963: 124).

19:17b. Chrysostom records the tradition that Adam was buried at Calvary (*Homily* 85.1; cf. Origen, *Commentary on Matthew* 27.33). Boehme declares that when the blood of Christ was shed, it cleansed the flesh of Adam (1945: 254). Ryle collates authorities to show that Calvary was not a hill (1873: 325) – though it can hardly have been the 'long and crooked valley' in which Idris Davies crucifies the 'father and the son' with a parodic application of 14:9 to the chronic sufferings of miners (1980: 200).

The Crucifixion

19:18. No colloquy with the thieves is reported, as at Luke 23:39–43. To Calvin these companions represent the whole race of sinners for whom Christ died (1961: 169), while Chrysostom sees a fulfilment of Isa 53:12 (*Homily* 85.1).

19:19. Chrysostom observes that the inscription (also at Matt 27:37, Mark 15:26, Luke 23:38) served to distinguish Christ from the thieves (*Homily* 85.1), and in the legend of Helena's finding of the Cross it serves to identify the relic (M. J. Edwards 2003: 88). Augustine sees a fulfilment of the prophecy in Ps 2:6 that God will set his king on the hill of Sion and of the rubrics to Ps 56 and 57, 'Thou shalt not corrupt the inscription of the title' (*Homily* 117.5). Cyril of Alexandria detects a reference to the inscription in 'the writing nailed against us' at Col 2:14 (3.83–5 Pusey).

19:20. The title 'King of the Jews' had been assumed by Herod the Great (Josephus, *Jewish War* 1.14.4). To Augustine the languages signify Jewish worship, Greek philosophy and Roman dominion (*Homily* 117.4); Theophylact makes Latin stand for practical wisdom, Greek for physics, Hebrew for theology (Aquinas 1997: 579). Westcott, however, prefers the reading 'Hebrew, Latin and Greek' – the native Aramaic followed by the official tongue and then by the *lingua franca* (1903: 274). In the concert of the three the assembled nations 'read their own reproach', as Hutcheson perceives (1972: 401).

19:21–2. Tertullian declares that Pilate had imbibed the spirit of prophecy (*Apology* 21), Augustine that 'he could not tear from his heart the thought that Christ was king of the Jews' (*Homily* 115.5). Though Brown produces a similar locution from 1 Macc 13:38 (1970: 902), Winter regards the inscription as the most 'stable fact' in the extant narratives of the Crucifixion (1961: 109).

The Spectators

19:23. Chrysostom reports that coats of quality in Palestine were woven from two strips (*Homily* 85.2). The four parts, according to Brown, will have been a

27 & 28. The Crucifixion and Lamentation. By The MASTER of the DOMINICAN EFFIGIES. Working 1337–45. Italian (Florentine) School. Presented by Mr. Harold Bompas, 1941.

Master of the Dominican Effigies, *Crucifixion and Deposition*. Ashmolean Museum, Oxford.

turban, an outer cloak, a girdle and either sandals or an undershirt (1970: 903). As Westcott remarks, an allusion to the high priest's seamless robe (Josephus, *Antiquities* 3.161) may be intended (1903: 275). The crosses of the two thieves are unusually prominent in Blake's picture of this scene (Fitzwilliam Museum, Cambridge).

19:24. An unusually accurate citation of Ps 22:18. To Augustine the division of the garments represents the distribution of the Church catholic 'over four quarters of the globe', while the seamless tunic stands for the 'unity of all the parts', which consist, in charity (*Homily* 118.4). Chrysostom makes it a symbol of the indivisible union of God and man in Christ (*Homily* 85.1). Such allegories are not out of place, for, as Barrett notices, Philo 'treats the tunic as a symbol of the Word' at *Flight* 110–112 (1955: 457).

19:25. Only here is the mother of Jesus said to have been present: 'Love thither had her brought, and misbelief / Of these sad news, which charg'd her mind to fears' (Drummond of Hawthornden, 1894: 161). Theophylact notes that the mockery does not weaken Christ's solicitude for his mother (Aquinas 1997: 584). Since Mark and Matthew tell us that the women stood at a distance, Augustine thinks it probable that they stood within sight of Jesus but further away from him than the centurion (*Gospel Harmony* 3.21). In Sayers' dramatization Mary Magdalene wins access to the foot of the Cross by renewing her old liaisons with the soldiers (1943: 303–5); at all events, the weaker sex prevails (Chrysostom, *Homily* 85.3).

Interlude: Mother and Son

Hoskyns counts four women here to match the Roman guard (1947: 530). The number may be reduced to three if (as Jerome tells us) Mary the wife of Cleophas is the same person as 'the sister of Christ's mother', who is unnamed throughout this Gospel; he adds that she was the wife of Alpheus, father of James and Joses. In Byzantine iconography the two most prominent figures are always 'John' and 'Mary' – one to the right and one to the left in an attitude suggesting reverence rather than emotion (Weitzmann 1982: 110, 163). Dürer retains this pattern in his *Crucifixion* of 1508, but the face of John is now a 'tragic mask' (Panofsky 1955: 146). He turns away in Fra Angelico's *Crucifixion with Thieves* (Museo di San Marco, Florence), while in a polyptych by Piero della Francesca he betrays his pain by throwing back his arms (Pinacoteca Comunale, San Sepulcro).

The mother of Jesus is silent here, but in the Orthodox Service of the Twelve Gospels she recites his deeds and titles, and it is she who urges Joseph of Arimathea to procure the corpse for burial (Ware 1978: 596, 599, 618). In the West her pangs inspired the *Stabat Mater*, which Vivaldi, Boccherini, Pergolesi and Rossini set to music in the manner of their own operas. Dvorak and Pärt are at their simplest, Haydn at his most majestic, Cornysh and Szymanowski at their most opulent. Grief makes Mary ingenious in an English meditation:

'Thogh he whom thou me yevest mayden be . . . / The weighte of him and thee nat is egale (Hoccleve 1981: 166, 168). It is, however, the love of the disciple that emboldens another poet:

> Quanne ic se on rode
> Jesu my lemman,
> And beside him stonden
> Marie and Johan.
>
> (Gray 1975: 33)

Don Maclean's line in *American Pie* – 'And while the king was looking down / the jester stole his thorny crown' – pays the tribute of parody to this famous scene.

Words from the Cross

19:26. Ambrose calls this Christ's last will and testament (Aquinas 1997: 584). Langkammer (1968) demonstrates that the scholastics were the first to cite the verse as proof of Mary's co-operation in the atonement. Bede supposes that Jesus loved 'John' specially on account of his virginity (Aquinas 1997: 585). But if Mary Magdalene is Mary of Bethany, the case for his being Lazarus, her brother, cannot be lightly put aside (Stibbe 1992: 79). Jesus' saying (an echo of 19:5) is represented by the third sonata, a sad but lyrical piece, in Haydn's *Seven Last Words from the Cross*. Augustine believes that this is the hour of which Jesus spoke so roughly at 2:4 (*Homily* 119.1); a medieval poet makes Christ continue, 'Blythe moder mictu be' (Gray 1975: 18).

    19:27a. This commission proves to Epiphanius that Mary had no other offspring, and thus vindicates her perpetual virginity (*Panarion* 78.9). To Chrysostom it shows, against the Marcionites, that Christ received his flesh from a human mother (*Homily* 85.2). For Santucci the substitution of the disciple for Christ is a 'lesson against the heresy of blood-ties' (1974: 176). Avancini cites the dictum at Matt 12:50 that Christ's brother is the one who does God's will (1950: 170).

    19:27b. It is Christ who comes **to his own home** (*eis ta idia*) at 1:11, his followers who flee to theirs at 16:32. Ancient witnesses (Irenaeus, *Against Heresies* 3.1–3; Papias at Eusebius, *Church History* 3.39; Polycrates at Eusebius, *Church History* 5.24) tell us that the apostle retired to Ephesus, where, according to Irenaeus, he wrote his Gospel.

    19:28. Cf. Ps 69:21. In the word **finished** Dodd suspects an allusion to sacrifice, and so to the consecration foretold at 17:19 (1953a: 437). Calvin says that this death annuls all sacrifices, prohibiting in advance the 'abomination of the Mass' (1961: 183). The thirst, as Augustine argues, is a symptom of his humanity (*Homily* 119.4), though Langland makes a trope of it – 'I faught so, me thirstes yet, for mannes soules sake' (*Piers Plowman* 18.368, 1987: 231) – and Herrick admits no motive but 'to show / what bitter cups had been thy due' (1884: 316, alluding to 18:11). In the fifth of Gubaidulina's *Seven Words*, it is represented by four minutes of tense interplay between slow and rapid sequences in the cello.

19:29. Cf. Mark 15:36, Matt 27:48. To Augustine the **vinegar** represents the soured wine of Jewry, the **hyssop** Christ's humility, which cleansed our sin (*Homily* 119.4). Cyril of Jerusalem notes that **hyssop** cements the covenant at Heb 9:19 (*Catechesis* 3.5). Crashaw hints that the **vinegar** is symbolic: 'Is tortured thirst itself too sweet a cup? / Gall, and more bitter mocks, shall make it up' (1927: 270). Brown calculates that 'eighteen different plants' have been identified with the **hyssop** (1970: 909). Hutcheson deduces from Mark 15:23 that Christ refused the narcotic of wine mixed with myrrh, but was willing that the bitterness of death should be enhanced by the vinegar (1972: 405).

19:30a. For Baur the ejaculation **It is finished** proclaims the annulment of the Old Covenant with the Jews (1878: 157). Yet the perfect tense of the verb *tetelestai* implies a consummation – the fulfilment of a prophecy, the performance of a sacrifice, or the payment of a debt (see Augustine, *Homily* 119.6). It is also a tragic motif, as Toynbee observes, citing Seneca, *Hercules on Oeta* 1340, 1457, 1472 (1938: 473). Haydn's accompaniment to this 'sixth word' is a slow sonata which seems always about to break into a dance. In the shortest of Gubaidulina's *Seven Words*, expectant percussion is followed by an acceleration in strings, release then silence. An anonymous German mystic detects a note of expostulation (Inge 1904: 57); for Pink, however, this is the word of victory, which ends Christ's suffering, seals the plan of history, announces Satan's overthrow, completes the atonement, and promises absolution (1978: 376–93).

The Body on the Cross

19:30b. From the words **gave up** Tertullian infers that Christ expired voluntarily (*Apology* 21), and Chrysostom treats the bowing as a motion of acquiescence (*Homily* 85.3). This verse reveals to Boehme that the death of Christ, experienced on behalf of all humanity, consists in the surrender of his selfhood to the Father (1945: 256). At Luke 23:46 the spirit (*pneuma*) is commended to the Father; Matt 27:50 and Mark 15:37 are content with the verb *exepneusen*. Origen, comparing Eccl 12:7, maintains that, while the spirit returned to God,

the soul descended to the dead (*Heraclides* 7–8). Pope Gregory, however, identifies 'spirit' with 'soul', and Theophylact infers that the souls of the righteous
ascend at death (Aquinas 1997: 587). A jubilant hymn succeeds this verse in
Stainer's *Crucifixion*.

19:31. Cf. Deut 21:22. Bede already saw that *paraskeuê* means the day
before the Sabbath (Aquinas 1997: 588); Barrett adds that even a Sabbath after
the eating of the lamb would have been a **great** one, as the Omer sheaf of Lev
23:11 was presented on that day (1955: 461).

19:32–4a. Here, as Chrysostom notices, unbelievers confirm the truth of
prophecy (*Homily* 85.3). *Acts of Pilate* 12.1 names the soldier as Longinus (*NTA*
1.469). His spear, as an appurtenance of the Grail, was credited in medieval
romance with the power of healing. By this time it had become an unwieldy
lance, as in the *Coup de Lance* of Rubens (Antwerp Museum). Evidence for the
piercing of the host, or eucharistic bread, in medieval liturgy is discovered in
the West by Fisher (1917: 75) and in the East by Peebles (1911: 62). The usual
cause of death in crucifixion, according to the medical authors cited by Craveri,
is slow suffocation brought on by the stagnation of the blood (1967: 402).
Stroud (1847) maintained that the issue from the wound and the rapid death
betoken a haemorrhage in the pericardial sac. Cardiglia, who devotes a whole
book to the question (1937: 265), favours 'traumatic shock and sudden
syncope' (Craveri 1967: 401). As v. 35 implies a miracle, Origen reads this 'sign
of life' as a foretaste of the Resurrection (*Against Celsus* 2.69).

Water and Blood

19:34b. Water cleanses Pilate, while blood placates the mob, pronounces Cyril
of Jerusalem (*Catechesis* 13.21). For Augustine the blood, as the seed of the
Church, is prefigured by the extraction of Eve from Adam's side, and also by
the door in the side of the Ark (*Homily* 120.2). Romanus hints that it purges
the sin to which Eve incited Adam (*Cantica* 27.27.18 at Maas 1963: 155). Since
blood and water are equally miraculous, Theophylact denounces those who
refuse to mingle water with wine in the eucharist (Aquinas 1997: 589). Daisenberger rejoices that the spear thrust opened the heart of Christ (1970: 114);
Julian of Norwich avers that it created a space in which the world can stand
(1966: 100), and that the flowing wound suckles us like mother's milk (1966:
168). Crashaw celebrates the wounds that hastened the Resurrection, 'With
blush of thine own Blood thy day adorning' (1927: 245). Even Marlowe's
Faustus derives vain hope from a vision of Christ's blood 'in the firmament'
(1955: 157). Cowper traces this 'fountain filled with blood' to Zech 13:1 (1905:

442), while Toplady assimilates the lacerated body to the rock of Num 20:8–11 and the cave of Adullam at 1 Sam 22:1:

> Rock of ages, cleft for me,
> Let me hide myself in thee.
> Let the water and the blood,
> From thy riven side which flowed,
> Be of sin the double cure;
> Cleanse me from its guilt and power.
>   (*A&M* 210)

Lindars notes that *Targum Pseudo-Jonathan* on Numbers links the miracle at Num 20:11 to the transformation of water into blood at Ex 4:9 (1972: 588). J. Lightfoot compares a rabbinic statement that the rock of Moses gushed out blood and water (1859: 440). 1 John 5:6 remembers that Christ came 'not only by water but by blood'; Ignatius declares that the blood 'purified the waters' (*Ephesians* 1.20). According to the *Golden Legend* it cleansed the skull of Adam, which was buried beneath the Mount (see v. 17b). To Hoskyns (1947: 533) the double flood prefigures the benefits received by one who is born again of water and the Spirit (3:3–5) and drinks the blood of the Son of Man (6:53–6).

19:35. The received view is Bengel's: the same man is identified first as apostle, then as evangelist (1850: 473). Barrett concludes that only recourse to a hypothetical Aramaic prototype would justify the view that the one who **saw** is a different man from the one who **knows** (1955: 463). If he is not the disciple, he may be, as Lindars proposes, the soldier who struck the blow (1972: 589). Erasmus records the theory that he is Christ, who thus endorses the veracity of the author (1535: 266).

19:36–7. Cf. Zech 12:10; as Jerome notes in his commentary on the text in Zechariah, the Evangelist does not quote the Septuagint but translates the Hebrew (Natalis Alexander 1840: 714). Though Lindars catches an echo of Ps 34:20 (1972: 590), v. 37 is surely a rough quotation of Ex 12:46, and thus an indication that the Saviour is conceived as the paschal lamb.

The Burial

19:38–9. The request for the body becomes a common motif in martyrology, though in the *Martyrdom of Polycarp* it is refused. Other Evangelists do not mention Nicodemus, though Chrysostom reckons Joseph among the seventy of Luke 10:1 (*Homily* 85.3). Sacy remarks that, while Nicodemus comes by night to Christ again, his faith is still imperfect, since the spices imply no expectation of a return from death (1840: 714). Whereas the Orthodox liturgy calls the anointing 'strange and new' (Ware 1978: 635), Bede maintains that the spices are those prescribed at Ex 30:34–8 (Aquinas 1997: 591). Their purpose is to embalm the body – not a Christian practice, says Augustine, but in sepulture the custom of the people should be followed (*Homily* 120). Hutcheson, however, declares that the funeral of Christ 'perfumes the graves' of all believers (1972: 408–9). J. Clarke observes that Ananias is buried in the same swathing bands at Acts 5:6 (1740: 170), and Theophylact exhorts the rich to feed the poor, as Joseph covered the nakedness of Christ (Aquinas 1997: 593).

19:40–2. Cf. Matt 27:60. Bede notes that by ecclesiastical custom the host is consecrated 'not on silk or gold', but on clean linen (Aquinas 1997: 592). Augustine compares the sepulchre to Mary's womb, which received no other visitant before or after Christ (*Homily* 120.5). So **new** is it in the Anglo-Saxon *Dream of the Rood*, the excavation begins when the corpse has already been lowered from the Cross (Gordon 1954: 236). Thus, says Hutcheson, it was impossible that anyone but Christ should rise from it (1972: 409). Chrysostom observes that the proximity of the sepulchre (v. 42) made it easier for the disciples to approach it (*Homily* 85.4), while Wesley points out that the bearers had no time to carry the corpse of Christ any further (*MCNT* at XX.42).

Epilogue: Why the Cross?

All churches of ancient pedigree agree that, while the work of Christ cannot be fully efficacious until we make it our own in faith and love, there would be no ground for such a response unless some 'objective' benefit accrued to us from his death. The New Testament describes his death as a sacrifice, whose function is perhaps to avert the wrath of God, as 1 Cor 5:7 seems to intimate, or else to propitiate it, as some infer from 1 John 2:2 or from Rom 3:25. 1 Pet 3:16 implies that Christ endured the punishment due to sinners, while Paul avers that the sinless one became sin for us and expiated the curse of the Jewish law (1 Cor 5:21, 3:13). Since he also writes that we were 'bought with a price' (1 Cor 6:20), and Christ speaks of his own death as a ransom at Mark 10:45, a number of early Christians held that, because sin had made us captives to the devil, it was necessary for God to pay the devil's fee with the priceless blood of Jesus (Rashdall 1919: 280–7). Anselm protests that the devil has no rights against God, and holds instead that Christ is the 'satisfaction' which is due to offended honour (Rashdall 1919: 350–7); Gustave Aulen (1931) has given unusual prominence to the triumph of the crucified Jesus over 'principalities and powers' at Col 2:14. And even if the subjective theory that Hastings Rashdall lays at the door of Abelard will not suffice (1919: 357–64), all the Gospels relate that at least one witness was converted, even before Christ's resurrection, by the mere manner of his death (Matt 27:54, Mark 15:39, Luke 23:42 and 47, John 10:35).

In the Fourth Gospel penal substitution is proposed by Caiaphas, and perhaps endorsed by the Evangelist (11:49–53). The aroma of Mary's offering at 12:3 hints at sacrifice, as perhaps does the exclamation *tetelestai* (**It is finished**) at 19:30; victory over Satan is cemented by the judgement on the 'prince of this world' at 12:31 and 16:11. Yet the accent in the Fourth Gospel falls, pervasively and distinctively, on the revelatory power of Christ as light of the world and Word of God. In keeping with this theme, the Cross is above all else a spectacle – to the world at 12:32, to the women and the disciple whom Jesus loved at 19:24, to the author or his informant at 19:35. Justin Martyr quotes Isa 65:2, 'I have spread out my hands to a stiff-necked people' (*1 Apology* 65.2), while Skelton turns the gesture into an invitation to the new elect: 'Lo, how I hold my arms abroad, / Thee to receive ready y-spread' (1959: 18).

What of the modern imagination? Is Jacob's ladder, as Francis Thompson fancied, 'pitched between heaven and Charing Cross' (1913: 350)? Not for Edith Sitwell, in whose *Rain* the 'nineteen hundred and forty nails upon the Cross' make up a calendar, in Roman style, of the years since the Nativity (1952: 32); and not for David Gascoyne, who avers that Jesus 'hangs and suffers still' with a swelling retinue of Negroes, Jews and other ruined peoples (1988: 93). Eliot's Madame Sesostris cannot find the 'Hanged Man' (1974: 64), while G. Hill seems not to recognize 'the Jesus-faced man walking crowned with flies' (1985: 147). In Jack Clemo's poetry, the Cornish clay pits teem with rugged gibbets, better witnesses than nature or the ecclesiastical crucifix to a God of wrath and blood:

> Just splintered wood and nails
> Were fairest blossoming for him who speaks
> Where mica-silt outbreaks
> Like water from the side of his own clay.
>
> (1964: 16)

Prologue: Can it be True?

Dodd divides traditions of Christ's posthumous appearances into two types, the compact and the circumstantial (1963: 143). This nomenclature accounts for all testimonies except the two preserved in the present chapter; for there is no other extant narrative in which a single witness is addressed by name and favoured with peculiar tokens of the Resurrection. This personal vocation is foreshadowed in the parable of the good shepherd and in the summoning of Lazarus – both passages in which the Redeemer pawns his life to purchase the lives of others. The doubts of Thomas might have been predicted from his pusillanimous sarcasm at 11:16. Mary Magdalene visits the sepulchre in other Gospels, and at Luke 8:2 is a woman out of whom Christ cast seven devils. The story that she was a penitent harlot is presupposed in a Gnostic text, the *Pistis Sophia*, where she represents fallen Wisdom and becomes a privileged pupil of the Saviour, who espouses her to the 'virgin' apostle John (Mead 1991: 193). Thomas too belongs to the inmost circle in such documents, and is sometimes fused with Judas, not Iscariot, the counterpart of Thaddeus in other Gospels. Whether his name was Thomas or Thaddeus, the Church of Edessa in Syria was armed with a stock of legends which purported to show that its aberrant Christianity had been planted there by this favourite of the Lord (Eusebius, *Church History* 1.13 etc.).

The Empty Tomb

20:1a. The Greek locution **first of the Sabbath** is explained by some as a Semitism meaning 'the next day after' (Barrett 1955: 467). Augustine decides that the narrative ignores the other women (Mark 16:1, Matt 28:1 and Luke 24:10) because the Magdalen was the most fervent and the only one not rendered dumb by fear at Mark 16:8. Comparing **while it was dark** with Mark's 'at sunrise', he argues that the dark lingers as the light begins to break (*Gospel Harmony* 3.24). To Kidder the discrepancy marks the interval between setting out and arriving at the tomb (1737: 94). Pope Gregory, however, posits a figurative darkness, caused by the absence of the Creator from his tomb (Aquinas 1997: 595).

   20:1b. For the stone cf. Mark 15:46 etc.; chapter 19 says nothing of it. The empty tomb gives Mary notice of Christ's resurrection and certifies it to others (Chrysostom, *Homily* 85.4). Marsh rejoices that the disappearance of the stone has prevented Christians from attempting to 'seek communion with their Lord through physical "relics" of his body' (1968: 633).

   20:2. **Loved** translates the Greek *ephilei*, which for Westcott connotes a personal affection, as at 11:3, but not the profounder love expressed at 13:23 by *êgapa* (1903: 289). The verb *phileo* recurs at 21:15. In a few manuscripts Mary says not **the Lord**, but 'My Lord' – a variant which Augustine thinks more moving (*Homily* 120.6). Chrysostom notes that a woman enjoys the praise of being first to spread the news (*Homily* 85.4). Ryle suggests that while she ran, the 'other women' tarried and saw the one angel whose appearance is recorded at Mark 16:5 and Matt 26:5 (1873: 397, 400). None the less, Hemans – in her day a woman of unique celebrity – credits Mary also with 'a task of glory all thine own' (1912: 528). In an early *Gospel of Mary* it is Levi who persuades Peter to believe her when she comes to bid the disciples 'dry their tears' (*NTA* 1.342–3).

William Blake, *The Angels Guarding the Body of Christ in the Tomb*. Victoria & Albert Museum, London.

20:3. To Theophylact the absence of guards corroborates the miracle at Matt 28:2–4 (Aquinas 1997: 595); there were, however, no guards in this Gospel. Noting that 'John' is omitted in Luke's account, Ryle adduces Luke 9:5, Mark 9:2 etc. to prove that he and Peter were always intimates (1873: 401, 403).

The Two Disciples

20:4. Mary, says Westcott, 'is naturally forgotten in the description' (1903: 289); at Luke 24:12 Peter is alone. From the victory of the beloved disciple, Avancini infers that we have 'need of prevenient grace to come to Jesus' (1950: 189). Pope Gregory identifies the disciple with the synagogue, and Peter with the Gentiles, who are slower in belief (Aquinas 1997: 597). Ryle argues simply that Peter was the elder, adding that artists have always made him appear so in their pictures of this scene (1873: 403).

20:5–7. Cf. 11:44 for the napkin, or *sudarion*; Dürer made an engraving of an angel spreading it out (Panofsky 1955: fig. 245). Chrysostom sees a proof that the body was risen and not stolen, as thieves would not have paused to unwrap the cloths (*Homily* 85.4). Schnackenburg concludes that the wrappings are left behind to signify the commencement of a 'heavenly existence' (1982: 31). The *Gospel to the Hebrews* relates that Christ presented his linen shroud to the 'servant of the priest' (cf. 18:10); some maintain that it reappeared as the heard-dress or mandulion of Edessa in the middle of the sixth century (Kersten and Gruber 1992: 102–62). Although it retained a portrait of the Saviour's face, it is not known whether this is the cloth that astonished Constantinople in 1203, or the relic known today as the Turin Shroud (Wilson 1978: 143–214).

20:8. To Pope Gregory, Peter's entrance foretells the conversion of the Jews; Theophylact takes the beloved disciple to represent the contemplative man who surpasses his practical neighbour in insight, but falls behind in fervour (Aquinas 1997: 598). Though Brown contrasts his seeing with the praise of those who have not seen at v. 29 (1970: 1005), Lindars considers him the first of those who possess the 'Resurrection faith' without a vision of Christ (1972: 602).

20:9–10. As at 1 Cor 15:4, no text is quoted to show that the miracle was predicted in **the scriptures**; Westcott suggests Ps 16:10 (1903: 290). In the words **to their own homes** (which surely echo both 1:11 and 16:32), Black discovers the trace of an Aramaic dative (1946: 102), while Barrett adduces parallels in Num 24:25 (Septuagint) and Josephus, *Antiquities* 8.14 (1955: 469).

Mary Seeks Christ

20:11. Temple compares the tears of Lazarus' sister, whom he takes to be the same Mary (1961: 361); Natalis Alexander is put in mind of the bride who seeks her beloved in the Song of Songs (1840: 742). While Celsus disdains the evidence of a 'hysterical woman' (Origen, *Against Celsus* 2.55), Augustine commends the steadfastness of the weaker sex (*Homily* 121.1), which men have honoured by giving her name to colleges in Oxford and Cambridge as well as to a chapel near the supposed site of the tomb (Murphy-O'Connor 1998: 53). Against those who assume, on the authority of the rabbis, that her testimony would have been inadmissible, Maccini points out that Josephus seems to respect a woman's oath (*Antiquities* 15.82–4), and that Deuteronomic legislation merely demands two witnesses (1996: 65–74, 228).

20:12. Luke 24:4 speaks of men, not angels; as Calvin remarks, it is not clear what Mary herself took them to be (1961: 196). Augustine deduces that one of them is the angel who removed the stone at Matt 28:5 (*Gospel Harmony* 3.24.69). Temple writes that the man who had been between two thieves was buried between two angels (1961: 361). Lindars suggests that two witnesses to the miracle are required, as at 8:17 (1972: 604). Ryle suggests that the angels adopt the position of the cherubim at the two ends of the mercy-seat in Ex 25:20 (1873: 418). Blake's picture of two angels guarding the body in the sepulchre (Victoria and Albert Museum, London) is illuminated by his own lines from *Vala*, 'Night VIII': 'two winged immortal shapes, one standing at his feet towards the east, one standing at his head towards the west'.

20:13. Cf. the use of **woman** at 19:26 and 20:15; to Chrysostom it signifies compassion (*Homily* 86.1). To harmonize the text with Luke 24:4, Augustine guesses that the angels rose to speak (*Gospel Harmony* 3.24).

20:14. Chrysostom suggests that Mary turned because she divined the presence of Jesus from the posture of the angels (*Homily* 86.1). In a water-colour by Blake, his radiant figure stands behind her as she gazes into the tomb (Yale Centre for British Art, New Haven).

20:15. Mary is lifted gradually to the knowledge that the angels possess already, says Chrysostom (*Homily* 86.1). Avancini, quoting Drogo, says that Christ hides himself to goad her love (1950: 191). Pope Gregory, looking back to 15.1, remarks that Christ is indeed the spiritual **gardener**, while T. Robinson evokes a more ancient parable in his versified life of the Magdalen:

> Shee thought her Lorde, ye gardiner had been:
> And keeper of a garden, sure, was he:
> Yet no such garden, where dead sculls are seen,

> But Paradise, where pleasures ever bee,
> And blisse deriued from lifes aye-liuinge tree.
>   (1899: 68)

Theophylact sees in Mary's question a hint that the gardener might have removed the body to protect it from the Jews (Aquinas 1997: 601–2). For the Jewish calumny that the body was removed by Joseph's gardener see Tertullian, *On the Shows* 30.5–6, and Horbury (1972).

20:16. Barrett compares the calling of the sheep by name at 10:3 (1955: 469). In the Towneley play of the Resurrection, Jesus echoes his own words to the Samaritan at 4:26 (Happé 1975: 589). Jesus is called 'Rabbi' at 1:38 and 3:2; the form *rabbuni* appears at Mark 10:51 and in Aramaic Targums (Black 1946: 21). The text implies that Mary has turned away again, so Chrysostom surmises that she turned back to the angels whose astonishment she had not yet understood (*Homily* 86.1). To Brodie her acknowledgement of Jesus represents the conversion of Israel (1993: 567).

20:17. The words **touch me not** (AV) are rendered 'Do not cling to me' in the NEB, since Christ consents to be touched at 20:27, Luke 24:39 and by Mary herself at Matt 24:9. Lagrange takes the text to mean 'yes indeed, I am not yet ascended [but am about to, therefore] take this message' (1948: 512). Ryle, however, quotes from Beza and Sherlock the interpretation: 'Do not touch me now, for I shall be with you another forty days', as at Acts 1:3 (1873: 426, 429). Torrey, by retranslation into Aramaic, derives the sense: 'Touch me not; but before I ascend, go to my brethren' (1923: 343). Some, with Bernard, support emendation to the Greek *mê ptoou*, 'do not fear' (1928: 2.670–1). In the subsequent words of Christ, which announce the Ascension foretold at 6:62 and recounted at Acts 1:9, Calvin detects an echo of Ps 22:22 (1961: 199). Hitherto in this Gospel, God is the **Father** of Christ alone. Augustine paraphrases: '**mine** by nature, **yours** by grace' (*Homily* 121.3).

Interlude: Christ and the Magdalen

Augustine contends that Mary 'is a type of the Gentiles, who did not believe until after the ascension' (*Homily* 121.3); Chrysostom understands Christ's prohibition as a warning that they cannot enjoy the same familiarity now as before his death (*Homily* 86.2). D'Angelo (1990) cites *Apocalypse of Moses* 31, where the dying Adam rejects the contaminating touch of Eve; Origen too implies at *Commentary* 6.37 that Christ feared pollution before his exaltation was complete. Such contact was especially to be feared if she was – as the medieval Church suspected and artists have always pruriently assumed – a repentant whore. Rilke makes her woo the risen Jesus with an earthy passion (Haskins 1994: 359–64); in a dialogue set to music by Charpentier she begs to touch his wounds, then to kiss them, then to grasp his feet, but is always met by the same refusal.

In the many Renaissance paintings of this scene the Magdalen is dressed in red, as a souvenir of her previous occupation. The outstretched hand and angled feet of Christ suggest a certain vacillation in Fra Angelico's *Noli me tangere* (Museo di San Marco, Florence), while in Giuliano Amidei's picture of the same name, he seems to beckon her even as he moves away (Pinacoteca Comunale, Sansepulcro). Botticelli's painting, in which the pair almost touch hands, is the third in a series of four panels, and the successor of one which shows the Magdalen bathing the feet of Christ (Philadelphia Museum of Art). In Rodin's sculpture *Christ and the Magdalen* (Musée Rodin, Paris) they are locked together, while in Eric Gill's *The Nuptials of God* (Victoria and Albert Museum, London) the two are naked except for the copious hair of the prostitute. The elongated figure of Mary shrinks from her Saviour even as she embraces him in David Wynne's *Christ Meeting Mary Magdalen* (Ely Cathedral). The notion that they had sexual intercourse after the Crucifixion shocked the audience of Scorsese's film *The Last Temptation*, yet a medieval legend makes them the ancestors of the Merovingian kings (Baigent et al. 1982). Begg maintains that statues of a black virgin in France attest the cult of Mary among the Templars as an emblem of Gnostic Wisdom (1985: 97–125). Wyatt appropriates the Latin words as a motto of female chastity: '*Noli me tangere*, for Caesar's I am / and wylde for to holde though I seem tame' (1949: 7).

Christ's Word of Peace

20:18. Pope Gregory exults that, whereas Eve transmitted the serpent's lie, so a woman is now the herald of good tidings (Aquinas 1997: 604). Calvin rejects the inference that such 'weak and contemptible instruments' could be apostles or ecclesiastical ministers (1961: 200).

20.19a. Rordorf contends that this episode presupposes a liturgical celebration of the Lord's day (1968: 40, 202). Theophylact suggests that Christ postponed his second appearance until the disciples were assembled (Aquinas 1997: 605). Calvin sees their gathering as an act of faith, their locking of the doors as a mark of weakness (1961: 201). Avancini draws the moral that we must lock the doors of sense before God can come into the heart (1950: 201). Henry maintains that this episode hallows the 'secondary ordinances' – 'the

Lord's day, solemn assembly, standing ministry' – by which Christ secures his teaching (1991: 2052, col. 3).

20:19b. Christ's passage through the locked door is prefigured, for Augustine, by his entry into a womb that remained inviolate (*Homily* 120.4). Some Catholics have derived an ingenious argument for transubstantiation in the eucharist from Christ's passage through the door;

> For since thus wondrously he pass'd, 'tis plain
> One single place two bodies did contain,
> And sure the same Omnipotence as well
> Can make one body in more places dwell.
> (Dryden 1910: 119)

Calvin retorts that the text does not tell how he **stood among them**, and allows that he may have caused the door to open (1961: 202). The conventional greeting **Peace be with you is** reminiscent here of 14:27, 16:33, etc.; Luther, who opines that Christ passed through the doors miraculously, compares the sudden irruption of the word into the heart (1983: 355).

20:20. Cf. Luke 24:17. To Chrysostom the conjunction of the words and the gesture show that the Cross is an instrument of peace (*Homily* 86.3). Barrett suggests that the feet are ignored because Christ was not nailed but bound to his Cross in the earliest accounts (1955: 473).

The Commissioning of the Disciples

20:21. Cf. 13:20, 17:18. This verse proclaims the origin of the apostolate (from the verb *apostellein*). The verb used of his own mission by Christ is *pempein*, and Westcott draws a distinction between the Father's charge to him and his delegation of that charge to the apostles (1903: 298). Brodie compares the sending of the blind man at 9:7 (1933: 568). Hopkins recollecting the descent of the dove at 1:32, declares that peace comes not to give us rest but to 'brood and sit' (1970: 85).

20:22. Here, according to Cyril of Alexandria, the second Adam replenishes and augments the infusion of the Holy Spirit at Gen 2:7. Henry, comparing the breath of God at Ezek 37:9, observes that that of Christ no longer signifies wrath as at Isa 11:4 and 30:33 (1991: 2053, col. 3). Pope Gregory adds that the spirit to love our neighbour is vouchsafed on earth, but the spirit to love God must be sent from heaven (Aquinas 1997: 607). The Church of England, while it claims no power to impart the Spirit by insufflation, prescribes the repetition of Christ's words in the ordination of ministers (Wordsworth 1857: 84–5, citing Hooker, *Ecclesiastical Polity* 5.77, etc.). Brown notes that this verse gave rise to the custom of 'filling a bag with the holy breath of the Coptic Patriarch of Alexandria' so that it might be used to consecrate the new ruler of the Church in Ethiopia (1970: 1023). Swinburne deplores the success of the apostles: 'Thou hast conquered, O pale Galilean; the world has grown grey with thy breath' (1917: 69).

20:23. Cf. Matt 16:19 and the commands to baptize for remission of sins at Mark 16:16, Matt 28:19. The motif is traced by Emerton (1962) to a Targum on Isaiah 22:22; other Jewish sources suggest to J. Lightfoot that the gift includes the power of exorcism (1859: 445–8). Calvin, who denies that the 'stinking breath' of 'mitred bishops' can impart the Spirit, insists that the insufflation is a proof that the Spirit proceeds from Christ, but not the institution of a third sacrament (1961: 504–6). Hoskyns, however, declares that 'as Christ washed the feet of his disciples, so must [the Church] remit the sins of the faithful' (1947: 545). Ryle admits that all ministers must determine when to pronounce or withhold the word of absolution, but denies that any Church can now profess the infallibility that is granted in this verse to the apostles (1873: 449). In Wesley's view the minister has power to excommunicate, but can only pronounce *the terms on which* a sinner is absolved (*MCNT* at XX.23).

Doubting Thomas

20:24. Characterizing Thomas, on the evidence of 11:16, as a 'saturnine' unbeliever, T. V. Moore judges that he was absent by his own fault (1981: 76–84). On his character see 11:16 and epilogue to chapter 14 above.

20:25. The reference to marks in the hands may have been inspired by Ps 22:16–17, since it would have been the wrists, not the palms, that bore the weight of the body on the Cross (Hewitt 1932). Chrysostom berates Thomas as the epitome of the carnal man, who cannot credit what he does not see (*Homily* 87.1). Pope Gregory says, however, that posterity learned more from his hesitation than from the immediate faith of the others (Aquinas 1997: 608).

20:26. Chrysostom construes the delay as a reprimand to Thomas, who should have believed what the others had witnessed and Christ himself foretold (*Homily* 87.1). We cannot impute to Christ the reluctance of Shakespeare's Coriolanus, who parades his scorn for the Roman electorate even as he courts them with his wounds (*Coriolanus*, Act 2, scene 3).

20:27. The Towneley play of the Resurrection counts 'four hundreth woundys and v. thowsand' (Happé 1975: 578). Augustine holds that Christ retained these tokens for the purpose of demonstration, though in heaven all such scars will be effaced (*On the Creed* 2.8). Martin of Tours is said to have repelled a diabolic impersonation of Christ by demanding to see the marks of his nails (Wiebe 1997: 28), while Francis of Assisi and many after him have been glad to bear these 'stigmata' on their own flesh as the wages of devotion (R. Brown 1958: 171–218). Oscar Wilde's selfish giant dies in peace when a child displays these 'wounds of love' (1990: 299–300).

20:28. In a jar from Palestine these words surmount a picture of Thomas touching the wounds (Grabar 1968: 124); in Byzantine iconography even the halo of Christ is less persuasive than this manual demonstration (Weitzmann 1982: 171). But did the doubter in fact put forth his hand? As Schnackenburg notes, the silence of the text divides the commentators (1982: 332). Cyril believes that Thomas was permitted to touch because, unlike the Magdalen at 20:17, he had received the Holy Spirit (3.135–6 Pusey); Wesley insists that Thomas believed 'without thrusting his hand into his side' (*MCNT* at XX.28). Nor is it clear whether precedents such as 1 Kings 18:39 or Ps 35:24 will explain his utterance, as Hoskyns would maintain (1947: 548); nowhere else in the Gospel, as Erasmus notes, is Christ openly called God (1535: 267). Lindars compares the worship of Domitian as 'our lord and god' at Suetonius, *Domitian* 13 (1972: 615). The word *theos* is applied to the Logos at 1:1, and perhaps to Christ at Titus 2:13, 1 John 5:20 and Rom 9:5, though all are subject to controversy; the letters of Ignatius, however, frequently invoke 'our God Jesus Christ'. Bengel rejects the thesis of Artemonius, that Christ is addressed as **Lord** and his Father as **God** (1850: 477). Theodore of Mopsuestia is also said to have held that the words **My God** are an exclamatory prayer to the Father; Bultmann, however, declares that in conjunction the terms make up a cultic title, reminiscent of Jer 38:18 etc. (1957: 538nn). Dodd relates **My Lord** to the Jesus of history, **My God** to the 'Christ of faith' (1953a: 430).

20:29. The first sentence may be a question or a statement (Barrett 1955: 477); cf. 1:50 on the credulity of Nathanael. Pope Gregory, comparing Heb 11:1, avers that 'we are included' in the blessing; Theophylact restricts it to the ten who believed without inspecting the wounds (Aquinas 1997: 612). Bultmann makes it a general rule that we ought to trust the Word without demanding evidence (1957: 539). J. Lightfoot cites a rabbinic dictum that the proselyte is superior to the Israelites who believed because of the spectacle at Sinai (1859: 448–9). Cf. also 2 Cor 5:7, but contrast Job 42:5.

20:30. Chrysostom understands this as a confession that the Evangelist had knowingly recorded less than others (*Homily* 87.1). Bultmann detects a conventional echo of Sir 43:27, 1 Macc 9:22, Philo, *Life of Moses* 1.213, ect. (1957: 540n). Dodd thinks that the Evangelist is confessing his selective use of a primitive tradition (1963: 216, 429); here and at 21:24, Hutcheson insists that nothing needful to salvation is omitted (1972: 426, 438). Against R. H. Light-foot (1956: 336) and Barrett (1955: 65), Brown denies that either the Crucifixion or the Resurrection is numbered among the signs (1971: 1059).

20:31. If the tense of the verb **believe** is present, it means 'that you may *continue* to believe'; if aorist, 'that you may *begin* to believe'. Wesley endorses the former, explaining that 'Faith cometh sometime by reading, though ordinarily by hearing' (*MCNT* at XX.31). Locke insists, against the clergy of all denominations, that the sole belief required of us is that **Jesus is the Christ, the Son of God** (1790: 101). Whereas Grotius considers this the intended peroration of the Gospel, attributing the next chapter to the Ephesian elders, Natalis Alexander thinks that the author wrote it in anticipation of an epilogue which symbolically ordains the observance of the eucharist (1840: 739–40).

Epilogue: Faith and the Resurrection

Is Jesus risen indeed, as the Church proclaims on Easter morning? If, despite the silence of Paul, we assume that there was a tomb and that it was empty, the conventional apologetic, exemplified by Morison (1930), seems decisive. The authorities had no reason to steal the body and would have produced it in rebuttal of Christian preaching; the soldiers, notwithstanding the lie imputed to them at Matt 28:15, would not have slept; even had the disciples stolen the body, they would not have suffered martyrdom to sustain a conscious fraud. Nevertheless, the case is built on partisan and anonymous testimony, and, as Hume observed, experience always teaches us to reject such affidavits rather than countenance a breach in nature's laws (1962: 113).

Some, who would rather accuse the four Evangelists of error than deceit, suspect that Jesus was not dead at the time of sepulture (Butler 1938: 140–88). Novelists such as Kazantzakis (1961), Lawrence (1929) and G. Moore (1952) have improved upon this conjecture, and Josephus, *Autobiography* 75, has been adduced to prove that living men could be taken from the cross (Strauss 1892: 737). This theory, however, implies that he died again, and does explain why he was visible only to those who desired his coming; while Origen was content to reply that a spiritual body is visible only to the eye of faith (*Against Celsus* 2.62–7), the *Gospel of Nicodemus* meets the objection by arranging a vision for Pilate and eliciting a testimony from Satan. Pannenberg is the most distinguished of the modern apologists who have undertaken to show that probability is on the side of the witnesses (1968: 86–106); yet others who are equally loth to deny the historicity of the Resurrection hold, with Barth, that if we attempt to penetrate the 'facts' behind the record, we can only produce an argument against faith (1956: 149–50). Bultmann goes so far as to deny that we can speak of the Resurrection as an event in contradistinction to the preaching or kerygma of Easter Day (1961: 38–43). Strauss, who regards the appearances as hallucinations fathered by the Messianic prophecies of the Old Testament, maintains that the Resurrection is the most important article of Christian faith because it is the one that belongs most purely to the category of myth (1892: 772).

Yet myths, whatever truths they may symbolically convey, are fictitious narratives. Dodd has attempted to show by formal analysis that the accounts depend on independent testimonies, and that where there is fabrication, they would more properly be characterized as legends (1995). This conclusion tacitly admits that the disparities between, and the ambiguities within, the accounts preclude the construction of a posthumous history for Jesus. The Fourth Gospel is as ever the most elusive, as it twice implies that he could be touched but never describes the contact. Green (1989) maintains that women favour a sensuous, and men an intellectual, explanation of such visions. John of the Cross, however, reprimands both Mary and Thomas for their sentimental clinging to the flesh (1991: 184). None the less, Charlotte Mew is not ashamed to plead for '[t]he spirit afterwards, but first the touch', although the touch be 'in the doorway of a dream' (1981: 27). Her lines express the schism in the modern soul, not merely the soul of woman. Wandering the 'sinful streets' of Naples, Clough persuades himself at last that 'Christ is risen', meaning not that he has come to believe the witnesses, but that

> Though he return not, though
> He lies and moulders low;
> In the true creed
> He is yet risen indeed.
>   (1974: 300)

The Final Commission: John 21

Prologue: Authorship and Function

The study of this chapter is commended to Bishop Blougram's interlocutor by Browning (1902: 542). Yet its provenance and its connection with the foregoing chapter have been debated even by the faithful. Westcott deems it genuine, yet extrinsic to the original 'design of the Evangelist' (1903: 299). Bultmann contends that it must be by another hand, as a number of words are not attested elsewhere in the Gospel, and this is the only chapter in which Christ imparts particular commissions to his disciples. Ruckstuhl (1987), however, argues that there is no more evidence of multiple authorship than in any other chapter, while Hoskyns holds that the purpose of this narrative is to harmonize the appearances in Jerusalem, recounted in Luke's Gospel, with the evidence of

Matthew and Mark that the risen Christ was manifested only in Galilee (1947: 554). Barrett suspects that the episode recounted here preceded the events of chapter 20 in the tradition (1955: 482), but in its present form the chapter reckons this as the third sign since the Resurrection. If we suppose, with Fortna (1988: 78–89), that this statement is a relic of a catalogue in which the episode figured as the 'third sign' of the ministry, we may be inclined to regard it as a variant of the miraculous draught at Luke 6:1–11. Yet, as they stand, the two are not homologous, for in the Fourth Gospel Christ does not approach the boat, and if there is a miracle, he performs it on the shore. Dodd holds that the two Evangelists are heirs to the same tradition (1963: 143–5), Shellard (1995: 91–8) that the Third has culled the labours of the Fourth. It is certainly not impossible that Luke has replaced a posthumous epiphany with a miracle in the earthly career of Jesus because he wished to restrict the testimonies of the Resurrection to Judaea.

Hence we may say, with J. A. T. Robinson (1978), that this chapter is provoked by some historical development, and not merely by a desire on the part of the author or his editor to make use of the unconsumed material in his source. The closing verses are evidently intended to dissociate Christ himself from the expectation that he would come again in the lifetime of the beloved disciple. Whether it was the death of the disciple that had falsified the prophecy, or he himself thought it prudent to anticipate disappointment by rebutting it before his death, we cannot now determine; and even if he lived to read this epilogue, he may not have been the author of it, let alone of the previous 20 chapters in a work that is commonly known as the Gospel of John.

The Fishing

21:1–2. Bultmann notes that one of the fishers must have been the disciple whom Jesus loved (1957: 547), but a similar episode in the *Gospel of Peter* names only Peter, Andreas, Philip and Levi. To Augustine the seven signify the time until the end of the world, by analogy to the seven days of the week (*Homily* 122.6). Eight are saved, including Noah, at 1 Pet 3:20. Acts 6:2–3 implies that twelve stands for Israel, seven for the nations (cf. Mark 8:19–20).

21:3. 'Catch not men but fish . . . He was not risen,' sings the despairing Clough (1974: 202); but Izaak Walton derives a plea for anglers from this episode (1939: 65–6), while Augustine cites 2 Thess 3:8 to show that evangelists may pursue a worldly trade (*Homily* 122.3). Pope Gregory, though he almost taxes Peter with turning back to his plough as at Luke 9:62, concludes that an occupation which was sinless before the resurrection of Christ is sinless now (Aquinas 1997: 616).

21:4–6. Jesus appears onshore at Mark 6:49 and Luke 24:16; Hutcheson comments that 'Christ is not only a God near at hand, but a God afar off also' (1972: 429). Sacy contrasts this manifestation of the immortal body with the elusiveness of his mortal flesh at 7:1–12 and 10:39 (1840: 752). The salutation **children** recurs at 1 John 2:1, etc., but the word *prosphagion* (**fish**) is rare in Greek and unparalleled in the New Testament (Barrett 1955: 482).

21:7. It is not clear that a miracle occurs here, as at Matt 14:9, although Bede guesses that it was either the draught of fish or the voice of Jesus which enabled **that disciple** to recognize him (Aquinas 1997: 617). R. H. Lightfoot observes that Peter approached the Lord through his companion at 13:23–6 and lagged behind him in awareness at 20:1–10 (1956: 342). Hutcheson maintains that while impetuous zeal is a virtue in him, the others would have sinned if they had followed him, thus abandoning the catch (1972: 431). Gee (1989) suggests that he leapt into the water to escape Christ, and that v. 11 shows him wading reluctantly to the land. Eisler concludes that the **two hundred cubits** in the Greek betoken penitence as at Philo, *On Genesis* 5.22, and that Peter has now 'put on Christ' to undergo the sacramental immersion foretold at 13:9–10 (1923: 110–18). Theophylact, however, writes that the tunic is the dress of Tyrian fishermen (Aquinas 1997: 617).

The Meal

21:8. To Augustine the fish caught on the right signify those worthy of resurrection, who cannot be numbered until they are brought to haven on the Last Day. The two measures of a hundred cubits stand for the circumcised and the uncircumcised in the kingdom (*Homily* 122.7). To Bede they signify the love of God and the love of neighbour, while the cooked fish is Christ himself (Aquinas 1997: 619).

21:9. Chrysostom detects a second miracle, and one that entails the creation of new materials where the first drew only on natural supplies (*Homily* 87.1). Eisler compares the customary meal of fish on the Sabbath, and maintains that the 'real Lord's supper' is represented by a picture in the catacombs of seven disciples dining on fish in the presence of the master (1923: 209, 215, 221–5).

21:10–11. This request, in Theophylact's view, is designed to show that the vision is no mirage (Aquinas 1997: 618). Christ declines to emulate the clairvoyance of Pythagoras, who is said to have numbered a draught of fish (not caught by any miracle) before it came to land (Eisler 1923: 121–2, citing Porphyry, *Life of Pythagoras* 25).

21:12. Who art thou? (AV) is the question of the Jews at 8:25 and of Paul at Acts 9:5. Augustine says that they dared not ask what was all too evident (*Homily* 123.1), Chrysostom that awe had trapped their tongues (*Homily* 87). They are equally reticent at 4:27.

21:13. This feast with seven disciples proves to Pope Gregory that only those endowed with the 'sevenfold grace of the spirit' receive eternal life (Aquinas 1997: 621). Chrysostom reflects that the Resurrection had deprived Jesus of the *need* to eat and drink, but not the *power* (*Homily* 87).

21:14. Augustine counts ten appearances in all: to the 'women' (i.e. Mary) at the sepulchre; to the women as they returned; to Peter alone; to two disciples on the road to Emmaus; to ten, excluding Thomas, in Jerusalem; to Thomas and the rest of the eleven; by the sea of Tiberias; on a mountain in Galilee; on the last occasion of eating with the disciples; and at the hour of his ascension (*Gospel Harmony* 3.26). He explains that the Evangelist reckons all occasions after the first two as one; more plausibly, Bernard sees here a rejoinder to Mark's intimation at 16:7 that the scene of the *first* appearances was Galilee (1928: 2.701). Ryle argues that the purpose of the sign is to remind us that a minister is to be a fisher of men (as at Mark 1:17), to predict the future judgement by the haling of the net to shore (as at Matt 13:49), and to anticipate the marriage feast of the Lamb (Luke 12:37) by supping with them (1873: 495).

Piscatory Interlude

The number 153, as Augustine notes, is the sum of the numbers from 1 to 17; he argues that the second figure represents the sum of the ten commandments and the sanctification of the seventh day (*Homily* 122.8). Jerome, in his commentary on Ezek 47:9–12, states that it symbolizes all the tribes of men, because ancient naturalists acknowledged 153 species of fish. Grant (1949) observes, however, that unless we omit three whales and a dolphin, the total in Jerome's source, the poet Oppian, is 157. In any case, only 24 species of fish have been discovered in this rich pasture, according to Hastings (1906: 599). Emerton (1958) also looks to Ezek 47:10, which asserts that the Dead Sea from En-gedi to En-eglaim will be a 'place for the spreading of nets'; he points out that by *gematria* (the substitution of numbers for letters), Gedi is equal to 17 and Eglaim to 153. Bultmann is not persuaded by the exercise of the same technique on the Hebrew *ha-'ôlām hab-bā*, 'age to come' (1957: 549n). Eisler obtains the sum by adding 76, the number of Simon in Greek, to 77, the number of *Ikhthus*, 'fish' (1921: 111). Westcott reports the calculations of Cyril of Alexandria (100 for the Gentiles, 50 for Israel, 3 for the Trinity), Rupert of Deutz (100 for the married, 50 for widows, 3 for virgins), Bruno Astensis (3 for the three known continents and 3 × 50 for emphasis), as well as Volmar's chimerical application of *gematria* to the name Simon bar Jona Kepha (1903: 306–7). Michell adds 1224, the number of *to diktuon* (net) to another 1224, the number of *ikhthues* (fishes), describing the aggregate 2448 as a 'great fish', which he then divides by 16 to obtain 153 (1973: 97). Brown is content to cite 2:6 as an instance of the author's predilection for accurate numbers (1970: 1075–6).

Chrysostom's assertion that the fish is Christ seems arbitrary, but the acronym *Ikhthus* (*Iesous Khristos Theou Huios Soter* – 'Jesus Christ, Son of God, Saviour') is attested in the icons and inscriptions of the early second century. The letters of this formula were employed in a verse acrostic that is now subsumed in the eighth of the *Sibylline Oracles*, but was quoted first in Constantine's *Oration to the Saints* (M. J. Edwards 2003: 42–3). The epitaph of Abercius Marcellus, a bishop and missionary of the late second century, proclaims that it was the fish that nourished him everywhere in his travels (Ramsay 1897: 722–3), and it functions as a eucharist in the story of the Grail (Matthews 1997: 186–8).

Peter's Task

21:15a. Christ employs the verb *agapas*, Peter *phileo*; to Chrysostom the first verb signifies love of God, the second love of neighbour (*Homily* 88.1). Westcott comments that 'the foundation of the apostolic office is laid in love and not belief' (1903: 302). The qualification **more than these**, ignored in Peter's reply, may mean 'more than these men love me', 'more than you love these others' (Erasmus 1535: 268), or 'more than you love your trade' (Lindars 1972: 635). Augustine presumes the first interpretation, and suggests that Peter omits the words in his answer because he cannot read the hearts of his companions (*Homily* 124.4).

21:15b. The injunction **feed my sheep** echoes 10:15–27. Milton denounces venal clerics, whose 'hungry sheep look up and are not fed' (1966: 146) and Erasmus warns the prelates of his day that the sheep are given to be pastured, not devoured (1535: 268). Pope Pius X's encyclical *Pascendi* ordains a diet of ecclesiastical doctrine (Denzinger 1957: 570). His claim to be Shepherd of Shepherds rests on a long tradition beginning with Jerome's letter to Pope

Damasus (15.2); Hobbes, however, argues that, with the ripening of God's plan for the world, the pastorate has devolved on Christian sovereigns (1973: 303). Barrett remarks that mutual stewardship is enjoined on all members of the body of Christ (1982: 165–6).

21:16. Peter replies, as before, with *phileo*, where the verb in the question was *agapas*. The lambs have been replaced by **sheep**, perhaps, as Theophylact argues, because the lambs are the new initiates, the sheep those who have been made perfect (Aquinas 1997: 624).

21:17a. Now Christ too substitutes *phileis* for *agapas*. Trench declares that Peter 'has triumphed', eliciting from his master a verb that denotes the warmth of sentiment that we feel for a parent rather than the esteem that we accord to a benefactor (1880: 43). Yet the two verbs are equivalent at 5:20, as at Josephus, *Life* 39.

21:17b. The Greek appears to say **little sheep** (*probatia*): to Brodie this word signifies the helplessness which supervenes on adulthood, the phase in which we have grown from lambs to sheep (1993: 591). In the threefold interrogation Theophylact sees a warrant for the threefold confession in baptism (Aquinas 1997: 624). Chrysostom sees that the three confessions purge the three denials (*Homily* 88.1). Bultmann finds a 'variant' of the promise to Peter at Matt 16:16–19 (1957: 551). Romanus, who believes that the verb *philein* enjoins on Peter an obligation to forgive as he is now forgiven, pronounces it fitting that he and the thief of Luke 23:43 should be the janitors of paradise for the fallen race of Adam (*Cantica* 31.5 at Maas 1963: 244).

The Destiny of Peter and the Beloved Disciple

21:18. Cf. 21:7b. Chrysostom reminds us that, while physical strength subsides with age, wisdom and virtue may grow more robust (*Homily* 87). Calvin remarks that Christ's prediction inverts the order of nature, which reserves old age for peace (1961: 221–2). Cullmann suspects, but cannot prove, that Jesus is adapting a current proverb (1962: 88–9). On the **stretching out of hands** as a synonym for crucifixion, cf. Letter of Barnabas 12.2 (on Isa 35:2) and 12.4 (on Ex 17:2). Barrett adds a pagan parallel from Epictetus 3.26.2 (1955: 487). Legend tells that Peter fled Rome under Nero's persecution, but was shamed into returning when he met Christ on his way to be crucified once more (*Acts of Peter* 35/7, *NTA* 2.318).

21:19. Tertullian takes this girding as an allusion to the crucifixion of Peter during Nero's persecution (*Scorpiace* 15). 1 Clement 5.7 is the earliest testimony to his martyrdom in Rome. Later legend has it that he was crucified upside-down (*Acts of Peter* 37/8, *NTA* 2.319), and in this posture he appears in a striking picture by Zurbarán.

21:20–1. Augustine holds that the author, by styling himself **the disciple whom Jesus loved**, is reinforcing the authority of his Gospel (*Homily* 124.4). Hutcheson regards it as a sign of love that he follows when only Peter has been summoned (1972: 437). Henry writes, 'the engaging of one brings others', citing Song of Songs 1:4: 'Draw me and we will follow' (1991: 2059, col. 3). Peter's question means, according to T. V. Moore, 'Am I to suffer alone, or this man also?' (1981: 114). Ryle opines that it may express both affection and curiosity, but refuses to follow other commentators in discerning a 'latent jealousy' (1873: 522).

21:22. Brodie observes that a similar construction (**'what have I to do with thee?'** at 2:4) is succeeded by a gift (1993: 594). Even in Theophylact's time there were some who maintained that John the beloved disciple was still alive, but would 'be killed by Antichrist, and will preach Christ's name with Elias' (Aquinas 1997: 628). Augustine records the tradition that he is sleeping, but not dead, in Ephesus (*Homily* 124.2). He adds that Peter's **following** stands for the active life, and the **remaining** of the other for the life of contemplation; or again, one stands for service in the present life and one in the world to come (*Homily* 124.5). Erasmus understands Christ to imply that Peter will die by violence, but the disciple will await the course of nature (1535: 268–9). He refutes a Latin variant which implies that Christ did promise to return before the death of the disciple; yet, 'certainly he did tarry till Christ came to destroy Jerusalem' (Wesley, *MCNT* at XXI.22). J. Clarke, advancing the same solution, adds that 'John' is one of the generation whose survival to witness the coming of the kingdom is foretold at Mark 9:1 (1740: 101).

The Purpose of This Book

21:23. These words might have been written to reconcile Christians to the death of the last apostle (Barrett 1955: 488), or to deprecate speculation in his lifetime. Stibbe, who believes the disciple to be Lazarus, suggests that his resurrection had given rise to the expectation of immortality (1992: 80). Brown argues that the term **brothers** in the Greek, which refers at 20:17 to the intimate disciples, has widened its meaning here to include all 'Christians of the Johannine community' (1970: 1110). Theophylact suggests that the **coming** of Jesus was the chastisement of Jerusalem in AD 70 – an event which John, but not Peter, lived to see (Aquinas 1997: 630). Ryle, who notes that others understood it to mean either death or the revelation of the visions which are recorded in the Apocalypse, concludes that Christ was simply teasing Peter with a hypothesis (1873: 525–6).

21:24. Cf. 3 John 12. Noting that John is said in ancient sources to have written at the behest of the other apostles, Hoskyns infers that they are the ones whom the author joins to himself with the pronoun **we** (1947: 559–60). Hengel contends, more plausibly, that the speakers are the editors who completed the unfinished Gospel (1989: 100). Chapman (1980) shows that members of the Johannine community resort to the plural pronoun when advancing testimony; Grotius ascribes this postscript to the elders of the Ephesian church, and Natalis Alexander has little authority for his reply that the substitution of 'we' for 'I' is a Hebraism (1840: 739–40). Dodd, however, suggests that the Greek verb *oidamen* means simply 'it is well known' (1953b), while Chrysostom appears to have read *oida men*, 'for my part, I know'. Brown argues that the pronoun **he** dissociates the dead apostle from the living community, which speaks on his behalf (1970: 1124). To Josipovici this verse betrays the 'anxiety' of one who can offer nothing but his own (unproven) truthfulness as surety for his tale (1988: 214).

21:25. Unless it is hyperbolical, says Augustine, this verse means not that the world lacks space for such writings, but that readers lack the capacity to digest them (*Homily* 124.8). Hoskyns compares the saying of Rabbi Johanan ben Zakkai that the heavens could not contain his own small portion of God's illimitable wisdom (1947: 561). Sacy maintains that the author has revealed all that would be of profit to the reader, while he has demonstrated his candour by exposing both the ignominies suffered by his master and the fallibility of the other disciples (1840: 762). The phrasing is all but identical with that of 20:31, but Roberts (1987) rejects the inference of J. A. T. Robinson (1985) that the author's plan included the epilogue even as he was writing the peroration of his main narrative.

Epilogue: The Author and his Community

In modern criticism of the New Testament, it has almost become a truism that each book was produced for its own community, and many would hold, with Ashton (1991), that the character of the Johannine community will always be more amenable to research than the identity of the author. Nevertheless, the word 'community' cannot be used in academic prose without some caveats to exclude a false construction. It cannot, for example, denote a congregation small enough to assemble in the hearing of the Evangelist, as then it would be a costly act of supererogation to write at all. Nor, at the other extreme, can it embrace everyone who thought or came to think like the Evangelist, for this community, being the creation of the Gospel, knows as little as we do of its date and authorship.

The existence of a circle about the author, which colluded in the transmission of his Gospel, can be inferred from the last two verses. Furthermore, the canon includes an epistle which, although it bears no name, has been attributed since antiquity to the John who is also commonly supposed to have been the Fourth Evangelist. The writer of the epistle says many things on his own authority which the Gospel ascribes to Christ; he uses the pronoun 'we' to include his audience, and assumes that they will join him in anathematizing not only the unbeliever but also the false believer who holds that Jesus is not the Christ (2:2, 5:1) and denies that the Son of God has been revealed in palpable flesh (1:1, 4:3, etc.). He pronounces that he who sins is of the devil (3:8), that certain offences cannot be forgiven (5:16), and that the apostates who differ from him have never been members of the Christian family (2:19). For all that, his cardinal tenet is that 'God is love' (4:8), and the application is that Christian brethren must show love to one another (though not to outsiders) if they would prove their love of God (3:16, etc.).

We cannot be certain that the epistolator was the author of the Gospel; he might, for example, have mastered the naïve and repetitive style of the Evangelist by listening to his sermons. It is possible, again, that he was the author of the epilogue alone, and again that Gospel, letter and epilogue issued from a single pen in the course of a changeful life. Ancient reports agree that the Evangelist penned his Gospel with the weight of years upon him, and Jerome's anecdote that as he expired he intoned the words 'little children, love one another' lends some weight to the notion that he had formed his own community. Brown (1979) contends that fissures and inconsistencies in the Gospel represent successive phases in the estrangement of this sect from the Jews, the world and other Christians; whereas he would posit as many as five redactions, Koester (1986) is content with three and Cullmann with only one (1976: 10). Hengel (1989) holds, on the one hand, that the community preserved a larger measure of historical information, and on the other, that its founder was not the apostle, but a different John who styles himself 'the Elder' in the second and third of the Johannine epistles. The Gospel at once encourages and annuls such divinations, since, although it appeals to witnesses, it implies that the words suggested by the Paraclete possess the same authority as those that were spoken by the Word on earth.

We need not assume that any modern theory is more veridical, simply because it is less poetic, than Browning's picture of the Evangelist expiring in the wilderness, with a sentinel to warn against the approach of persecutors and his followers pressing wine to his lips in the hope of calling forth a final testimony. What follows is at once a vindication of his Gospel and a reprimand to those who reduce all truth to the intransigent facts of history:

> The statuary, ere he mould a shape
> Boasts a like gift, the shape's idea, and next
> The aspiration to produce the same;
> So, taking clay, he calls his shape thereout,
> Cries ever, 'Now I have the thing I see':
> Yet all the while goes changing what was wrought,
> From falsehood like the truth, to truth itself.
>
> (1902: 592)

Bibliography

Works cited by standard chapter divisions

The following can be consulted in Library of the Ante-Nicene Fathers (Edinburgh and Grand Rapids Mich.), Post-Nicene Fathers (Edinburgh and Grand Rapids Mich.): the *Didache*, Ignatius, Justin Martyr, Irenaeus, Hippolytus (*Refutation*), Tertullian, Clement of Alexandria, Origen (*First Principles*), Eusebius, Athanasius, Cyril of Jerusalem (*Catechetical Homilies*), Hilary, Basil, Gregory Nazianzen, Chrysostom, Ambrose, Augustine, Athenagoras, Barnabas, Cyprian.

The following can be consulted in the Loeb Classical Library (Cambridge, Mass.): Ignatius (in *Apostolic Fathers*), Jerome's Letters, Josephus, Philo, Prudentius, all pagan authors.

Other ancient or medieval works not in these series, cited by chapter or Migne pagination:

Apocryphal Acts and Gospels, best consulted in *NTA* or in *The Apocryphal New Testament*, ed. M. R. James and J. K. Elliott (Oxford, 1993).

Cyril of Alexandria, *Commentarium in Evangelium Johannes*, ed. J. E. Pusey, 3 vols (Oxford, 1876).

Dante, *Tutte le Opere*, ed. E. Moore (Oxford, 1944).

Epiphanius of Salamis, *Panarion*, ed. K. Holl, 3 vols (Leipzig, 1915).

Eriugena, J., *Opera quae supersunt*, ed. J.-P. Migne, Patrologia Latina 122 (Paris, 1853). Includes fragments on John's Gospel.

Jerome, *Opera*, in J.-P. Migne (ed.), Patrologia Latina 23 (Paris, 1845). Includes *Adversus Pelagianos*.

——*Epistulae*, vol. 1, ed. I. Hilbert (Vienna, 1996).

Optatus of Milevis, *Against the Donatists*, tr. M. J. Edwards (Liverpool, 1997).

Origen, *Commentary on John*, with fragments, ed. A. Brooke, 2 vols (Oxford, 1896).

——*On the Pasch, Dialogue with Heraclides*, tr. R. J. Daly (New York, 1992).

Radulphus Ardens, in J.-P. Migne, (ed.), Patrologia Latina 155 (Paris, 1880). Includes sermons on New Testament texts.

Victor of Vita, *History of the Vandal Persecution*, tr. J. Moorehead (Liverpool, 1992).

Works cited by page number of modern editions

Where two dates are given in parentheses, the first is that of original publication, the second that of the edition whose pagination is employed in the present volume.

Abbott, J. 1906: *Johannine Grammar*. London.

Abse, D. 1998: *Arcadia, One Mile*. London.

Agrippa, Cornelius 1993: *Three Books of Occult Philosophy* (1533), tr. J. Freake (1651), ed. D. Tyson. St Paul, Minn.

Andrewes, L. 1887: *Seventeen Sermons on the Nativity*. London.

Andreyev, L. 1947: *Judas Iscariot, the Christians, the Phantoms*, tr. B. Robb. London.

Aquinas, Thomas 1997: *Catena Aurea: A Commentary on the Four Gospels*, vol. 4: *St John*, tr. J. H. Newman. Southampton.

Arnold, E. 1910: *The Light of the World*. London.

Arnold, M. 1889: *God and the Bible*. London.

——1950: *Poems*, ed. C. B. Tinker and H. F. Lowry. Oxford.

Ashe, G. 1967: *King Arthur's Avalon*. Glasgow.

Ashton, J. 1991: *Understanding the Fourth Gospel*. Oxford.

——1994: *Studying John*. Oxford.

Aulen, G. 1931: *Christus Victor*, tr. A. G. Hebert. London.

Avancini, N. 1950: *The Life and Teachings of our Lord Jesus Christ* (1750), tr. K. Mackenzie. London.

Bacon, B. W. 1933: *The Gospel of the Hellenists*. New Haven.

Bacon, F. 1972: *Essays*. London.

Baigent, M., with R. Leigh and H. Lincoln 1982: *Holy Blood, Holy Grail*. New York.

Baldensperger, W. 1898: *Der Prolog des Vierten Evangeliums*. Tübingen.

Ball, D. M. 1996: '*I am*' *in John's Gospel: Literary Function, Background and Theological Implications*. Sheffield.

Bammel, E. 1984: Jesus as a political agent in a version of the Josippon. In E. Bammel and C. F. D. Moule (eds), *Jesus and the Politics of his Day*, Cambridge, 197–209.

Barnabas, Gospel of 1907: tr. L. and L. Ragg. Oxford.

Barrett, C. K. 1955: *The Gospel According to John*. Cambridge.

——1982: *Essays on John*. London.

Barrow, I. 1859: *The Pope's Supremacy*. London.

Barth, K. 1956: *Church Dogmatics*, vol. 4.1: *The Doctrine of Reconciliation*, tr. G. W. Bromiley. Edinburgh.

——1975: *Church Dogmatics*, vol. 1.1: *The Doctrine of the Word of God*, tr. G. W. Bromiley. Edinburgh.

Bauckham, R. 1996: Nicodemus and the Gurion family. *JTS* 47, 1–37.

Baur, F. C. 1844: Über die Composition und Charakter des johanneische Evangeliums. *Theologische Jahrbuch*, 1–191, 397–475, 615–700.

——1878: *The Church History of the First Three Centuries*, tr. A. Menzies, vol. 1. London.

Beatrice, P. F. (ed.) 2001: *Anonymi Monophysitae Theosophia*. Leiden.

Beaumont, J. 1967: *Poems*, ed. A. C. Grosart, 2 vols. New York, reprint.

Begg, E. 1985: *The Cult of the Black Virgin*. London.

Bell, D. 1996: *Many Mansions*. Kalamazoo, Mich.

Bengel, J. A. 1850: *Gnomon* (1740), 2 vols. London.

Benoit, P. 1969: *The Passion and Resurrection of Jesus Christ*. New York.

Berger, K. 1984: *Formgeschichte des Neuen Testaments*. Heidelberg.

Berkeley, G. 1837: *Works*, 1 vol. ed. London.

Bernard, J. H. 1928: *A Critical and Exegetical Commentary on the Gospel According to St. John*, 2 vols. Edinburgh.

Berriman, Dr 1737: *The Gradual Revelation of the Gospel*. In G. Burnet (ed.), *A Defence of Religion Natural and Revealed*, vol. 4, London, 92–256.

Betz, H. D. 1992: *The Greek Magical Papyri in Translation*. Chicago.

Beutler, J. 1991: Der alttestamentliche-judische Hintergrund der Hirtenrede in Johannes 10. In J. Beutler and R. T. Fortna (eds), *The Shepherd Discourse of John 10 and its Context*, Cambridge, 18–32.

Birdsall, J. N. 1960: John X.29. *JTS* 11, 342–4.

Black, M. 1946: *An Aramaic Approach to the Gospels and Acts*. London.

Blair, H. 1824: *Sermons*. London.

Blake, W. 1969: *Complete Writings*, ed. G. Keynes. Oxford.

Boehme, J. 1656: *The Aurora*, tr. J. Sparrow. London.

——1945: *Personal Christianity*, ed. F. Hartmann. New York.

Borgen, P. 1972: Logos was the True Light. *NT* 14, 115–30.

——1976a: The use of tradition in John 3.13–14. *NTS* 23, 18–35.

——1976b: Reply to B. Lindars, 'The Place of the Old Testament in the Formation of New Testament Theology'. *NTS* 23, 66–75.

Borsch, F. H. 1967: *The Son of Man in Myth and History*. London.

——1970: *The Christian and Gnostic Son of Man*. London.

Brandon, S. G. F. 1968: *The Trial of Jesus of Nazareth*. London.

Bream, N. H. 1969: No need to be asked questions: a study of Jn. 16:30. In *Search the Scriptures – NTS in Honour of Raymond T. Stamm* (Leiden), 49–74.

Bridges, R. 1953: *Poems*. Oxford.

Brodie, T. L. 1993: *The Gospel According to John: A Literary and Theological Commentary*. New York.

Bromiley, G. W. 1953: *Zwingli and Bullinger*. Philadelphia.

Brown, R. (tr.) 1958: *The Little Flowers of St Francis*. New York.

Brown, R. E. 1962: The *Gospel of Thomas* and St John's Gospel. *NTS* 9, 155–77.

——1966: *The Gospel According to John*, vol. 1. New York.

——1967: The Paraclete in the Fourth Gospel. *NTS* 13, 113–32.

——1970: *The Gospel According to John*, vol. 2. New York.

——1979: *The Community of the Beloved Disciple*. New York.

Browning, R. 1902: *Poetical Works*. London.

Buchanan, G. 1968: The Samaritan origins of the Gospel of John. In J. Neusner (ed.), *Religions in Antiquity: Essays in Memory of E. R. Goodenough*, London, 149–75.

Buchanan, G. W. 1978: *Revelation and Redemption: Jewish Documents of Deliverance from the Fall of Jerusalem to the Death of Nahmanides*. Dillsboro, NC.

Buchanan, R. 1882: *Selected Poems*. London.

Bulgakov, M. 1967: *The Master and Margarita* (1938), tr. M. Glenny. London.

Bultmann, R. 1925: Die Bedeutung der neuerschlossenen mandäischen und manichäischen Quellen fur das Verständnis der Johannesevangeliums. *Zeitschrift für neutestamentliche Wissenschaft*, 24, 100–46.

——1952: *Theology of the New Testament*, vol. 1. London.

——1955: *Theology of the New Testament*, vol. 2. London.

——1957: *Johannesevangelium*. Göttingen.

——1961: The New Testament and mythology. In H. W. Bartsch (ed.), *Kerygma and Myth*, Princeton, 1–44.

Bunyan, J. 1868: *Works, Allegorical, Figurative and Symbolical*, ed. G. Offord. London.

Burgon, J. W. 1998: *Causes of Corruption of the New Testament Text* (1896). Lafayette, Ind.

Burkitt, F. C. 1915–16: The Last Supper and the Fourth Gospel. *JTS* 17, 291–7.

Burridge, R. 1992: *What are the Gospels?* Cambridge.

Buse, I. 1954–5: John V.8 and Johannine-Marcan Relationships. *NTS* 1, 134–6.

——1958: St John and the Marcan Passion Narrative. *NTS* 4, 215–20.

Busse, U. 1991: Open questions on John 10. In J. Beutler and R. T. Fortna (eds), *The Shepherd Discourse of John 10 and its Context*, Cambridge, 6–17.

Butler, S. 1938: *The Fair Haven*. London.

——1985: *Notebooks*, ed. H. F. Jones. London.

Caldwell, T. 1959: *Dear and Glorious Physician*. New York.

Calvin, J. 1959: *The Gospel According to St. John*, vol. 1 (1553), tr. T. H. L. Parker. Grand Rapids, Mich.

—— 1961: *The Gospel According to St. John*, vol. 2 (1553), tr. T. H. L. Parker. Grand Rapids, Mich.

—— 1970: *Three French Treatises*, ed. F. M. Higman. London.

Cardiglia, J. G. 1937: *Unolpo di laucia al cuorp di Cristo*. Milan.

Carmichael, M. 1979–80: Marriage and the Samaritan woman. *NTS* 26, 332–46.

Catchpole, D. 1998: The Beloved Disciple and Nathanael. In C. Rowland and C. H. T. Fletcher-Louis (eds), *Understanding, Studying, Reading: New Testament Essays in Honour of John Ashton*, Sheffield, 69–92.

Causley, C. 1975: *Collected Poems 1951–1975*. London.

Cawley, A. C. 1974: *Everyman and Mediaeval Miracle Plays*. London.

Chapman, J. 1980: We know that his testimony is true. *JTS* 31, 379–87.

Charlesworth, J. H. 1995: *The Beloved Disciple: Whose Witness Validates the Gospel of John?* Valley Forge, Pa.

Chillingworth, W. 1841: *Works*. Philadelphia.

Church, W. R. 1930: The dislocations in the eighteenth chapter of John. *Journal of Biblical Literature*, 49, 375–83.

Clark, K. 1988: *Leonardo da Vinci*, rev. M. Kemp. Harmondsworth.

Clarke, D. (ed.) 2000: *Isabella Whitney, Mary Sidney and Aemilia Lanyer: Renaissance Women Poets*. Harmondsworth.

Clarke, J. 1740: *Complete History of the Bible*, vol. 2. London.

Claudel, P. 1960: Mort de Judas/Death of Judas. In W. Fowlie (ed.), *French Stories/Contes Français*, New York, 172–95.

Clemo, J. 1964: Selections in *Penguin Modern Poets* 6. Harmondsworth.

Clough, A. H. 1974: *The Poems of Arthur Hugh Clough*, ed. F. L. Mulhauser. Oxford.

Coakley, J. F. 1995: Jesus' messianic entry into Jerusalem (John 12.12–19 par.). *JTS* 46, 461–82.

Cohn-Sherbok, D. 1992: *Many Mansions*. London.

Coleridge, H. 1908: *The Complete Poetical Works*, ed. R. Colles. London.

Coleridge, S. T. 1972: *Lay Sermons*. Princeton and London.

—— 1974: *Poems*, ed. John Beer. London.

—— 1983: *Biographia Literaria* (1817), ed. J. Engell and W. Jackson Bate. Princeton.

Conybeare, F. C. 1910: *Myth, Magic and Morals: A Study of Christian Origins*. London.

Corelli, M. 1935: *Barabbas: The Tragedy of the World* (1893), 57th ed. London.

Cowley, A. 1881: *Complete Works*, ed. A. B. Grosart, vol. 2. Blackburn.

Cowper, W. 1905: *Poems*, ed. H. Milford. London, Edinburgh and Glasgow.

Cox, H. 1988: *Many Mansions: A Christian's Encounter with Other Faiths*. Boston.

Crashaw, R. 1927: *Poems*, ed. L. C. Martin. Oxford.

Craveri, M. 1967: *The Life of Jesus: An Assessment through Modern Historical Evidence*, tr. C. L. Markmann. London.

Crossan, J. D. 1980: A structuralist analysis of John 6. In R. Spencer (ed.), *Orientation by Disorientation*, Pittsburgh, 235–52.

Cullmann, O. 1962: *Peter: Apostle, Bishop, Martyr*. Philadelphia.

—— 1976: *The Johannine Circle*. London.

Cyril of Jerusalem 2000: Selections ed. E. J. Yarnold. London.

Daisenberger, J. A. 1970: *The Oberammergau Passion Play*. Oberammergau.

D'Angelo, M. R. 1990: A critical note: John 21.17 and Apocalypse of Moses 31. *JTS* 41, 529–36.

Daniélou, J. 1957: *Les Manuscrits de la Mer Morte et les origins du Christianisme*. Paris.

Danker, F. W. 1960–1: The υιος phrases in the New Testament. *NTS* 7, 94.

Daube, D. 1956: *The New Testament and Rabbinic Judaism*. London.

Davies, I. 1980: *Collected Poems*. Llandysul, Wales.

De la Potterie, I. 1960: Jesus, roi et juge d'après Jn 19.13: *ekathisen epi bematos*. *Biblica*, 41, 217–47.

—— 1963: The Truth in Saint John, tr. J. Ashton. In *The Interpretation of John*, London 1986, 53–66.

—— 1975: χαρις paulinienne et χαρις johannique. In E. P. Ellis and E. Grasser (eds), *Jesus und Paulus*, Gottingen, 256–82.

—— 1983: 'Nous adorons, nous, ce que nous connaîssons, car le salvation vient des Juifs': histoire de l'exégèse et interpretation de Jn 4.22. *Biblica*, 64, 74–115.

Denzinger, H. 1957: *Enchiridion Symbolorum*. Barcelona, Fribourg and Rome.

Derrett, J. M. D. 1960–1: Dives and Lazarus and the preceding sayings. *NTS* 7, 364–80.

—— 1963–4: Law in the New Testament: the story of the woman taken in adultery. *NTS* 10, 1–26.

Dickinson, E. 1970: *Complete Poems*, ed. T. H. Johnson. London.

Dodd, C. H. 1935: *The Bible and the Greeks*. London.

—— 1953a: *The Interpretation of the Fourth Gospel*. Cambridge.

—— 1953b: Note on John 21.24. *JTS* 4, 212–13.

—— 1955: The appearances of the risen Christ: an essay in form-criticism. In D. Nineham (ed.), *Studies in the Gospels: Essays in Honour of R. H. Lightfoot*, Oxford, 9–36.

—— 1961: *Parables of the Kingdom*. London.

—— 1963: *Historical Tradition in the Fourth Gospel*. Cambridge.

Dodds, E. R. 1951: *The Greeks and the Irrational*. Berkeley.

Donne, J. 1929: *Complete Verse and Selected Prose*. London.

—— 1958: *The Sermons of John Donne*, selected by T. Gill. New York.

Doré, G. 1995: *Engravings*. London.

Dowding, L. 1943: *Many Mansions*. London.

Drummond, H. 1953: *The Greatest Thing in the World*. London and Glasgow.

Drummond of Hawthornden, W. 1894: *Poems,* vol. 2, ed. W. M. C. Ward. London.

Drury, J. 1979: *The Pot and the Knife*. London.

Dryden, J. 1910: *Poems*, ed. J. Sargeaunt. London.

Duffy, C. A. 1999: *The World's Wife*. London.

Dunderberg, I. 1998: *Thomas*' I-sayings and the Gospel of John. In R. Uro (ed.), *Thomas at the Crossroads*, Edinburgh, 33–64.

Dunkerley, R. 1958–9: Lazarus. *NTS* 5, 321–7.

Eckhart 1958: *Selected Treatises and Sermons*, tr. J. M. Clark and J. V. Skinner. London.

—— 1977: *Treatises and Sermons*, vol. 2, tr. M. O'C. Walshe. Shaftesbury, Dorset.

Edersheim, L. 1897: *The Life and Times of Jesus the Messiah*, vol. 2. London.

Edwards, H. E. 1953: *The Disciple who Wrote these Things*. London.

Edwards, J. 1830: *Works*, vol. 7, ed. S. B. Dwight. New York.

Edwards, M. J. 2003: *Constantine and Christendom*. Liverpool.

Eisler, R. 1923: *Orpheus – the Fisher: Comparative Studies in Orphic and Early Christian Cultic Symbolism*. London.

Eliot, T. S. 1974: *Collected Poems 1909–1962*. London.

Elsley, H. 1844: *Annotations on the Gospels and the Acts of the Apostles*. London.

Emerton, J. A. 1958: The one hundred and fifty three fishes at John XXI.11. *JTS* 9, 86–9.

—— 1962: Binding and Loosing – Forgiving and Retaining. *JTS* 13, 325–31.

—— 1966: Melchizedek and the gods: fresh evidence for the Jewish background of John X.34–6. *JTS* 17, 399–401.

Ephraem Syrus 1990: *Hymns on Paradise*, tr. S. Brock. New York.

Erasmus, D. 1535: *Annotationes in Novum Testamentum*. Basle.

Eslinger, L. 1987: The wooing of the woman at the well. *Literature and Theology*, 1, 167–83.

Evans, C. A. 1995: Predictions of the destruction of the Herodian Temple in the Psende-pigcapha, Qumran Scrolls and related texts. In J. H. Chevlesworth (ed.), *Qumran Questions*, Sheffield, 92–150.

Ezekiel, the tragedian 1983: *The Exagoge*, ed. H. Jacobson. Cambridge.

Farrar, F. W. 1901: *The Life of Christ* (1874). London.

Fennema, D. 1985: God the Only Son. *NTS* 31, 124–35.

Feuillet, A. 1966: L'heure de la femme (Jn 16.21) et l'heure de la Mère de Jesus (Jn 19.25–27). *Biblica*, 47, 169–84, 361–80, 557–73.

Ficino, Marsilio 1559: *Theologia Platonica*, repr. 1995. Zurich, Hildesheim and New York.

Fisher, L. A. 1917: *The Mystic Vision in the Grail Legend and in the Divine Comedy*. New York.

Fitzmyer, J. 1981: *To Advance the Gospel*. Grand Rapids, Mich., and Cambridge.

Fortna, R. T. 1970: *The Gospel of Signs*. Cambridge.

—— 1988: *The Fourth Gospel and its Predecessor*. Edinburgh.

France, A. 1892: Le procurateur de Judée. In *idem*, *L'Étui de Nacre*, Paris.

Frazer, J. G. 1914: *The Golden Bough*, vol. 6: *The Scapegoat*. London.

Freed, E. D. 1965: *Old Testament Quotations in the Gospel of John*. Leiden.

—— 1970: Did John write his Gospel partly to win Samaritan converts? *NT* 12, 241–56.

—— 1982: *Ego Eimi* in John VIII.24 in the light of its context and Jewish messianic belief. *JTS* 33, 163–7.

Gascoyne, D. 1988: *Collected Poems*. Oxford.

Gaster, T. 1923: *The Samaritans*. London.

Gee, D. H. 1989: Why did Peter spring into the sea? (John 21.7). *JTS* 40, 481–9.

Germanus of Constantinople 1984: *On the Divine Liturgy*, ed. and tr. P. Meyendorff. New York.

Giblin, C. H. 1980: Suggestion, negative response and positive action in St John's portrayal of Jesus. *NTS* 80, 197–211.

Ginzberg, L. 1998: *The Legends of the Jews*, vol. 6. Baltimore.

Girard, R. 1972: *Le Violence et le Sacré*. Paris. Tr. Patrick Gregory. Baltimore.

—— 1978: *Des Choses Cachés depuis la Fondation du Monde*. Paris.

Glasson, T. F. 1963: *Moses in the Fourth Gospel*. London.

Goethe, J. W. 1962: *Faust: Der Tragödie erster und zweiter Teil*. Munich.

Goguel, M. 1928: *Jean-Baptiste*. Paris.

Goodenough, E. R. 1953: *Jewish Symbols in the Greco Roman Period*, vol. 4: *The Problem of Method*. Princeton.

Gordon, R. K. 1954: *Anglo-Saxon Poetry*. London.

Gore-Booth, E. 1925: *The Shepherd of Eternity and Other Poems*. London.

Gottfried von Strassburg 1977: *Tristan* (1210), ed. K. Marold and W. Schroeder. Berlin and New York.

Goulder, M. 1977: The two roots of the Christian myth. In J. Hick (ed.), *The Myth of God Incarnate*, London, 64–86.

Grabar, A. 1968: *Christian Iconography: A Study of its Origins*. Princeton.

Grant, R. M. 1949: One hundred fifty three fish. *HTR* 42, 273–5.

Grassi, J. A. 1972: The wedding at Cana (John II 1–11): a pentecostal meditation? *NT* 14, 131–6.

Graves, R. 1986: *Selected Poems*, ed. Paul O'Prey. Harmondsworth.

Gray, D. 1975: *A Selection of Religious Lyrics*. Oxford.

Greban, A. 1962: *Le Vray Mystère de la Passion*, ed. R. Cluny. Paris.

Green, D. 1989: *Gold in the Crucible*. Longmead.

Grelot, P. 1988/9: Jean 8.56 et Jubilés 16.16–29. *Revue de Qumran*, 13, 621–8.

Gresswell, E. 1830: *Dissertations on the Principles and Arrangement of a Harmony of the Gospels*, vol. 3. Oxford.

Grigsby, B. 1985: Washing in the pool of Siloam: a thematic anticipation of the Johannine cross. *NTS* 27, 227–35.

Grundmann, W. 1984: The decision of the Supreme Court to put Jesus to death (John 11: 47–57) in its context: tradition and redaction in the Gospel of John. In E. Bammel and C. F. D. Moule (eds), *Jesus and the Politics of his Day*, Cambridge, 295–318.

Gunn, T. 1993: *Collected Poems*. London.

Gunther, J. J. 1981: The relation of the Beloved Disciple to the Twelve. *Theologische Zeitschrift*, 37, 129–48.

Guyenot, L. 2002: Fire, water and faith: the Holy Spirit and early Christian polemics against the Baptists. *Downside Review*, 240, 80–100.

Hall, J. 1906: *Divine Poems*. In G. Saintsbury (ed.), *Minor Poets of the Caroline Period*, vol. 2, Oxford, 213–25.

Hamburger, J. F. 2002: *St John the Divine: The Deified Evangelist in Mediaeval Literature and Art*. Berkeley.

Hanson, A. T. 1965: John's citation of Psalm LXXXII. *NTS* 11, 158–62.

—— 1967: John's citation of Psalm LXXXII reconsidered. *NTS* 13, 363–7.

—— 1976–7: John 1.14–18 and Exodus XXXIV. *NTS* 23, 90–101.

—— 1991: *The Prophetic Gospel*. Edinburgh.

Happé, P. (ed.) 1975: *English Mystery Plays*. Harmondsworth.

Harris, J. R. 1893: *Memoranda Sacra*. London.

Harrison, J. 1963: *Themis: A Study in the Social Origins of Greek Religion*. London.

Harvey, A. E. 1976: *Jesus on Trial: A Study in the Fourth Gospel*. London.

Haskins, S. 1994: *Mary Magdalen: Myth and Metaphor*. San Francisco.

Hastings, J. (ed.) 1906: *A Dictionary of Christ and the Gospels*, vol. 1. Edinburgh.

—— (ed.) 1913: *A Dictionary of Christ and the Gospels*, vol. 2. Edinburgh.

Hawker, R. S. 1904: *Cornish Ballads and Other Poems*. London and New York.

Haydon, B. R. 1950: *Autobiography and Journals*, ed. R. Elwin. London.

Heer, F. 1970: *God's First Love: Christians and Jews over Two Thousand Years*. London.

Heliand 1992: tr. G. Ronald Murphy. New York.

Hemans, F. 1912: *Poetical Works*, ed. W. M. Rosetti. London, Melbourne and Toronto.

Hengel, M. 1989: *The Johannine Question*, tr. J. Bowden. London.

Henry, M. 1991: *Commentary on the Whole Bible* (1706). Peabody, Mass.

Herbert, G. 1974: *The English Poems of George Herbert*, ed. C. A. Patrides. London.

Herrick, R. 1884: *Hesperides, or Works both Human and Divine*, ed. H. Morley. London.

Hewitt, J. W. 1932: The use of nails in crucifixion. *HTR* 25, 29–45.

Hill, C. E. 1998: What Papias said about John (and Luke). *JTS* 49, 582–630.

Hill, G. 1985: *Collected Poems*. Harmondsworth.

—— 1996: *Canaan*. Harmondsworth.

Hippolytus 1897: *Werke*, vol. 1, ed. N. Bonwetsch and H. Achelis. Leipzig.

Hobbes, T. 1973: *Leviathan* (1651), ed. K. R. Minogue. London.

Hoccleve, T. 1981: *Selections*, ed. M. C. Seymour. Oxford.

Hölderlin, J. C. F. 1961: *Selected Poems*, ed. and tr. M. Hamburger. Harmondsworth.

Hopkins, G. M. 1970: *The Poems*, ed. W. H. Gardner and N. H. Mackenzie. Oxford.

Horbury, W. 1972: Tertullian on the Jews in the light of *De Spectaculis* XXX.5–6. *JTS* 23, 455–9.

—— 1982: The Benediction of the Minim and Early Jewish–Christian Controversy. *JTS* 33, 19–61.

—— 1984: Christ as brigand. In E. Bammel and C. F. D. Moule (eds), *Jesus and the Politics of his Day*, Cambridge, 183–97.

Hoskyns, E. 1947: *The Fourth Gospel*, ed. Noel Davey. Oxford.

Housman, A. E. 1939: *Collected Poems*. London.

Hughes, Ted 1972: *Crow: From the Life and Songs of the Crow*. London.

—— 2000: *Poems*, selected by Simon Armitage. London.

Hugo, V. 1886: *Dieu. Fin de Satan*. Edinburgh, London and Paris.

Hume, D. 1962: *Enquiries Concerning the Human Understanding and Concerning the Principles of Morals* (1748), ed. L. A. Selby-Bigge. Oxford.

Hunter, R. B. 1977: *The English Spenserians*. Salt Lake City, Utah.

Huntingford, T. 1829: *Testimonies in Favour of the Separate Existence of the Soul*. London.

Hutcheson, G. J. 1972: *Exposition of the Gospel according to John* (1657). London.

Ibbot, Dr 1737: *The True Notion of the Exercise of Private Judgment or Free-thinking*. Repr. in G. Burnet (ed.), *A Defence of Natural and Revealed Religion*, London, vol. 3, 1–104.

Inge, W. R. 1904: *Light, Life and Love: Selections from the German Mystics of the Middle Ages*. London.

Isaac of Stella 1979: *Sermons on the Christian Year*, vol. 1, tr. H. McCaffery. Kalamazoo, Mich.

James, M. R. 1893: *Apocrypha Anecdota*. Cambridge.

James, W. 1960: *The Varieties of Religious Experience* (1905), ed. A. D. Nock. London.

Jeremias, J. 1957: *The Eucharistic Words of Jesus*, 2nd edn. London.

—— 1969: *Jerusalem in the Time of Jesus*. Philadelphia.

Jocz, J. 1962: *The Jewish People and Jesus Christ*. London.

John of the Cross 1979: *Poems*, tr. R. Campbell. London.

—— 1991: *Collected Works*. Washington, D.C.

Johnston, G. 1970: *The Spirit-Paraclete in the Gospel of John*. Cambridge.

Jones, D. 1952: *Anathemata*. London.

Jones, G. 1996: *Collected Poems*, ed. M. Stephens. Cardiff.

Josipovici, G. 1988: *The Book of God: A Response to the Bible*. New Haven.

Julian of Norwich 1966: *Revelations of Divine Love*, tr. C. Wolters. Harmondsworth.

Jülicher, A. 1910: *Die Gleichnisreden Jesu*. Tübingen.

Jung, C. G. 1967: *Alchemical Studies*. London.

—— 1968: *Aion: Researches into the Phenomenology of the Self*. London.

Jungkuntz, R. 1964: An approach to the exegesis of John 10.34–6. *Concordia Theological Monthly*, 35, 556–65.

Käsemann, E. 1968: *The Last Testament of Jesus*. London.

—— 1969: The structure and purpose of the prologue to John's Gospel. In *New Testament Questions of Today*, London, 138–67.

Kazantzakis, N. 1961: *The Last Temptation*, tr. P. A. Bien. London.

Kelly, J. N. D. 1972: *Early Christian Creeds*. London.

Kermode, F. 1979: *The Genesis of Secrecy: On the Interpretation of Narrative*. Cambridge, Mass., and London.

Kersten, H. and Gruber, E. R. 1992: *The Jesus Conspiracy: The Turin Shroud and the Truth about the Resurrection*. Shaftesbury, Dorset.

Kidder, B. 1737: *A Demonstration of the Messias*. Abridged in G. Burnet (ed.), *A Defence of Natural and Revealed Religion*, vol. 3, London, 72–119.

Kieckhefer, R. 1998: The Devil's contemplatives: the *Liber Iuratus*, the *Liber Visionum* and Christian appropriation of Jewish occultism. In C. Fanger (ed.), *Conjuring Spirits: Texts and Traditions in Medieval Ritual Magic*, Stroud, Glos., 250–65.

Kiefer, R. 1980: Two types of exegesis with a linguistic basis. In H. Küng and J. Moltmann (eds), *Conflicting Ways of Interpreting the Bible*, New York, 9–16.

Kierkegaard, S. 1954: *The Sickness unto Death* (1849), with *Fear and Trembling*, tr. W. Lowrie. New York.

—— 1962: *The Present Age*, and *On the Difference between a Genius and an Apostle*, tr. Alexander Dru. London.

—— 1967: *Edifying Discourses*, tr. W. Lowrie. Princeton.

King, H. 1921: *Poems*. In G. Saintsbury (ed.), *Minor Poets of the Caroline Period*, Oxford, vol. 3, 161–273.

Knight, G. W. 1968: *Shakespearian Production*. London.

Koester, H. 1986: The history of religions school, Gnosis and the Gospel of John. *Studia Theologica*, 40, 115–36.

—— 1990: *Ancient Christian Gospels: Their History and Development*. London.

Kokkinos, N. 1989: Crucified in A.D. 36 – the keypoint for dating the birth of Jesus. In J. Vardaman and E. Yamauchi (eds), *Chronos, Kairos, Christos*, Winona Lake, 355–81.

Kraemer, R. 1999: Jewish women and Christian origins. In R. Kraemer and M. di Angelo (eds), *Women and Christian Origins*, Oxford and New York, 35–49.

Kragerud, A. 1959: *Der Lieblinsjunger im Johannesevangelium*. Oslo.

Kysar, R. 1986: *John*. Minneapolis.

Lagerkvist, P. 1952: *Barabbas*, tr. A. Blair. London.

Lagrange, M. 1948: *L'Evangile selon S. Jean*. Paris.

Lamarche, P. 1964: The prologue of John. *Revue des Sciences Religieuses*, 52, 497–537; tr. John Ashton in *The Interpretation of John*, Philadelphia and London, 1986, 39–52.

Lampe, G. W. H. 1977: *God as Spirit*. London.

Lane Fox, R. 1991: *The Unauthorised Version*. Harmondsworth.

Langkammer, H. 1968: Christ's 'Last Will and Testament' (Jn 19, 26.27) in the interpretation of the Fathers of the Church and the scholastics. *Antoniamum*, 43, 99–109.

Langland, W. 1987: *The Vision of Piers Plowman* (1387): *A Complete Edition of the B Text*, ed. A. V. C. Schmidt. London.

Laurentin, A. 1972: *Doxa I: Problèmes de Christologie. Commentaires patristiques sur Jean 17.5*. Paris.

Lawrence, D. H. 1929: *The Escaped Cock*. Paris. Repr. as *The Man who Died*, London, 1931.

—— 1972: *Selected Poems*, ed. K. Sagar. Harmondsworth.

Lee, E. H. 1957: St Mark and the Fourth Gospel. *NTS* 3, 50–8.

'Levi' 1964: *The Aquarian Gospel of Jesus Christ*, by Levi H. Dowling. London.

Lewis, C. S. 1994: *Poems*, ed. W. Hooper. London.

—— 1996: *The Magician's Nephew* (1955). London.

—— 1997: *The Voyage of the Dawn Treader* (1955). London.

Liddon, H. P. 1880: *University Sermons*. London.

—— 1906: *The Divinity of our Lord*. London.

Liechty, D. 1994: *Early Anabaptist Spirituality*. London.

Lightfoot, J. 1859: *Commentary on the New Testament from the Talmud and Hebraica*, vol. 3: *Luke–John* (1684). Oxford.

Lightfoot, J. B. 1904: *Biblical Essays*. London.

Lightfoot, R. H. 1956: *St John's Gospel: A Commentary*. Oxford.

Lindars, B. 1971: *Behind the Fourth Gospel*. London.

—— 1972: *The Gospel of John*. London.

Lloyd-Jones, D. M. 1996: *Life in the Spirit*. Eastbourne.

Locke, J. 1790: *The Reasonableness of Christianity as Demonstrated in the Gospels* (1695). London. Repr. Bristol, 1997.

Loewe, R. 1981: 'Salvation' is not of the Jews. *JTS* 32, 341–68.

Loisy, A. 1903: *Le Quatrième Évangile*. Paris.

Longfellow, H. W. 1925: *Poetical Works*. Oxford.

Loomis, R. S. 1963: *The Grail from Celtic Myth to Christian Symbol*. Cardiff.

Lowe, M. 1976: Who were the Ιουδαιοι? *NT* 18, 101–30.

Luther, M. 1953: *Early Theological Writings*, ed. J. Atkinson. Philadelphia.

—— 1961: *Selected Writings*, ed. J. Dillenberger. New York.

—— 1983: *Sermons*. Grand Rapids, Mich.

Maccini, R. 1996: *Her Witness is True: Women as Witnesses according to John*. Sheffield.

Macdonald, J. 1964: *The Theology of the Samaritans*. London.

McGrath, J. 1998: A rebellious son? Hans Odeberg and the interpretation of John 5.18. *NTS* 44, 470–5.

Maeterlinck, M. 1910: *Mary Magdalene*. London.

Mahoney, A. 1965: A new look at an old problem (John 18, 12–14, 19–24). *Catholic Biblical Quarterly*, 27, 137–44.

Maier, P. L. 1968: Sejanus, Pilate and the date of the Crucifixion. *Church History*, 37, 3–13.

Mâle, E. 1986: *Religious Art in France*, 2 vols. Princeton.

Malina, B. and Rohrbaugh, R. 1998: *Social-Science Commentary on the Gospel of John*. Minneapolis.

Manson, T. W. 1943: *The Teaching of Jesus*. Cambridge.

—— 1951: The cleansing of the Temple. *Bulletin of the John Rylands Library*, 33, 276–80.

Marlowe, C. 1955: *Poems and Plays*, ed. M. R. Ridley. London.

Marsh, J. 1968: *Saint John*. Harmondsworth.

Martyn, J. L. 1976: We have found Elijah. In R. Hamerton-Kelly and R. Scroggs (eds), *Jews, Greeks and Christians*, Leiden, 181–219.

—— 1979: *History and Theology in the Fourth Gospel*, 2nd edn. Nashville, Tenn.

Marvell, A. 1952: *Poems*, ed. H. MacDonald. London.

Masefield, J. 1923: *Collected Poems*. London.

—— 1925: *The Trial of Jesus*. London.

Mastrantonis, G. 1982: *Augsburg and Constantinople*. Brookline, Mass.

Matera, F. J. 1982: *The Kingship of Jesus: Composition and Theology in Mark* 15. Chico, Calif.

Matheson, P. 1981: *The Third Reich and the Christian Churches*. Edinburgh.

Matthews, J. 1997: *Sources of the Grail*. Edinburgh.

Maurice, F. D. 1857: *The Gospel of St. John*. London.

Mead, G. R. S. 1921: *Pistis Sophia*. London.

Meeks, W. 1966: Galilee and Judaea in the Fourth Gospel. *Journal of Biblical Literature*, 85, 159–69.

—— 1967: *The Prophet-King: Moses Traditions and the Johannine Christology*. Leiden.

—— 1972: The man from heaven in Johannine sectarianism. *Journal of Biblical Literature*, 91, 44–92.

Metzger, B. 1975: *A Textual Commentary on the Greek New Testament*. Oxford.

Mew, C. 1981: *Collected Poems and Prose*, ed. V. Warner. London and Manchester.

Meyendorff, J. 1975: *Christ in Eastern Christian Thought*. New York.

Meynell, A. 1923: *Poems*. London.

Michell, J. 1973: *City of Revelation*. London.

Millar, F. G. 1990: Reflections on the trials of Jesus. In P. R. Davies (ed.), *Essays in Honour of Geza Vermes*, Sheffield, 133–63.

Milton, J. 1966: *Poetical Works*, ed. Douglas Bush. Oxford.

—— 1973: *On Christian Doctrine*, in *Collected Works*, vol. 6, tr. J. Carey. London and NewHaven.

Moltmann, J. 1967: *Theology of Hope*. New York.

—— 1990: *The Way of Jesus Christ*. London.

Montefiore, H. 1962: Revolt in the desert? *NTS* 8, 135–41.

Moore, G. 1952: *The Brook Kerith* (1916). Harmondsworth.

Moore, G. F. 1922: Intermediaries in Jewish theology. *HTR* 15, 41–85.

Moore, T. V. 1981: *The Last Days of Jesus* (1858). Edinburgh.

More, H. 1662: *Enthusiasmus Triumphatus*. London. Repr. Los Angeles, 1966.

Morison, F. 1930: *Who Moved the Stone?* London.

Moule, C. F. D. 1954: A note on 'under the fig-tree' in John 1.48, 50. *JTS* 5, 210–11.

Mozley, J. B. 1876: *University Sermons*. London, Oxford and Cambridge.

Murphy, R. E. 1958: Šahat in the Qumran literature. *Biblica*, 39, 60–6.

Murphy-O'Connor, J. 1998: *The Holy Land*, 4th edn. Oxford.

Murray, L. 1980: *Michelangelo*. London.

Natalis Alexander 1840: *In Sanctum Ioannem* (1724), ed. J-P. Migne. Paris.

Nelli, R. 1968: *Écrits Cathares*. Paris.

Neusner, J. 1991: *Jews and Christians: The Myth of a Common Tradition*. London.

Newman, J. H. 1838: *Tracts for the Times 85: Lectures on the Scripture Doctrine of the Church*. London.

—— 1982: *Who is a Christian? Selections from Parochial and Plain Sermons*. Denville, NJ.

Newton, J. 1979: *Out of the Depths: An Autobiography* (1822). Chicago.

Nicklas, T. 2000: 'Unter dem Feigenbaum': die Rolle des Lesers im Dialog zwischen Jesus und Natanael (Joh 1.45–50). *NTS* 46, 193–205.

Nietzsche, F. 1908: *Ecce Home*. Berlin.

Nonnus 2002: *Parafrasi del Vangelio de S. Giovanni*, Canto 1, ed. C. de Stefani. Bologna.

North, W. E. S. 2001: *The Lazarus Story within the Johannine Tradition*. Sheffield.

Noyes, A. 1920: *Collected Poems*, vol. 2. London.

Odeberg, H. 1929: *The Fourth Gospel Interpreted in its Relation to Contemporaneous Religious Currents in Palestine and the Hellenistic-Oriental World*. Chicago.

O'Neill, J. 1999: Jesus of Nazareth. *JTS* 50, 135–42.

Origen 1992: *On the Pasch* and *Dialogue with Heraclides*, tr. R. J. Daly. New York.

Owen, J. 1850: *Works*, vol. 1: *The Glory of Christ*. London.

Owen, W. 1985: *Poems*, ed. Jon Stallworthy. London.

Paffenroth, K. 2001: *Judas: Images of the Lost Disciple*. London.

Painter, J. 1991: Tradition, history and interpretation in John 10. In J. Beutler and R. T. Fortna (eds), *The Shepherd Discourse of John 10 and its Context*, Cambridge, 53–74.

Pannenberg, W. 1968: *Jesus – God and Man*. London.

Panofsky, E. R. 1955: *The Life and Art of Albrecht Dürer*. Princeton.

Peebles, R. J. 1911: *The Legend of Longinus*. Baltimore.

Pink, A. W. 1978: *The Seven Sayings of the Saviour from the Cross*. In *Four Great Works*, Grand Rapids, Mich., 277–406.

Plath, S. 1965: *Ariel*. London.

Purvis, J. D. 1975: The Fourth Gospel and the Samaritans. *NT* 17, 161–96.

Rahner, K. 1975: *A Rahner Reader*, ed. G. A. McCool. London.

Raine, K. 1956: *Collected Poems*. London.

Ramsay, W. M. 1897: *Cities and Bishoprics of Phrygia*, vol. 1, pt 2. Oxford.

—— 1994: *Letters to the Seven Churches of Asia* (1904), ed. M. Wilson. Peabody, Mass.

Rankin, O. 1930: *The Origin of the Festival of Hannukah*. Stuttgart.

Rashdall, H. 1919: *The Idea of Atonement*. London.

Renan, E. 1927: *The Life of Jesus* (1861). London.

Richard of St Victor 1979: *The Mystical Ark*, etc., tr. G. Zinn. London.

Ridderbos, H. 1966: The scope and character of the prologue to the Gospel of John. *NT* 8, 180–201.

Ridler, A. 1994: *Collected Poems*. Manchester.

Roberts, C. H. 1987: John 20:30–31 and 21:24–25. *JTS* 38, 409–10.

Robertson, F. M. 1905: *Sermons on Christian Doctrine*. London.

—— 1906: *Sermons on Bible Subjects*. London.

Robinson, E. A. 1997: *Selected Poems*. Harmondsworth.

Robinson, J. A. 1988: *The Nag Hammadi Library*. Leiden and San Francisco.

Robinson, J. A. T. 1962: *Twelve New Testament Studies*. London.

—— 1978: *Redating the New Testament*. London.

—— 1984: 'His witness is true': a test of the Johannine claim. In E. Bammel and C. F. D. Moule (eds), *Jesus and the Politics of his Day*, Cambridge, 453–76.

—— 1985: *The Priority of John*. London.

Robinson, T. 1899: *The Life and Death of Mary Magdalene* (1620), ed. H. O. Sommer. London.

Rodgers, W. R. 1952: *Europa and the Bull*. London.

Romanus the Melodist 1963: *Cantica Genuina*, ed. P. Maas and C. A. Trypanis. Oxford.

Rooke, D. W. 2000: A woman's plight and the later Fathers. In L. Kreitzer and D. W. Rooke (eds), *Ciphers in the Sand: Interpretations of the Woman Taken in Adultery (John 7.53–8.11)*, Sheffield, 83–104.

Rordorf, W. 1968: *Sunday*. London.

—— 1979: Christ als Logos und Nomos. In A. M. Ritter (ed.), *Kerygma und Logos*, Göttingen, 424–34.

Rossetti, C. 1995: *Works*. Ware, Herts.

Ross, J. F. 1962: The prophet as Yahweh's messenger. In B. W. Anderson and W. Harrelson (eds), *Essays in Honour of John Muilenberg*, London, 98–107.

Rostovtzeff, M. (ed.) 1934: *The Excavations at Dura-Europos*. New Haven.

Ruckstuhl, E. 1987: *Die literarische Einheit des Johannesevangeliums*, 2nd edn. Freiburg.

Rudolph, K. 1960: *Die Mandäer*, vol. 1: *Das Mandäerproblem*. Göttingen.

Rupp, G. and Watson, P. S. 1969: *Luther and Erasmus on Free Will*. Philadelphia and London.

Rutherford, Mark 1925: Judas – what can be said for him? In H. Milford (ed.), *Selected Modern Essays*, Oxford, 3–19.

Ryle, J. 1866: *Expository Thoughts on John*, vol. 1. London.

—— 1869: *Expository Thoughts on John*, vol. 2. London.

—— 1873: *Expository Thoughts on John*, vol. 3. London.

Sacy, Maistre de (i.e. L.Isaac) 1840: *Sur S. Jean* (1684), ed. J.-P. Migne. Paris.

Sanday, W. M. 1905: *The Interpretation of the Fourth Gospel* (1874). London.

Sanders, E. P. 1985: *Jesus and Judaism*. London.

—— 1993: *The Historical Figure of Jesus*. Harmondsworth.

Sanders, J. N. 1954–5: Those whom Jesus loved. *NTS* 1, 29–41.

Santucci, L. 1974: *Wrestling with Christ*. London.

Sayers, D. L. 1943: *The Man Born to be King*. London.

Schenke, H.-M. 1986: The function and background of the beloved disciple in the Gospel of John. In C. W. Hedrick and R. Hodgson (eds), *Nag Hammadi, Gnosticism and Early Christianity*, Peabody, Mass., 111–25.

Schnackenburg, R. 1968: *The Gospel According to John*, vol. 1. New York.

—— 1980: *The Gospel According to John*, vol. 2. New York.

—— 1982: *The Gospel According to John*, vol. 3. New York.

Schneiders, S. 1991: A case study: a feminist interpretation of John 4: 1–42. In *The Revelatory Text*, San Francisco, 180–99.

Scholem, G. 1971: *The Messianic Idea in Judaism and other Essays on Jewish Spirituality*. New York.

Schürer, E. 1979: *History of the Jewish People in the Age of Jesus Christ*, rev. G. Vermes, F. Millar and M. Black, vol. 2. Edinburgh.

Schüssler Fiorenza, E. 1983: *In memory of Her: A Feminist Theological Reading of Christian origins*. New York.

Schweitzer, A. 1954: *The Quest for the Historical Jesus* (1906), tr. W. Montgomery. London.

Scobie, C. 1964: *John the Baptist*. London.

Scot, R. 1972: *Discoverie of Witchcraft* (1584), ed. Montague Summers. Mineola, NY.

Scott, J. 2000: The one that got away. In L. Kreitzer and D. W. Rooke (eds), *Ciphers in the Sand*, Sheffield, 30–41.

Scott, M. 1992: *Sophia and the Johannine Jesus*. Sheffield.

Seeley, J. 1895: *Ecce Homo*. London.

Sexton, A. 1991: *The Selected Poems of Anne Sexton*. London.

Shellard, B. 1995: The relation of Luke and John: a fresh look at an old problem. *JTS* 46, 71–98.

Sherwin-White, A. N. 1963: *Roman Law and Roman Society in the New Testament*. Oxford.

Simonis, A. J. 1967: *Die Hirtenrede im Johannes-Evangelium*. Rome.

Sisam, C. and Sisam, K. 1970: *The Oxford Book of Mediaeval Verse*. Oxford.

Sisson, C. H. 1990: *Selected Poems*. Manchester.

Sitwell, E. 1952: *Selected Poems*. Harmondsworth.

Skelton, J. 1959: *Complete Poems, 1460–1529*, ed. P. Henderson. London.

Smart, C. 1954: *Jubilate Agno*, ed. W. H. Bond. London.

Smith, M. 1985: *Jesus the Magician*. Wellingborough.

Smith, J. Z. 1987: Dying and rising gods. In M. Eliade (ed.), *The Encyclopedia of Religion*, New York and London, vol. 4, 521–7.

Smith, S. 1978: *Selected Poems*. Harmondsworth.

Södering, T. 2000: 'Was kann aus Nazareth schon Gutes kommen?' (Joh 1.46). *NTS* 46, 21–41.

Soyinka, W. 1973: *Collected Plays*, vol. 1. Oxford.

Sparks, H. F. D. 1985: *The Apocryphal Old Testament*. Oxford.

Spenser, E. 1970: *Poetical Works*, ed. E. de Selincourt. Oxford.

Spiegel, S. 1969: *The Last Trial*, tr. J. Goldin. Princeton.

Squire, J. C. 1921: *Selections from the Modern Poets*. London.

Stanton, E. C. 1985: *The Woman's Bible* (1892–5). Edinburgh.

Steiner, G. 1996: *No Passion Spent: Essays 1978–1996*. London.

Stibbe, M. W. G. 1992: *John as Storyteller: Narrative Criticism and the Fourth Gospel*. Cambridge.

Strauss, D. F. 1892: *The Life of Jesus*, 4th edn, tr. G. Eliot. London.

Stroud, J. C. 1847: *The Physical Cause of the Death of Christ*. London.

Sturge Moore, T. 1932: *Poems*, vol. 2. London.

Suggitt, J. 1984: John XVII.17, *Ο ΛΟΓΟΣ ΣΟΣ ΑΛΗΘΕΙΑ ESTIN*. *JTS* 35, 104–17.

Swedenborg, E. 1933: *The True Christian Religion* (1771). London.

Swinburne, A. C. 1917: *Songs and Ballads: First Series* (1866). London.

Talbert, C. H. 1975/6: The myth of a descending-ascending redeemer in Mediterranean antiquity. *NTS* 22, 418–43.

Tanner, N. P. and Alberigo, J. 1990: *The Decrees of the Ecumenical Councils*, 2 vols. Edinburgh.

Taylor, J. 1850: *Unum Necessarium: On the Doctrine and Practice of Repentance* (1655). In *Collected Works*, vol. 7, London.

Taylor, R. 1831: *The Devil's Pulpit, or Astro-Theological Sermons*. London.

Taylor, T. M. 1956: The beginnings of Jewish proselyte-baptism. *NTS* 11, 193–8.

Temple, W. 1961: *Readings in John's Gospel*. London.

Tennyson, A. 1953: *The Complete Works*. Oxford.

Teresa of Avila 1957: *Life* (1565), tr. J. M. Cohen. Harmondsworth.

Theissen, G. 1978: *The First Followers of Jesus*, tr. J. Bowden. London.

Theobald, M. 1988: *Die Fleischwerdung des Logos*. Münster.

Thomas, D. 1952: *Collected Poems 1934–1952*. London.

Thomas, K. 1973: *Religion and the Decline of Magic*. Harmondsworth.

Thomas, R. S. 1993: *Collected Poems 1945–1990*. London.

Thompson, F. 1913: *Poems*. London.

Tolstoy, L. 1936: *The Kingdom of God and Peace Essays* (1896), tr. A. Maude. Oxford.

Torrey, C. C. 1923: The Aramaic origins of the Gospel of John. *HTR* 16, 305–45.

Toynbee, A. 1938: *A Study of History*, vol. 6: *The Disintegration of Civilisations*. Oxford.

Traherne, T. 1980: *Selected Writings*, ed. D. Davis. Manchester.

Trench, R. C. 1880: *Synonyms of the New Testament*. London.

——1904: *Notes on the Miracles of the Gospels*. London.

Troje, L. 1916: *Adam und Zoe; eine Szene der altchristlichen Kunst in ihren religions-geschichtliche Zusammenhange*. Heidelberg.

Turner, J. D. 1991: The history of religions background of John 10. In J. Beutler and R. T. Fortna (eds), *The Shepherd Discourse of John 10 and its Context*, Cambridge, 33–52.

Turner, V. 1959: *Jesus and his Sacrifice*. London.

Underwood, T. L. 1999: *The Acts of the Witnesses: The Autobiography of Lodowick Muggleton and other Early Muggletonian Writings*. Oxford and New York.

Urquhart, C. 1984: *My Father is the Gardener*. London.

Van der Horst, P. W. 1994: The Birkat ha-Minim in Recent Research. *Expository Times*, 105, 363–8.

Vaughan, H. 1914: *Poems*, ed. L. C. Martin, vol. 2. Oxford.

Vawter, B. 1964: Ezekiel and John. *Catholic Biblical Quarterly*, 26, 450–8.

Vermes, G. 1973: *Jesus the Jew*. London.

——1975: *The Dead Sea Scrolls in English*. Harmondsworth.

Vissen't Hooft, W. A. 1957: *Rembrandt and the Gospel*. London.

Voltaire, F. M. Arouet de 1961: *Mélanges*. Paris.

Von Balthasar, H. U. 1989: *The Glory of the Lord*, vol. 7: *Theology: The New Covenant*, tr. B. McNeil. Edinburgh.

Vurtheim, J. 1920: The miracle of the wine at Dionysus' advent. *Classical Quarterly*, 14, 92–6.

Walton, I. 1939: *The Compleat Angler* (1653). New York.

Ware, K. T. 1978: with Mother Mary, *The Lenten Triodion*. London.

Webb, J. F. (tr.) 1965: *Lives of the Saints*. Harmondsworth.

Weitzman, K. (ed.) 1982: *The Icon*. London.

Wesley, C. 2001: *Sermons*, ed. K. Newport. Oxford.

Wesley, J. 1876: *A Collection of Hymns for the Use of the People Called Methodists*. London.

——1944: *Forty-Four Sermons*. London.

Westcott, B. F. 1903: *The Gospel According to St. John*. London.

Whitefield, G. 1958: *Selected Sermons*. Edinburgh.

Wickham, A. 1984: *The Writings of Anna Wickham, Free Woman and Poet*, ed. R. D. Smith. London.

Wieand, D. 1965–6: John V.2 and the pool of Bethesda. *NTS* 12, 392–404.

Wiebe, P. H. 1997: *Visions of Jesus*. Oxford and New York.

Wilde, O. 1990: *Complete Works*. Leicester.

Wiles, M. F. 1960: *The Spiritual Gospel*. Cambridge.

Wills, L. M. 1997: *The Quest of the Historical Gospel: Mark, John and the Origins of the Gospel Genre*. London.

Wilson, I. 1978: *The Turin Shroud*. Harmondsworth.

Winter, P. 1961: *The Trial of Jesus*. Berlin.

Wolfe, H. 1925: *The Unknown Goddess*. London.

——1927: *Requiem*. London.

Wordsworth, C. 1857: *Theophilus Anglicanus*. London.
Wroe, A. 1999: *Pilate: The Biography of an Invented Man*. London.
Wücherpfennig, A. 2002: *Heracleon Philologus*. Tübingen.
Wyatt, T. 1949: *Poems*, ed. K. Muir. London.
Yeats, W. B. 1990: *The Poems*, ed. D. Albright. London.
Young, A. 1985: *The Poetical Works*, ed. Edward Lowbury and Alison Young. London.

Index